Influence, Belief, and Argument

An Introduction to Responsible Persuasion

Douglas Ehninger

The University of Iowa

Scott, Foresman and Company
Glenview, Illinois   Brighton, England

Preface

Influence, Belief, and Argument: An Introduction to Responsible Persuasion is addressed to the reader who wishes to sharpen his skills as a maker and critic of written or spoken arguments. To this end, it views an argument as a unit of proof consisting of three separate but interrelated parts, *evidence, warrant,* and *claim.* The role each of these parts plays in the generation of proofs and the standards it must meet if an argument is to be sound are explained and illustrated.

Because it envisions arguments as occurring in informal as well as formal situations, *Influence, Belief, and Argument* omits the complex classical treatments of organization, case building, and rebuttal usually found in textbooks on public discussion and debate. Because it is concerned with the ways proofs work to gain assent from a reader or listener, it is more than just a book on how to think straight. Finally, *Influence, Belief, and Argument* is not a sophisticated handbook of formal logic: technical terms and notational symbols are avoided, only the most elementary concepts of logic are presented, and these are considered primarily in terms of their rhetorical or persuasive impact.

In addition to the characteristics just noted, *Influence, Belief, and Argument* has several additional features which render it unique. Among these are a fresh classification of the forms or types of argument (Chapter VI), a discussion of standard lines and patterns of proof (Chapter VII), and an analysis of counterfeit proofs as they occur in a communicator's language, thought, or manner of presentation (Chapter VIII). Chapter I explores the nature and uses of argument, and contrasts argument with other methods of influencing belief or behavior.

Library of Congress Catalog Card Number: 73-91028
ISBN: 0-673-07867-1

Regional offices of Scott, Foresman and Company are located in Dallas, Texas; Glenview, Illinois; Oakland, New Jersey; Palo Alto, California; Tucker, Georgia; and Brighton, England.

Each of the chapters in *Influence, Belief, and Argument* is accompanied by an extensive list of exercises and assignments. Many of these require the examination of arguments or pseudo-arguments found in newspaper stories, editorials, advertisements, letters to the editor, court decisions, and the like. Together with other assignments, such sample passages implement one of the principal assumptions on which the book rests: that while a knowledge of rules and principles is useful, the only way one actually learns to make and judge arguments is through extended practice. Further materials for study and analysis are provided in a number of extended arguments and case-study situations in the appendixes.

During the more than four decades in which I have been actively engaged in the study and teaching of argument, I have accumulated more debts than I can adequately acknowledge here. *Influence, Belief, and Argument* owes much to the hundreds of undergraduate and graduate students who have passed through my classes, and who in so doing have exerted a major influence on my thinking. I also have been influenced by dozens of colleagues who have challenged my thinking, and by countless treatises on rhetoric and argumentation dating from classical times to the present. In particular, I owe a debt of gratitude to the writings of James H. McBurney, Henry W. Johnstone, Jr., Chaim Perelman, Charles L. Stevenson, and Stephen Toulmin. Wilma Ebbitt and my sometime coauthor Wayne Brockriede were kind enough to examine my manuscript during the course of its preparation and to suggest many improvements. Whatever defects in doctrine or style remain are due to my ineptness rather than their lack of discernment, and are far fewer than they would have been without such excellent counsel.

D. E.
Iowa City, Iowa

Contents

Chapter 1.
Influence, Belief, and Argument

Each of us, every day of our lives, is bombarded by dozens of written and oral appeals aimed at influencing our beliefs or directing our behavior.[1]

In the morning, as we awaken and switch on the radio, we are greeted by an orotund voice urging us to buy fabrics at Fabs, keep healthy with Geritol, fly United to Honolulu, or insure our automobiles with Allstate.

At breakfast we find in the editorials, syndicated columns, and sometimes even in the news stories of our daily paper statements designed to influence our thinking about race relations, daycare centers, the drug traffic, or defense spending.

[1]Here, and throughout, the term *belief* is used to refer to a judgment concerning how some things are ("Mary is fundamentally a shy person"; "Mary is beautiful"), or how they should be ("Mary should make more friends").

Because it is a judgment, a belief is to be distinguished from a mere item of knowledge or information ("Mary is five feet tall"). It is also, however, to be distinguished from an attitude, which upon analysis will usually be found to rest upon a group or cluster of beliefs ("I like [have a favorable attitude toward] Mary because she is [I believe her to be] kind and generous").

An argument as a single capsule or unit of proof characteristically seeks to influence a belief, as here defined. Arguments grouped together into organized patterns may, however, implant or alter an attitude by addressing themselves to the various beliefs upon which the attitude rests. (*Argument I:* "Because Mary is thoughtful of those about her, she is kind." *Argument II:* "Because Mary gives freely of her time and money, she is generous." *Conclusions of Arguments I and II used as support for attitude:* "Because Mary is kind and generous, I like [have a favorable attitude toward] her.")

As we walk to campus, we pass a billboard on which a handsome man or incredibly beautiful woman recommends that we pick a six-pack, smoke a Salem, or buy a Chrysler.

In our nine o'clock survey of American literature, the instructor contends that Hemingway was the greatest of all modern novelists, and at ten o'clock we listen to an economics lecture on the need for tax reform.

Later in the day, a student senator asks us to sign a petition urging the abolishment of letter grades, a class representative requests a contribution to the Heart Fund, and a smooth-talking salesman wheedles us into subscribing to *Harpers* and *Sports Illustrated.*

In the evening we turn on television, where a candidate for local office appeals for votes in a coming election and the interviews on the late-night "talk shows" are interrupted every few minutes by back-to-back commercials advertising toothpaste, dog food, cosmetics, and floor wax.

In addition to being targets at which persuasive appeals of many sorts are constantly directed, we in turn spend a considerable portion of our own time and energy trying to influence the beliefs and actions of others. We write home asking for a larger allowance or assuring our parents that, for today's college student, apartments are preferable to dormitories. We advise our friends to take Professor Smith's course in physical geography, but warn them to avoid Dr. Brown's section of Chemistry I. We send letters to the college paper and make persuasive speeches in classes and at meetings of clubs and organizations. During rap sessions over coffee at the union or beer at the campus bar, we defend vigorously our views on abortion, marijuana, or recycling.

Uses of Persuasive Appeals

The efforts people make to influence the beliefs and actions of their fellows return important dividends both to the persons involved and to society as a whole. In a world as varied and complex as ours, we are in countless ways dependent upon others for advice and guidance. We, as individuals, cannot subject to laboratory tests all of the hundreds of items of food, hardware, drugs, and clothing we must buy. We cannot study every bill introduced into Congress or examine in detail every provision of our state and county budgets. We cannot visit in person each of the world's potential trouble spots or talk to all of the statesmen concerned. We do not, in fact, even possess the expert knowledge or technical equipment necessary to tell us accurately how well our own bodies are functioning.

Yet as consumers we must make judgments among products, as voters we must support policies, and as individuals we must act to maintain or restore our physical well-being. In all of these matters, and many others besides, we must be guided by the recommendations of persons who are experts in their respective fields.

But besides supplying advice and guidance, persuasive appeals perform a second important function. Through their aid, people are able to engage in innumerable tasks and achieve innumerable goals that lie beyond the reach of the individual working alone. The teacher who wishes to reform the educational system in her school or community must first persuade a sufficient number of her colleagues that present practices are deficient and that the action she proposes would provide an acceptable remedy. The citizen who would rewrite laws or modify public institutions must first persuade the voters to elect him to office and then must lead the thinking of his fellow legislators along the lines he desires. The modern medical or scientific researcher requires, more often than not, the support of dozens or hundreds of skilled technicians welded together into a functioning team. Even "socialization" itself—that broad and gradual process by which the child comes to acquire the patterns, values, and lifeways of the culture into which he is born—is, in the final analysis, the result of influences consciously exerted upon him by such institutions as the home, the school, and the church.

Finally, it may be observed that efforts to influence the thoughts and behavior of others have a moral as well as a pragmatic justification. The individual who, as a result of experience or study, knows what is best for another has not only the right, but under normal circumstances also the obligation, to keep that person from straying into error. A traveller who learns that a bridge is unsafe but does not attempt to persuade his friend to avoid it is clearly delinquent in his duty. The physician who understands the dangers inherent in a given diet but fails to warn his patient is similarly delinquent. As responsible men and women, each of us has a double obligation to those about us: first, to listen to the advice and recommendations addressed to us by persons whose knowledge or judgment deserves respect; and second, to offer to others the benefit of our own knowledge when we have reason to believe it sound and useful.

For these reasons, to legislate the abolishment of all attempts on the part of one person to influence the thinking or behavior of another would have consequences that are clearly undesirable. Besides depriving us of the guidance we need if we are to live happy and productive lives, it would abrogate a responsibility every person owes to those whose training or experience are inferior to his own.

Abuses of Persuasive Appeals

While neither the individual nor the social order in which he lives could easily survive if all attempts to influence belief and behavior were suddenly outlawed, it has long been recognized that persuasive appeals may serve illegitimate as well as legitimate ends and that they may employ ethically dubious as well as ethically acceptable means.

Abuses in the Ends Served

All too often persuasive appeals are made not to achieve what is best for the person or group addressed, but rather to serve the selfish ends of the agent who advances them. Attempts on the part of unprincipled persuaders to exploit readers or listeners for selfish purposes—to make them buy things they don't need, endorse principles they don't understand, or fight wars of aggression masquerading as wars of defense—are as old as the race itself.

More than twenty-five hundred years ago the Greek philosopher Plato, observing the misuses to which the art of persuasion was put in the Athens of his day, urged that it be abandoned in favor of the painstaking brand of dialectical inquiry illustrated in his dialogues. In recent decades advances in the science of "engineering consent" have opened to the unprincipled advertiser, politician, or propagandist a new and vastly increased arsenal of potent persuasive appeals. At the same time, developments in the electronic media of communication have made possible the dissemination of these appeals to millions of persons with a rapidity hitherto undreamed of.

As a result, exploitation of the individual has, in large measure, given way to the calculated enslavement of entire populations for purposes of commercial advantage or political control. Indeed, it is easy to imagine how skillfully framed appeals emanating from a diabolical message source and transmitted over wide areas with lightning speed might some day lead to the nightmare of total thought control depicted in such books as George Orwell's *1984*.

Abuses in the Means Employed

Abuses in the means used to effect persuasion arise when appeals are made in such a way that they bypass the understanding of the individuals addressed and elicit responses of an unreflective or "trigger" nature.

Appeals of this sort may trade upon prejudice or superstition; they may assert without proof that doing as prescribed will satisfy a deep-seated wish or desire; they may invite a reaction biased by the heat of anger or the chill of fear; they may subtly "identify" a product or proposal with a condition that is especially prized. In all these cases the aim is the same. By exerting upon the unwary subject some psychic or social pressure that produces an automatic response, the understanding is circumvented and belief springs from causes of which the believer is not himself aware.

Experts in the field of mass persuasion have developed to a high degree the art of inducing "trigger" responses through the presentation of hidden but powerful belief- and action-producing stimuli. Today such appeals are widely used not only to sell goods and services, but also to muster support for public policies, to create favorable "images" for corporations, and even to "package and merchandise" candidates for high national office.

Argument as a Mode of Appeal

Aware of the important role the persuasive interchange of ideas plays in the life of the individual and the maintenance of the social structure, men have sought to devise a way of exerting influence that would be free of the evils and abuses we have just surveyed. The result of their efforts is argument, the method of influence that is the subject of this book.

Although argument is frankly an instrument for affecting belief or behavior, and is, therefore, to be classed among the modes of persuasive appeal, one crucial difference sets it apart from other instruments designed for this purpose. Instead of seeking assent of an unreflective or uncritical nature, argument seeks assent that is, in the fullest sense, deserved or warranted. To this end, it confronts the understanding of the reader or listener directly, laying out for his inspection and analysis the facts and reasons upon which the appeal is based.

The convictions that result from argument are, therefore, self-convictions. Rather than being impressed upon the individual from without, they grow and develop from within. The person addressed, no less than the person making the appeal, is an active participant in the process by which convictions are formed or actions chosen. The awareness of why a given appeal merits endorsement is bound to the endorsement itself.

All this, of course, does not mean that argument as an instrument of persuasion is free of limitations or that it may not sometimes be misused. Because the development of a conviction from within is a gradual process, argument is more time-consuming than the quick-fire methods of suggestion or emotional appeal. Because it conscientiously avoids coercion in favor of self-persuasion, argument may not always produce the result the persuader desires. Because unsound or inadequate proofs may through skillful handling be made to appear sound, argument often is at the mercy of those who would abuse it.

Nor does the superiority of argument over alternative methods for arriving at beliefs and decisions mean there is no place in life for emotion and impulse or for the play of the imagination. Our existence would be dreary and prosaic indeed if all feeling and desire and all excursions of the fancy were ruled out in favor of a coldly rational approach to even the most trivial situations.

Even with its limitations, however, argument can still claim both practical and philosophical superiority over other methods for forming beliefs and arriving at decisions.

The Superiority of Argument

Practical Considerations

There are at least three practical reasons for asserting the superiority of argument. First, a belief that results from argument, since it rests upon a careful examination of relevant facts and data, is more apt to represent an accurate appraisal of a situation than is a belief rooted in emotion, desire, or suggestion.[2] Hence it is more useful both to the individual who holds it and to those persons or groups his actions are likely to affect. It works out better when put to the test of practice; it withstands more resolutely the strains of attack and criticism; it is, as a rule, more productive of additional insights and fresh knowledge.

Beliefs based upon faith, impulse, or desire are held blindly. When they accord with the facts or work out in practice, it is by accident rather than

---

[2]*Suggestion* may conveniently be thought of as the process of implanting an idea in the marginal fields of attention so as to set off a habitual or predetermined response.

Suggestion may lie in the connotation of a term ("juvenile delinquent" vs. "problem child"), in the way a statement is made or a question asked ("You wouldn't, by any chance, be interested in joining our club, would you?" vs. "I'm sure that if you joined our club, you would find it interesting"), in the tone of voice, appearance of the speaker, or a wide variety of other sorts of sensory stimuli.

For an older but still useful discussion of suggestion as it relates particularly to the problems and processes of written and oral persuasion, see Lew Sarett and William Trufant Foster, *Basic Principles of Speech* (Boston: Houghton Mifflin Co., 1936), pp. 306–22.

design. When they prove true or fruitful, it is because of a happy guess rather than an informed decision. Only beliefs and actions based upon an understanding of the reasons that justify them share the twin qualities of reliability and responsibility—those qualities argument is designed to promote.

In addition to being more accurate and, therefore, more productive, beliefs based on arguments have a flexibility that beliefs of other sorts commonly lack. Convictions anchored in authority, prejudice, or desire are locked into place by stubbornness, indolence, superstition, or fear. They are clung to rigidly, despite the fact that conditions which once justified them may have long since passed away. Beliefs that grow out of arguments, on the other hand, because they are attuned to the facts, change as the facts change. When new situations arise or new problems are encountered, belief patterns appropriate to them are searched out and developed. Beliefs resting on uncritical grounds often go out of date long before they are abandoned; beliefs resting on arguments are always relevant.

Third, from a practical point of view, argument is superior to alternative methods of decision making because actions undertaken as a result of argument are generally carried out with a willingness and persistence that actions impelled by other means of inducement frequently lack. The person who acts out of the self-convincing process of argument understands not only what he is to do, but also why he is to do it; he acts on his own volition rather than at the bidding of someone else. Common sense, practical observation, and experimental evidence combine to suggest that if one wishes an individual or group to carry out a task willingly and with persistence, one is well advised to invest the time and energy entailed in persuasion through argument.[3]

Philosophical Considerations

Philosophically, there are simple but compelling reasons why argument is to be preferred over alternative methods for influencing belief and behavior.

Because he believes the proper way to influence others is to bring those persons to see for themselves the rightness or justness of the claims he presents, the advocate who chooses argument as his instrument treats his readers or listeners not as things to be manipulated, but as persons to be reasoned with, as responsible, rational beings whose judgment deserves respect and whose integrity must be honored. Modes of persuasive appeal which seek to circumvent or benumb the understanding are disrespectful of the individuals addressed; they degrade the listeners or readers by endeavoring to produce the automatic, instinctive sort of response characteristic of animals, rather than the considered, judgmental sort of response humans alone are capable of making. Argument, in contrast, is respectful of people and of those distinctive qualities of reason, understanding, and reflection which mark them off as "human." Instead of addressing the biological individual, it addresses the person as thinker.

The role of argument as a humane and humanizing instrument does not, however, stop here. In proportion as the arguer respects the humanity of others by treating them as persons rather than as things, he asserts and

---

[3]See, for example, Lester Coch and John R. P. French, Jr., "Overcoming Resistance to Change," *Human Relations*, 1 (1948), 512–32.

reinforces his own humanity, becomes more humane himself. "Person-making," the German philosopher Martin Buber was fond of remarking, is a distinctly reflexive process. The qualities of freedom and responsibility that make one a person are not absolutes. They cannot be attained or maintained in isolation, but only in relationship to others. Humanity is something we gain for ourselves only insofar as we willingly grant it to those about us. The more skilled we become in the use of emotion, prejudice, or suggestion as instruments of persuasion, the farther we depart from the ideals which ought to govern our relations with our fellows; the more skilled we become in the use of argument, the closer we approach these ideals.

Finally, as in our daily contacts we show respect for one another by resorting to such humanizing instruments as argument, we gradually create a society in which peace, tolerance, and mutual appreciation flourish, a society in which the maximum development of each person and of the group as a whole becomes possible—the sort of society, in short, in which we all wish to live.

Clearly, then, for philosophical reasons, no less than for practical ones, it is important that we gain as much skill as we can in making and evaluating arguments.

Exercises

1. Collect five newspaper columns or editorials aimed at influencing the beliefs or actions of the reader. Analyze these materials carefully. Do they present facts and reasons in an effort to invite self-conviction, or do they attempt to win agreement by methods that bypass the under-standing? Present your findings orally or in writing.

2. Collect from popular magazines five advertisements which seek to win an automatic or "trigger" response from the reader. Describe in each case the nature of the appeal employed.

3. Make a list of some of the ways in which your friends and associates have sought to influence your thinking or behavior during the past few days. Then make a list of all of the ways in which you have endeavored to influence others.

   Study the lists you have drawn up, noting in how many cases the appeal was addressed to the understanding and in how many cases some other means of persuasion was employed.

4. Make an honest appraisal of two or three of your most cherished beliefs concerning education, politics, or some other subject in which you are especially interested. To what extent can you fairly say your beliefs have grown out of a careful examination of pertinent facts and reasons, and to what extent are they rooted in desire, prejudice, and the like?

5. This chapter suggests that any appeal which bypasses or short-circuits the understanding is basically unethical. Is this, in your judgment, too

rigid a standard to employ? Would you, for example, be willing to regard as ethical an appeal to honor, love, duty, or altruism?

6. Do you agree that persons who are confident they know what is best for another have a moral obligation to prevent him from straying into error? If so, in discharging this obligation are they justified in using nonargumentative means of persuasion?

7. If a person *appears* to be laying out for objective examination and analysis the facts and reasons upon which an appeal is based, but actually is suppressing or manipulating these factors so as to mislead the recipient, would you call his appeal an argument? If not, how would you designate it?

8. This chapter is clearly an attempt to influence the thinking of the reader concerning the nature and importance of argument as a method of persuasive appeal. Would you say that, in all cases, the chapter itself meets the criteria of argument, or does it at times resort to assertion, suggestion, or emotional appeal?

9. The term *argument* is sometimes used in senses other than the one emphasized here. What are some of these senses, and how do they relate to the view here presented?

10. Give examples of beliefs or practices rooted in authority, tradition, or custom that are still clung to, even though the conditions that once justified them no longer obtain.

11. Jonathan Swift once wrote to a friend, "I have got materials towards a treatise proving the falsity of the definition *animal rationale* [i.e., that man is a rational animal], and to show that it should be only *rationis capax* [i.e., capable of reason]." In light of your experience, which of these definitions do you think is more accurate? Give examples to substantiate your choice.

Writing or Speaking Assignment

Prepare a short speech or essay on one of the following subjects, or on a subject suggested by one of these:

Big-Time Advertising: Curse or Blessing?
The Moral Obligation to Persuade
How to Analyze a Persuasive Appeal
Socrates' Crusade for Examined Ideas and Beliefs
Persuading Ethically
Self-Persuasion as an Ideal
The Mass Media as Socializing Instruments
Argument and the Ideal Society
Suggestion as a Persuasive Device

Emotional Appeals in the Speaking of Billy Graham (or some other well-known speaker)

Argument as a Humanizing Instrument

Why the Proofs of Mathematics Do (or Do Not) Meet the Criterion of Self-Conviction

For Additional Reading

Ehninger, Douglas. "Argument as Method: Its Nature, Its Limitations, and Its Uses." *Speech Monographs*, 37 (June 1970), 101–10.

Ehninger, Douglas, and Wayne Brockriede. *Decision by Debate.* New York: Dodd, Mead & Co., 1963. Chapter I, "Choosing and Deciding Critically."

Eisenberg, Abne M., and Joseph A. Illarde. *Argument: An Alternative to Violence.* Englewood Cliffs, N.J.: Prentice-Hall, Inc., 1972. Chapter I, "An Orientation to Argument"; Chapter II, "Why People Argue."

Fisher, Walter, and Edward M. Sayles. "The Nature and Functions of Argument." In *Perspectives on Argumentation,* ed. Gerald R. Miller and Thomas R. Nilsen. Glenview, Ill.: Scott, Foresman and Co., 1966. Pp. 2–22.

Hook, Sidney. "The Ethics of Controversy." *New Leader,* February 1, 1954, pp. 12–14. Reprinted in *Readings in Argumentation,* ed. Jerry M. Anderson and Paul J. Dovre. Boston: Allyn & Bacon, Inc., 1968.

Johnstone, Henry W., Jr. "Some Reflections on Argumentation." *Logique et Analyse,* 6 (1963), 30–39. Reprinted in *Philosophy, Rhetoric, and Argumentation,* ed. Maurice Natanson and Henry W. Johnstone, Jr. University Park, Penn.: Pennsylvania State University Press, 1965. Pp. 1–9.

Mills, Glenn E. *Reason in Controversy.* Boston: Allyn & Bacon, Inc., 1964. Chapter I, "Introduction to Argumentation."

Ruby, Lionel. *The Art of Making Sense.* Philadelphia: J. B. Lippincott Co., 1954. Chapter I, "On Being Logical."

St. Aubyn, Giles. *The Art of Argument.* New York: Emerson Books, Inc., 1962. Chapter I, "Irrational Man."

Chapter II.
The Parts of
an Argument

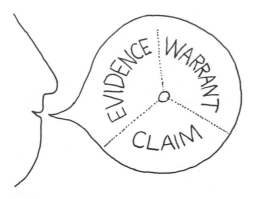

Arguments vary widely in the subjects they concern, the forms they take, the premises they employ, and the degrees of conclusiveness they produce. They may be about politics, religion, economics, literature, sports, or morals. They may be compressed into three or four words or extended over a long speech or essay. They may be drawn from precedents, based on assumptions, or grounded on a careful study of facts and data. They may establish the truth of a matter beyond all reasonable doubt or merely show it to be probable or possible.

Every argument, however, whatever subject it concerns, whatever form it assumes, whatever purpose it serves, or whatever degree of proof it attains, always consists of three basic parts or elements. For reasons which will become clear in a moment, we shall label these parts *E, W,* and *C.*

Part *E* consists of one or more items of belief or knowledge the person addressed is willing to accept or, at least for the moment, assume to be true. Part *C* consists of one or more similar items the person addressed does not accept or is not willing to assume as true. Part *W* asserts that a relationship of some sort exists between what is accepted or assumed and what is not accepted or assumed. It makes clear why, if one endorses Part *E* of an argument, he is also in reason called upon to endorse Part *C.*

The element in the argument the person addressed already accepts or is willing to assume (Part *E)* is known as the *evidence.* The element in the argument the person addressed does not accept or is unwilling to assume (Part *C*) is called the *claim.* The third element in the argument, which shows that, if one accepts the *evidence* (Part *E*), he is also in reason called upon to accept the *claim* (Part *C*), is named the *warrant* (Part *W*).[1]

Viewed functionally, the evidence (*E*) is the ground upon which the argument rests, the base from which it starts, the matters of fact or opinion to which it ultimately appeals. The claim (*C*) is the conclusion toward which the argument points, the goal it seeks, the contention it attempts to establish or make believed. The warrant (*W*) has for its purpose bringing the evidence (*E*) to bear upon the claim (*C*). It shows why, if a reader or listener endorses the evidence, the author of the argument is also justified in asking him to endorse the claim. Thus, when we put its three parts together, an argument reads: Given *E,* and in view of *W,* therefore *C.*

The three parts or elements of an argument, considered in terms of the functions or operations they perform in producing proof, may be likened to the parts of a bridge over a river. The *evidence,* as the foundation upon which the argument rests, is comparable to the pilings planted on the riverbed. The *warrant,* as the part of the argument which applies or carries the *evidence* to the *claim,* is comparable to the steel superstructure which rises from the pilings and supports the roadway over which traffic passes. And, finally, the *claim,* as the contention the argument is intended to establish and support, is comparable to the roadway itself as it rests jointly upon the pilings and the superstructure of the bridge.

(C) **Claim** $\rightarrow$

(W) **Warrant** $\longrightarrow$

(E) **Evidence** $\longrightarrow$

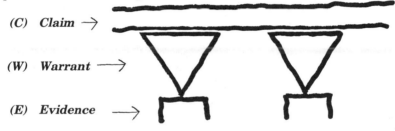

Arranged in the customary order of *evidence* (pilings), *warrant* (superstructure), *claim* (roadway), a complete argument would appear as follows:

(E) **Evidence**   John is an honors graduate of Webster High School.

(W) **Warrant**   Since honors graduates of Webster High School invariably do well in college,

(C) **Claim**   John may be expected to do well in his college work.

By first citing the recognized fact that John is an honors graduate of Webster High School and then showing how this fact is related to the quality of college work, the argument justifies us in proceeding beyond the evidence as given to assert that John will do well in college.

In the example just given, the parts of the argument appear in their natural or normal order—evidence, warrant, claim. Moreover, each of the parts is

---

[1]The terms *claim* and *warrant* are borrowed from Stephen Toulmin, *The Uses of Argument* (London: Cambridge University Press, 1958), Chapter III passim. As readers familiar with that work will recognize, the analysis of argument here presented draws heavily upon the same source.

explicitly stated. Arguments as they occur in everyday life, however, frequently appear in irregular form and often have one of their parts omitted. In addition, they sometimes are more complicated than our discussion to this point would suggest. Let us first examine some of the variant forms in which arguments may occur and then explore the more complicated patterns or formats they sometimes exhibit.

Variant Forms of Argument

Our sample argument about John and his probable success in college may appear not only in the form stated above (*Form 1*), but also in the forms that follow.

Form 2

(C)	*Claim*	John may be expected to do well in his college work.
(W)	*Warrant*	For honors graduates of Webster High School invariably do well in college,
(E)	*Evidence*	And John is an honors graduate of that high school.

Form 3

(C)	*Claim*	John may be expected to do well in his college work.
(E)	*Evidence*	After all, he is an honors graduate of Webster High School,
(W)	*Warrant*	And honors graduates of Webster High School invariably do well in college.

Form 4

(W)	*Warrant*	Since honors graduates of Webster High School invariably do well in college,
(E)	*Evidence*	And since John is an honors graduate of that high school,
(C)	*Claim*	John may be expected to do well in college.

Upon rare occasions our argument might even appear in these more awkward, but equally valid, forms:

Form 5

(E)	*Evidence*	John is an honors graduate of Webster High School.
(C)	*Claim*	Therefore, he may be expected to do well in his college work,

(W) **Warrant**   Because honors graduates of Webster High School invariably do well in college.

Form 6

(W) **Warrant**   Since honors graduates of Webster High School invariably do well in college,

(C) **Claim**   John will do well in his college work.

(E) **Evidence**   After all, he is an honors graduate of that school.

Not only may the parts of an argument be arranged in the various ways we have just surveyed, but sometimes one of the parts may be omitted as superfluous. If, for example, the person addressed is well acquainted with the success honors graduates of Webster High School enjoy in college, the *warrant* need not be specifically mentioned. In this case, the argument would read:

(E) **Evidence**   John is an honors graduate of Webster High School.

(C) **Claim**   Therefore, he may be expected to do well in college.

Or the *evidence* and *claim* may even be compressed into a single sentence: Since John is an honors graduate of Webster High School (*E*), he may be expected to do well in college (*C*).

On the other hand, if the person addressed knows that John is, indeed, an honors graduate of Webster High School, the *evidence* may be omitted. Then the argument would take this form:

(W) **Warrant**   Since honors graduates of Webster High School invariably do well in college,

(C) **Claim**   John may be expected to do well in his college work.

Or, again, expressed in a single sentence: John, as an honors graduate of Webster High School, may be expected to do well in college.

If the *evidence* and *warrant* are stated, but the reader or listener is left to draw for himself the *claim* to which they jointly point, the argument becomes: With respect to John's prospects in college, I need only remark that he is an honors graduate of Webster High School (*E*), a school whose honors graduates invariably do well in college (*W*).

More Complicated Arguments

While there are some cases in which the *warrant* may be omitted as superfluous, there are also instances in which, though present, it is not accepted by the reader or listener as proper warrant for the claim advanced. The listener may, for example, say, "I know that John is an honors graduate of Webster High School, but I have never been shown what you seem to assume: namely, that honors graduates of this school invariably do well in their college work. How do you know that this is so?"

In such a case the person advancing the argument is called upon to prove that the statement he offers as warrant for his claim is indeed justified, that it truly represents an existing condition or state of affairs. To do this he must add a fourth element to his argument, *support for the warrant.* When this is added to the three basic elements of *evidence, warrant,* and *claim,* the argument appears as follows.

(E) Evidence   John is an honors graduate of Webster High School.

(W) Warrant   Since honors graduates of Webster High School invariably do well in college, and

(SW) Support for Warrant   Because studies show that no honors graduate of Webster High School ever had a cumulative GPA of less than 3.0 in his first year of college work,

(C) Claim   John may be expected to do well in college.

Under these circumstances, it should be observed, the three basic parts of the argument—*evidence, warrant,* and *claim*—continue to perform their usual functions. The purpose of the new element—the *support for the warrant*—is merely to assure us that the warrant makes a statement that is factually true and, therefore, that it constitutes a valid justification for the claim asserted. By assuring us upon the basis of the supporting data presented that honors graduates of Webster High School do indeed do well in college, it enables us to proceed with confidence in relating our known information concerning John to his probable success in doing college work. In order to have an argument, however, here as always we still require *evidence* in the form of something believed or assumed by the person to whom the argument is addressed, a *claim* in the form of a proposition which that person disbelieves or doubts, and a *warrant* in the form of a statement which asserts the existence of a relationship between the evidence and the claim.

Chains of Arguments

Thus far we have viewed an argument as an independent and self-contained unit of proof, capable in its own right of establishing the claim in question. Sometimes, however, the claim the author of an argument wishes to establish is of such a nature that no single unit of proof is equal to the task. When this situation arises, it becomes necessary to employ a series or chain of arguments or to group a number of arguments together into a cluster.

When arguments are arranged in a series or chain, each unit of proof save the first one is preceded by a similar unit, the conclusion or claim statement of which serves as evidence for the argument that follows. In this way, evidence in the form of facts or values that at first glance seem remote from the final claim the arguer wishes to establish may be brought to bear in its support.

Let us suppose, for example, that the claim the arguer seeks to establish is that the nation can look forward to a round of strikes in the basic industries.

And let us further suppose that the evidence upon which he bases this prediction is that the cost of living is rising rapidly. By constructing the following chain of intermediary arguments, this evidence may be brought to bear upon the claim.

Argument 1.   *(E)*   Reliable government indexes show that the cost of living is rising rapidly.

                (W)   Since through long experience we know that a rapid rise in the cost of living leads to demands for increased wages by workers in the basic industries,

                (C)   We may expect that these workers will seek pay boosts.

Argument 2.   *(E)*   For the reasons just given, the prospect is that in the months ahead workers in the basic industries will demand increased wages.

                (W)   Since management, caught in the cost-price squeeze characteristic of periods of rising prices, undoubtedly will resist these demands,

                (C)   A period of labor-management strife may be expected to ensue.

Argument 3.   *(E)*   For the reasons just given, a period of labor-management strife is in prospect.

                (W)   Since in such periods workers in the basic industries have usually enforced their demands by striking,

                (C)   We may expect a round of strikes in these industries.

Just as one of the steps in an individual argument or unit of proof may be omitted as superfluous or the language condensed so as to avoid unnecessary repetition or formalism, so may these same modifications be made in an argumentative chain. The point to be emphasized, however, is that when a chain of arguments is presented in its complete form, without any of the links omitted, the conclusion or claim statement of each unit in the chain serves as the evidential basis for the unit that follows. In this way successive arguments are linked together until the admitted facts or recognized values from which the chain of reasoning starts are successfully related to the final claim which it is the purpose of the chain to establish.

Clusters of Arguments

Sometimes the claim an arguer wishes to advance can be established neither by a single argument nor by a chain of arguments moving progressively from an initial body of evidence to a final claim or conclusion. Under these circumstances, a number of independent arguments or chains of arguments may be grouped together into a cluster, or bundle, of proofs, the cumulative effect of which is to support the claim in question.

Let us take as our example here the claim "Come next November's election, the 'ins' should be replaced by the 'outs.'" It would, of course, be possible to ground this claim on a single piece of evidence in the form of a general rule or principle the person addressed is willing to endorse—say, the principle that a change in administrations every four years is a healthy thing for the country. Usually, however, something more specific or concrete in the way of proof is demanded.

To meet this demand, the person advancing the claim might show through a cluster of independent arguments, each supported by its own evidence and warrant, the failure of the incumbent administration on the economic front, in the area of foreign affairs, in the fight against crime and corruption, and the like. In addition he might, if he chose, develop a parallel cluster of arguments to show that the party not presently in office is likely to do a better job in each of these areas.

Within argumentative clusters of this sort, individual arguments or units of proof, instead of growing one out of the other in a chainlike manner, retain their autonomous status. Each, acting as an independent element, contributes a certain measure of credibility to the claim the arguer seeks to establish. Since, however, no one unit of proof is judged sufficient to establish this claim alone and unaided, it is joined with others of a similar or related nature.

The difference between arguments arranged so as to form a chain and arguments grouped together into a cluster of independent proof units may be illustrated as follows:

A Chain of Arguments

Given as *evidence   (M)*
Since *warrant   (N)*
Therefore, *claim   (O)*

Given as *evidence   (O)*
Since *warrant   (P)*
Therefore, *claim   (Q)*

Given as *evidence   (Q)*
Since *warrant   (R)*
Therefore, *claim   (S)*

A Cluster of Arguments

Evidence (M)	*Evidence (P)*	*Evidence (S)*
Warrant (N)	*Warrant (Q)*	*Warrant (T)*
Claim (O)	*Claim (R)*	*Claim (U)*

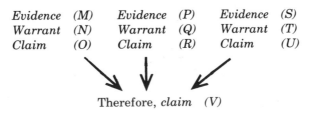

Therefore, *claim   (V)*

Exercises

1. Explain in your own words the roles that evidence and warrant play in substantiating a claim. As part of your explanation, give examples other than those used in this chapter.

2. Given the fact that the barometer is falling rapidly and the knowledge that a rapidly falling barometer is a sign of the approach of a severe storm, compose an argument in the pattern *EWC* to substantiate the claim "We shall have a severe storm." Then recast this argument into each of the following patterns: *CWE, CEW, WEC, ECW, WCE.*

3. Restate the six arguments developed in answer to the preceding question, adding a statement designed to support the warrant step.

4. Under what circumstances should the author of an argument state first the claim he wishes to advance, and under what circumstances should he set forth first the evidence and warrant upon which the claim is based?

5. Make clear the differences between a chain of arguments and a cluster of arguments, and frame a hypothetical example of each.

6. The English philosopher Stephen Toulmin says that when a person is presented with a claim which he disbelieves or doubts, he characteristically asks two questions of the claim's author: (1) "What have you got to go on?" (2) "How do you get there?" To which parts of an argument do these questions refer?

7. Study each of the following excerpts carefully. Keeping in mind the criteria set forth in this chapter and the preceding one, decide first whether the excerpt is an argument or an attempt to influence belief or instigate action by some nonargumentative means.

   Next go back over the excerpts you have judged to be arguments and cast each into the pattern *EWC*. Remember that in some cases not all of the parts of the argument may be explicitly stated, and will, therefore, have to be supplied in order to complete the pattern.

   Do not worry about whether the arguments you are analyzing seem to be sound or unsound, strong or weak. You are asked only to decide which of the following are arguments, and to break those selected down into their respective parts.

   a. The blood pumped out by a man's heart in a single hour is greater than his own weight. Since the heart obviously cannot create this much blood hour after hour, it must follow that the blood circulates through the body and reenters the heart. *Adapted from William Harvey.*

   b. All laws are promulgated for this end: that every man may know his duty; and therefore the plainest and most obvious sense of the words is that which must be put on them. *Sir Thomas More.*

c. Education at Its Best

From kindergarten to doctoral study, Tulsa has it now and has had it all along. Two Tulsa high schools are among only 38 in America to be ranked Superior in National Merit Scholarship competition. Such quality secondary education is why Tulsa's graduating seniors earn more than $1 million in college scholarships annually. It's no small wonder, since more than 40 percent of our teachers have advanced degrees.

Tulsa has two four-year universities and a new state-supported junior college whose curriculum is responsive to the needs of the local business community.

The University of Tulsa, founded in 1894, is one of the 50 major private universities in the nation, and offers bachelor's, master's, and doctoral degrees in almost 100 areas of academic study.

Oral Roberts University, a four-year liberal arts institution, has the most sophisticated visual aids equipment west of the Mississippi.

Tulsa Junior College has university-parallel programs in preprofessional and general education, occupational and technical programs.

In the field of specialized training, Tulsa vocational-technical schools have flexible curriculums keyed to day-to-day needs of the business and industrial community.

In education, Tulsa gives you more than you would expect from a metropolitan city of half a million.

Get the whole story on Tulsa, the city that has it now! Write or call the Metropolitan Tulsa Chamber of Commerce, 616 South Boston Avenue, Tulsa, Oklahoma 74119, (918) 585–1201. *Advertisement in* Fortune *Magazine, 86 (August 1972), 24B.*[2]

d. Parent to child: "You had better be good because Santa Claus is coming soon."

e. No one has ever been able to explain why the Doric temple at Paestum is more beautiful than a glass of cold beer except by bringing in considerations that have nothing to do with beauty. Beauty is a blind alley. It is a mountain peak which once reached leads nowhere. . . . *W. Somerset Maugham.*

f. As to [the] conquest [of the American colonies], my Lords, I repeat it is impossible. You may swell every expense and every effort still more extravagantly; pile and accumulate every assistance you can buy or borrow; traffic and barter with every little pitiful German prince that sells and sends his subjects to the shambles of a foreign war; your efforts are for ever vain and impotent—doubly so from the mercenary aid on which you rely, for it irritates, to an incurable resentment, the minds of your enemies, to over-run them with the mercenary sons of rapine and plunder, devoting them and their possessions to the rapacity of hireling

---

[2]Reprinted with permission of the Metropolitan Tulsa Chamber of Commerce.

cruelty. If I were an American, as I am an Englishman, while a foreign troop was landed in my country, I would never lay down my arms—never—never—never! *Lord Chatham, "Address to the Throne" (1777).*

g. Says "Housewife" Must Be Happy

OKLAHOMA CITY, OKLA. (AP)—A top Agriculture Department official said Friday that retail food prices are not too high, because if they were "the housewife would back out of the marketplace and the cost would go down."

J. Phil Campbell, undersecretary of agriculture, stopped short, however, of advocating that the housewife practice this sort of price control.   Des Moines Register, *February 24, 1973, p. 7.*[3]

h. "If you don't take pocket-handkerchers and watches," said the Dodger, "some other cove will; so that the cove what loses them will be all the worse and you'll be all the worse, too, and nobody half a ha'porth the better, except the chaps what gets 'em—and you've just as good a right to them as they have." *Dickens*, Oliver Twist.

i. The most dramatic evidence of the relationship between educational practices and civil disorder lies in the high incidence of riot participation by ghetto youth who have not completed high school. Our survey of the riot cities found that the typical riot participant was a high school dropout.   Report of the National Advisory Commission on Civil Disorders, *p. 236.*

j. DEAR ABBY:

May I share my happiness with the world? I threw away my girdle about two months ago, and now I am free, free, free! I can't understand how I ever put up with that uncomfortable harness for so many years.

Now I just slip into a pair of pantyhose and I'm ready to go! What a time-saver! It used to take me 20 minutes to struggle into my girdle.

FREE AGAIN

DEAR FREE:
Congratulations. I'd have to see you before sharing your enthusiasm. Any woman who needs 20 minutes to "struggle" into a girdle needs one.
Abigail Van Buren, "Dear Abby" (Chicago Tribune-New York News Syndicate, Inc.), The Miami News, *August 14, 1969, p. 22D.*[4]

k. *Socrates.* I know, Meno, what you mean. . . . You argue that a man cannot enquire either about that which he knows, or about that which he does not know; for if he knows, he has no need to enquire; and if not, he cannot; for he does not know the very subject about which he is to enquire. *Plato, "Meno,"* The Dialogues of Plato.

---

[3]Reprinted with permission of the Associated Press.

[4]Reprinted with permission.

l. The peculiar evil of silencing the expression of an opinion is, that it is robbing the human race: posterity as well as the existing generation: those who dissent from the opinion, still more than those who hold it. If the opinion is right, they are deprived of the opportunity of exchanging error for truth: if wrong, they lose, what is almost as great a benefit, the clearer perception and livelier impression of truth, produced by its collision with error. *John Stuart Mill,* On Liberty.

m. You're Never Too Old to Hear Better!

Des Moines, Ia.—A free offer of special interest to those who hear but do not understand words has been announced by Beltone. A tiny, *non-operating* model of the smallest Beltone all-in-the-ear aid ever made will be given absolutely free to anyone answering this ad.

Try it and see *how it is worn* in the privacy of your own home without cost or obligation of any kind. It's yours to keep free. It weighs less than a third of an ounce, and it's all at ear level in one unit. No wires lead from the body to head.

These models are free, so we suggest you write for yours now. Again, we repeat, it is a *non-operating* model, there is no cost and no obligation. For further information, write or call Beltone Hearing Aid Service, 906 Grand, Des Moines, Iowa 50309. Phone 515-282-0451, or in Carroll, 405 West 7th St., Phone 792-9224.   Des Moines Register, *April 8, 1973.*[5]

n. If you ask me, the Beavers have little chance of winning a pennant this year. Their new manager, Casey Smith, is not enforcing strict rules against gambling among the players. Unless such rules are enforced, they will play for higher and higher stakes as the season progresses. This, in turn, will lead to hard feelings and, instead of pulling together when they are on the field, the losers will try to get even with the winners. This is what happened to the Centerville Eagles.

o. Ambition is like choler; which is an humour that maketh men active, earnest, full of alacrity, and stirring, if it be not stopped. But if it be stopped, and cannot have his way, it becometh adust, and thereby malign and venomous. So ambitious men, if they find the way open for their rising, and still get forward, they are rather busy than dangerous; but if they be checked in their desires, they become secretly discontent, and look upon men and matters with an evil eye, and are best pleased when things go backward; which is the worst property in a servant of a prince or state. Therefore it is good for princes, if they use ambitious men, to handle it so as they be still progressive and not retrograde; which because it cannot be without inconvenience, it is good not to use such natures at all. For if they rise not with their service, they will take order to make their service fall with them. *Francis Bacon, "Of Ambition."*

[5]Reprinted by permission of Beltone Electronics Corporation and Mr. Ronald J. Richer, Richer Hearing Service, Inc.

p. What is the first business of one who practices philosophy? To part with self-conceit. For it is impossible for anyone to learn what he thinks he already knows. *Epictetus.*

q. It is settled, at least so far as this court is concerned, that works of physiology, medicine, science, and sex instruction are not within the [obscenity] statute, though to some extent and among some persons they may tend to promote lustful thoughts. . . . We think the same immunity should apply to literature as to science, where the presentation, when viewed objectively, is sincere, and the erotic matter is not introduced to promote lust and does not furnish the dominant note of the publication. The question in each case is whether a publication taken as a whole has a libidinous effect. The book before us [*Ulysses,* by James Joyce] has such portentous length, is written with such evident truthfulness in its depiction of certain types of humanity, and is so little erotic in its result, that it does not fall within the forbidden class. *Judge Augustin N. Hand in the Majority Opinion of the Circuit Court of Appeals, No. 459, Second Circuit, August 7, 1934. 72 Federal Reporter, 2nd Series, pp. 705–711.*

r. The more you study, the more you learn; the more you learn, the more you forget. So why study?

s. Equal justice to the South, it is said, requires us to consent to the extending of slavery to new countries [the Kansas-Nebraska Territory]. This is to say, inasmuch as you do not object to my taking my hog to Nebraska, therefore, I must not object to your taking your slave. Now, I admit this is perfectly logical, if there is no difference between hogs and Negroes. But while you thus require me to deny the humanity of the Negro, I wish to ask whether you of the South yourselves, have ever been willing to do as much? . . . The great majority, South as well as North, have human sympathies, of which they can no more divest themselves than they can of their sensibility to physical pain. These sympathies in the bosoms of the Southern people, manifest in many ways their sense of the wrong of slavery, and their consciousness that, after all, there is humanity in the Negro. In 1820, you joined the North, almost unanimously, in declaring the African slave trade piracy, and in annexing to it the punishment of death. Why did you do this? If you did not feel that it was wrong, why did you join in providing that men should be hung for it? The practice was no more than bringing wild Negroes from Africa, to sell to such as would buy them. But you never thought of hanging men for catching and selling wild horses, wild buffaloes, or wild bears. *Abraham Lincoln in a speech at Peoria, Illinois, October 16, 1854.*

t. Doubts One Person Killed J.F.K. After Autopsy Study
    PITTSBURGH, PA. (AP)—A forensic pathologist who examined the records and materials of the autopsy performed on President John F.

Kennedy said Saturday that accused assassin Lee Harvey Oswald could not have acted alone.

Dr. Cyril Wecht, Allegheny County coroner, said at a news conference a two-day examination of the autopsy materials at the National Archives in Washington, D.C., convinced him that it was "physically impossible" for only one gunman to have slain Kennedy.

Wecht's findings were in direct contradiction not only with the Warren Report conclusion that a single assassin was responsible for Kennedy's death, but also with a report by Dr. George K. Lattimer, the first private physician to examine the X-rays.

Wecht said: "The fact is that the physical evidence shows that not any one person could have been a shooter. There had to have been at least two people shooting."

Wecht charged that the single-assassin finding of the lengthy Warren Report hinges on the theory that one bullet fired from a single gun wounded President Kennedy in the back seat of his limousine, and also wounded and passed through former Texas Gov. Connally, who was riding in the front seat.

He declined to say how many gunmen he thought were involved.

Wecht, a long-time critic of the Warren Report, said he based his findings on an examination last week of X-rays, photographs, films, bullets and bullet fragments.

Wecht said several "extremely relevant" items—including microscopic slides and Kennedy's brain, which he said was to have been preserved—were not made available to him.

"Looking at the X-rays," he said, "I discovered a dark, brownish, black object inside the brain . . . nobody ever mentioned this previously. Nobody ever described it."

He did not say if he thought the object was a bullet.

Wecht said he will submit to Burke Marshall, executor of the Kennedy estate, a proposal for a full review of the autopsy materials by a team of experts.

Wecht, who is also director of the Institute of Forensic Sciences at Duquesne University, was granted permission by Marshall to study the autopsy materials.   Des Moines Register, *August 27, 1972, p. 4A.*[6]

u. Food prices are not "excessively high" by any reasonable standard of comparison. Food prices have risen less than the general index of living costs since 1967 and far less than the cost of services. Food prices are up 19 percent, services up 32 percent, and all living costs together up 23 percent. . . .

Even with all the extra costs of packaging and processing that now go into the food bill, the American consumer spent only about 16 percent of his income for food in 1971—a *decline* from 20 percent in 1960 and from 17 percent in 1967. The average American spends only about 12.6 percent of his income for food consumed at home.

[6]Reprinted with permission of the Associated Press.

Food "excessively high"? In comparison with what? *From editorial "Ignorance About Food Prices,"* Des Moines Sunday Register, *April 16, 1972, p. 8C.*[7]

v. Political economy begins with the fact of private property; it does not explain it. It conceives the *material* process of private property, as this occurs in reality, in general and abstract formulas which then serve it as laws. It does not *comprehend* these laws; that is, it does not show how they arise out of the nature of private property. Political economy provides no explanation of the basis for the distinction of labour from capital, of capital from land. When, for example, the relation of wages to profits is defined, this is explained in terms of the interests of capitalists; in other words, what should be explained is assumed. Similarly, competition is referred to at every point and is explained in terms of external conditions. Political economy tells us nothing about the extent to which these external and apparently accidental conditions are simply the expression of a necessary development. We have seen how exchange itself seems an accidental fact. The only motive forces which political economy recognizes are *avarice and the war between the avaricious, competition. Karl Marx.*

w. First, we must know that all substances in general—that is to say, all those things which cannot exist without being created by God—are by nature incorruptible and can never cease to be, unless God Himself, by denying them His usual support, reduces them to nothingness. And secondly, we must notice that body, taken in general, is a substance, and that it therefore will never perish. But the human body, however much it may differ from other bodies, is only a composite, produced by a certain configuration of members and by other similar accidents, whereas the human soul is not thus dependent upon any accidents, but is a pure substance. For even if all its accidents change—as, for example, if it conceives of certain things, wills others, and receives sense impressions of still others—nevertheless it still remains the same soul. But the human body becomes a different entity from the mere fact that the shape of some of its parts has been changed. From this it follows that the human body may very easily perish, but that the mind or soul of man, between which I find no distinction, is immortal by its very nature. *Réné Descartes,* Meditations on First Philosophy *(Indianapolis: The Bobbs-Merrill Co., Inc., 1960), pp. 14–15.*[8]

x. If we think to regulate printing, thereby to rectify manners, we must regulate all recreations and pastimes, all that is delightful to man. No music must be heard, no song be set or sung but what is grave and Doric. There must be licensing dancers, that no gesture, motion or deportment be taught our youth but what by their allowance shall be

[7]Reprinted with permission of the *Des Moines Register.*

[8]Reprinted with permission of the publisher.

thought honest. It will ask more than the work of twenty licensers to examine all the lutes, the violins and the guitars in every house; they must not be suffered to prattle as they do, but must be licensed what they may say. And who shall silence all the airs and madrigals that whisper softness in chambers? The windows also and the balconies must be thought on; there are shrewd books, with dangerous frontispieces, set to sale; who shall prohibit them? Shall twenty licensers? The villages must also have their visitors to inquire what lectures the bagpipe and the rebec reads, even to the ballatry and the gamut of every municipal fiddler. . . .

Next, what more national corruption . . . than household gluttony? Who shall be the rectors of our daily rioting? And what shall be done to inhibit the multitudes that frequent those houses where drunkenness is sold and harboured? Our garments also should be referred to the licensing of some sober workmasters, to see them cut into a less wanton garb. . . . Lastly who shall forbid and separate an idle resort, all evil company? These things will be, and must be; but how shall they be least hurtful, how least enticing, herein consists the grave and governing wisdom of a state. *John Milton,* Areopagitica.

y. The reader may possibly have heard of a peculiar theory of the emotions, commonly referred to in psychological literature as the Lange-James theory. According to this theory, our emotions are mainly due to those organic stirrings that are aroused in us in a reflex way by the stimulus of the exciting object or situation. An emotion of fear, for example, or surprise, is not a direct effect of the object's presence on the mind, but an effect of that still earlier effect, the bodily commotion which the object suddenly excites; so that, were this bodily commotion suppressed, we should not so much *feel* fear as call the situation fearful; we should not feel surprise, but coldly recognize that the object was indeed astonishing. One enthusiast has even gone so far as to say that when we feel sorry it is because we weep, when we feel afraid it is because we run away, and not conversely. Some of you may perhaps be acquainted with the paradoxical formula. Now, whatever exaggeration may possibly lurk in this account of our emotions (and I doubt myself whether the exaggeration be very great), it is certain that the main core of it is true, and that the mere giving way to tears, for example, or to the outward expression of an anger-fit, will result for the moment in making the inner grief or anger more acutely felt. There is, accordingly, no better known or more generally useful precept in the moral training of youth, or in one's personal self-discipline, than that which bids us pay primary attention to what we do and express, and not to care too much for what we feel. If we only check a cowardly impulse in time, for example, or if we only *don't* strike the blow or rip out with the complaining or insulting word that we shall regret as long as we live, our feelings themselves will presently be the calmer and better, with no particular guidance from us on their own account. Action seems to follow feeling, but really action and feeling go together; and by regulating the action, which is under the more direct control of the will, we can indirectly regulate the feeling, which is not.

Thus the sovereign voluntary path to cheerfulness, if our spontaneous cheerfulness be lost, is to sit up cheerfully, to look round cheerfully, and to act and speak as if cheerfulness were already there. If such conduct does not make you soon feel cheerful, nothing else on that occasion can. So to feel brave, act as if we *were* brave, use all our will to that end, and a courage-fit will very likely replace the fit of fear. Again, in order to feel kindly toward a person to whom we have been inimical, the only way is more or less deliberately to smile, to make sympathetic inquiries, and to force ourselves to say genial things. One hearty laugh together will bring enemies into a closer communion of heart than hours spent on both sides in inward wrestling with the mental demon of uncharitable feeling. To wrestle with a bad feeling only pins our attention on it, and keeps it still fastened in the mind: whereas, if we act as if from some better feeling, the old bad feeling soon folds its tent like an Arab and silently steals away. *William James, "The Gospel of Relaxation,"* Talks to Teachers on Psychology: and to Students on Some of Life's Ideals *(New York: Holt, Rinehart and Winston, Inc., 1915), pp. 199–200.*

z. John Jocob Astor bought goat farms, empty lots and swampy marshes on an island. The island is Manhattan.

Astor's success with Manhattan land purchases was essentially based on his ability to see a given piece of land, not for what it was, but for what it could be.

Land in the predeveloped stage may still look like a cutover forest, or a sagebrush-covered desert, but in real estate circles it is being referred to as an "impact area." An area just beginning to feel the impact of economic forces that will generate the demand for land.

This partial description of predeveloped land is one of the three stages of land development defined in our new booklet, "What You Should Know Before You Buy Land." It's only 12 pages, but in it you'll find answers to the questions you'll be asking yourself as a prospective landowner. Such as, "Can I afford to buy land?" and "What are my objectives?" Then we go on to describe the various classifications of land and good development practices. And we supply you with a handy "Land Buyer's Checklist" of the questions you should ask and the reports you should read prior to purchasing any land.

The one thing you won't find in our booklet is a commercial for Horizon Corporation or the land we own. Because we're not trying to sell anything with this booklet. Our aim is to make potential land-buyers more knowledgeable about how, when, where and what to buy. It's to your advantage to know all the facts. And, frankly, it's to our advantage too. Because the more you know about land, the more you'll appreciate what Horizon Corporation has to offer.

If you would like one or more copies sent to you, your friends, or civic and business groups, please fill out and mail the coupon. Or, for even faster action, call the phone number listed below. Des Moines Sunday Register, *April 8, 1973, p. 5B.*[9]

---

[9]Reprinted with permission of the Horizon Corporation.

Writing or Speaking Assignment

Report orally or in writing the contents of one or more of the chapters suggested below for additional reading.

Rather than reproducing in detail everything the author says, select what appear to be his leading ideas. Wherever possible, compare or contrast these ideas with the materials presented in this chapter. Take as your purpose supplementing your reader's or listener's understanding of what an argument is and how it works.

Strive particularly to make your discussion clear and easy to understand. To this end, define any technical terms in simple language, relate one idea to another by means of carefully drawn transitions, and supply meaningful examples.

Your effort will be judged on how successfully you communicate the contents of the chapter you report and how interesting your talk or essay is.

For Additional Reading

Beardsley, Monroe. *Practical Logic.* Englewood Cliffs, N.J.: Prentice-Hall, Inc., 1950. Chapter 1, "Sizing Up an Argument."

Castell, Alburey. *A College Logic: An Introduction to the Study of Argument and Proof.* New York: The Macmillan Co., 1935. Chapter 1, "The Nature of Argument"; Chapter 7, "The Nature of Proof."

Ehninger, Douglas, and Wayne Brockriede. *Decision by Debate.* New York: Dodd, Mead & Co., 1963. Chapter 8, "The Unit of Proof and Its Structure."

Olson, Robert G. *Meaning and Argument: Elements of Logic.* New York: Harcourt Brace Jovanovich, Inc., 1969. Chapter 9.

Ruby, Lionel. *The Art of Making Sense.* Philadelphia: J. B. Lippincott Co., 1954. Chapter 8, "Putting Up an Argument."

Toulmin, Stephen. *The Uses of Argument.* London: Cambridge University Press, 1958. Chapter 3, "The Layout of Arguments."

Chapter III.
Claims

In Chapter II we saw that the purpose of an argument is to win assent to a claim. While from an analytical point of view the claim is the third or final step in an argument, in practice it is frequently stated first—the arguer advancing a thesis or assertion he then proceeds to support by facts and reasoning. The claim is also the part of the argument a critic should examine first, for unless he has clearly in mind the scope and nature of the thesis set forth, he cannot reasonably judge the sufficiency of the evidence or the appropriateness of the warrant.

Is the claim tentative or categorical? Does it apply to selected members of a class or make an assertion concerning the class as a whole? Does it affirm or deny the existence of a state of affairs, or does it evaluate that state of affairs or urge a course of action relative to it? Is the claim single or compound, simple or complex? As our study progresses, we will come to recognize that attention to these questions constitutes the first step in the making and criticism of arguments.

Claims as Propositions

The first important fact to note about claims is that they are propositions. This means that, unlike questions or exclamations, they are sentences that make assertions or declarations, that say something about something else.

Questions and exclamations, although they are groups of words that convey meanings, do not assert anything. Hence they are not susceptible of proof, are not something with which a reader or listener can agree or disagree. Propositions, on the other hand, because they do make statements about one or more given items of knowledge, are in theory at least always capable of being supported by proofs of one sort or another. They can be shown to be true or probable or untrue or improbable upon the basis of facts and reasoning. They invite acceptance or rejection.

Terms

Because a claim is a proposition and because a proposition makes an assertion, it always must contain at least two constituent elements: a subject and a verb. "John smokes," "I exist," "Money talks," "Time flies" are propositions because they meet this requirement. More generally, however, a proposition consists of three elements, a subject, a verb, and an object (or predicate adjective or noun). "Might makes right," "Love conquers all," "Gentlemen prefer blondes" are propositions of this second sort.

The subject and object of a three-part proposition are known as its *terms.* A term may, as in the examples given above, consist of a single word. Often, however, it consists of two or more words which combine to produce a single unit of meaning. The italicized words in the following propositions are terms: "*April showers* bring *May flowers.*" "*A college education* is *a good long-term investment.*" "*All persons over forty years of age* should have *an annual medical checkup.*"

A claim is, then, first of all a proposition. It is a statement which, because it asserts something about something else, is in theory always capable of being proved true or false. A proposition must at a minimum contain a subject and a verb. Usually it consists of a subject, a verb, and an object. The subject and object, whether they are made up of one word or several, are the claim's terms.

Types of Claims

The claims advanced in arguments fall, as a rule, into one of four broad categories or types:

1. Assertions that something was/is/will be the case (or not the case).

2. Assertions that something was/is/will be of a certain sort (or not of that sort).

3. Assertions that something was/is/will be good/desirable/praiseworthy (or bad/undesirable/blameworthy).

4. Assertions that something should be done (or should not be done).

These are known respectively as *declarative claims, classificatory claims, evaluative claims,* and *actuative claims.*

If we conceive of a claim as an answer to a question, declarative claims may be said to answer questions of a factual nature; classificatory claims answer questions concerning how a thing should be interpreted or defined; evaluative claims answer questions concerning the worth or value of something; and actuative claims answer questions concerning the course of action that is to be followed. Let us now examine each of these types of claims individually.

Declarative Claims

Declarative claims are so named because in advancing them the author of an argument declares a certain state of affairs to have existed (or not existed) in the past, to exist (or not exist) at present, or as likely (or not likely) to exist in the future.

Past   The sculptured bust recently dug up near Athens was (was not) carved by Praxiteles.

Present There is (is not) life on Venus.

Future   In 1985 one quarter of the citizens of the United States will (will not) be over sixty-five years of age.

Declarative claims are, in principle, verifiable by direct recourse to data. That is, they can be established by observation or experiment or by referring the doubter to an appropriate source of printed information. In practice, however, this mode of verification is not always practical. We cannot, for example, talk directly with Praxiteles or question his contemporaries. We cannot at present visit Venus and make direct observations concerning conditions on that planet. We cannot project ourselves into the future so as to be able to make an actual count of the number of United States citizens who in the year 1985 will be over sixty-five years of age. Deprived of these resources, we must, by marshaling such relevant information as we do possess, reason our way to the best estimate we can make of the degree of credence which these claims deserve.

Naturally, where more direct and reliable means of verification are available, argument as a method of proof need not and should not be resorted to. This still leaves, however, a large number of factual questions which it is important to settle, and which, because of the limitations just noted, must be settled by nonempirical means.

Classificatory Claims

Whereas declarative claims are concerned with what was/is/will be the case, classificatory claims are concerned with how something that is recognized to be the case should be classified or defined, with the genus or category into which it properly falls. Here are some typical examples:

Germany's occupation of Austria in March 1938 was (may be defined or classified as) a clear case of unprovoked aggression.

Alcoholism is (to be defined or classified as) a disease.

If the legislature passes a law denying the right of public employees to bargain collectively, its action will be (classifiable as) unconstitutional.

Evaluative Claims

Evaluative claims are concerned not with whether something was/is/will be the case or with how something that is recognized to be the case should be defined or classified. Instead, they are concerned with the attitude we should adopt toward a given action or state of affairs, with how we should appraise or evaluate it. Consider the following:

The Roundheads acted justly in putting Charles I to death.

For medium-sized cities the council-manager form of government is best.

The consequences stemming from this action will be undesirable from both a personal and a social point of view.

Actuative Claims

Declarative, classificatory, and evaluative claims make assertions about states of affairs known or assumed to exist; actuative claims have as their purpose to bring new states of affairs into existence. They assert that some present policy or procedure should be replaced by a new way of doing or ordering things. Note the recommendation for change embodied in each of the following examples.

The present county property tax should be replaced by a graduated income tax.

The federal government should give unrestricted bloc grants to accredited institutions of higher learning to help defray increased costs of operation.

Designated student representatives should be made full voting members of all standing committees of the college.

The distinction between evaluative and actuative claims is sometimes difficult to grasp. There are, however, two important differences. First, evaluative claims call only for judgment—for mental assent or agreement on the part of the persons toward whom they are directed. Actuative claims, on the other hand, seek more than mental assent. As their name implies, they ask the persons addressed to enter upon a course of action designed to bring about a new or altered order of things. Second, evaluative claims, as we have seen, may invite judgments concerning the past or present as well as the future, concerning what has been or now is as well as what ought to be the case. Actuative claims, by contrast, because they recommend actions which the person advancing the claim wishes to have performed, concern only the future.

The Forms Claims Take

These declarative, classificatory, evaluative, and actuative claims may appear in many forms. Considered in terms of form, claims are simple or complex, unqualified or qualified, unconditional or conditional, universal or restricted, and affirmative or negative.

Simple or Complex

A simple claim makes a single, one-part assertion.

Declarative   Civil disobedience is increasing.

Classificatory   Civil disobedience is willful disobedience of the law
for the purpose of making one's convictions evident.

Evaluative   Civil disobedience is morally wrong.

Actuative   Persons who engage in civil disobedience should be
tried in special courts.

A complex claim asserts more than one thing about the matter in question.

Declarative   Civil disobedience is increasing and becoming more
violent in nature.

Classificatory   Civil disobedience is not only a willful violation of
the law, but also a transgression of the basic constitutional rights of others.

Evaluative   Civil disobedience is wrong morally and religiously.

Actuative   Persons who engage in civil disobedience should be
tried in special courts and denied all right to bail.

Complex declarative and evaluative claims, it should be observed, sometimes take the form of comparative statements.

Declarative   Civil disobedience is increasing more rapidly than
crimes of violence.

Evaluative   Civil disobedience is a worse crime than drug
running.

While in theory classificatory and actuative claims may also be comparative,
in practice this is seldom the case.

Unqualified or Qualified

Unqualified claims make flat, uncircumscribed assertions.

Civil disobedience is increasing.

Civil disobedience is morally wrong.

Qualified claims make tentative or limited assertions, or recognize exceptions to what they declare to be the case.

Civil disobedience is probably increasing.

Civil disobedience is morally wrong, except in those situations in which
public officials turn a deaf ear to all legitimate means of protest.

Unconditional or Conditional

Unconditional claims assert that something is or should be made the case
irrespective of other conditions or developments.

Persons who engage in civil disobedience should be tried in special courts.

Conditional claims state certain conditions under which the judgment or recommendation embodied in the claim is to apply. Often conditional claims are of the actuative type.

If our present courts continue to disregard the rights of persons accused of civil disobedience, such persons should be tried in special courts.

Universal or Restricted

Universal claims make assertions concerning all of the members of a given class.

All persons who commit acts of civil disobedience are (to be classified as) criminals.

Restricted claims make assertions concerning fewer than all of the members of a given class.

Most persons who commit acts of civil disobedience are (to be classified as) criminals.

John's act of civil disobedience makes him (classifiable as) a criminal.

Affirmative or Negative

Affirmative claims state what the person advancing the claim believes (or presumably believes) to be the case, or what he thinks (or presumably thinks) should be made the case.

Persons who commit acts of civil disobedience are criminals.

Persons who commit acts of civil disobedience should be tried in special courts.

Negative claims state what the person advancing the claim does not believe (or presumably does not believe) to be the case, or what he does not wish (or presumably does not wish) to be made the case.

Persons who commit acts of civil disobedience are not criminals.

Persons who commit acts of civil disobedience should not be tried in special courts.

Combined Forms

Obviously, in many cases a claim exhibits two or more of the forms just described. It may be both conditional and qualified, universal and negative, simple and restricted, etc. Always, however, regardless of the category into which it falls or the form in which it appears, a claim retains its basic nature as a statement which, because it asserts that something is or should be made the case, is capable of being supported by evidence and reasoning, and hence of being proved true or false.

Exercises

1. Distinguish in your own words between sentences and propositions. Are all propositions claims? Explain your answer.

2. Underline the terms in the following claims:

Good students study long and hard.

A brisk walk on a frosty morning is the very best form of exercise.

If you are interested in good government, you would do well to vote for Jones.

People who adhere to established practices and values are conservatives.

Getting one's work done quickly is not always the same as doing it well.

3. Which of the following sentences are claims and which are not? Defend your answers.

According to this morning's paper, federal expenditures for welfare have nearly doubled in the past five years.

A penny saved is a penny earned.

Come here at once!

Am I my brother's keeper?

What a beautiful morning!

John loves Mary.

Empirical knowledge is knowledge derived through the senses.

Helen ought to know better than to contradict her father.

George is captain of the soccer team.

Congress should always support the foreign policy decisions of the President.

If elected, I will serve the people of this district faithfully.

The more, the merrier!

All peaceful lay the sparkling sea.

4. Classify each of the following claims as (a) declarative, classificatory, evaluative, or actuative; (b) simple or complex; (c) qualified or unqualified; (d) universal or restricted; (e) affirmative or negative.

Simple pleasures probably bring more joy to more people than do the most expensive entertainments and pastimes.

Unless John has accumulated at least thirty hours of credit, he is not a sophomore.

Some forms of mental illness are, as a rule, not as serious as is generally believed.

Only the brave deserve the fair.

If you want to feel better, stop smoking and get more exercise.

Whales are mammals.

It will very likely rain tomorrow.

Economics is not, strictly speaking, a social science.

Love conquers all.

Iron bars do not a prison make.

Some professional football players smoke pot.

Students ought to respect their teachers even though they disagree with them.

5. Explain the conditions under which declarative claims become subjects for arguments, and give several examples of declarative claims which meet these conditions.

6. Restate each of the following claims affirmatively without changing its essential meaning:
   Carol is not a good bridge player.
   Parking violations are not felonies.
   The proof of the pudding is not always in the eating.
   You should not sign documents that you have not read carefully.
   Thomas is not taller than Henry.
   That is not the best way to do a job of this sort.
   As a rule, men do not live as long as women.
   A person should never believe all that he is told.
   It is not true that enlisted men in the armed services do not have to salute officers.
   A robust appearance is not a sign that a person is in good health.

7. Convert the following conditional (i.e., qualified) claims into declarative form:
   If a metal is heated, it will expand.
   I'll get there in time, provided I drive all night.
   Williams will start at quarterback on Saturday unless Brown's leg heals rapidly.
   Depending on his sales record, Smith will be promoted at the end of the year.
   If the rain starts before seven it will quit before eleven.
   If you want my vote, you must promise to cut taxes.
   If the market rises, sell; if it falls, buy.

8. Can all conditional claims be converted to declarative claims without altering their essential meaning? Give examples to support your answer.

9. Restate each of the following as a claim having a subject and predicate:
Fire!	Right on!
It snows.	What a beautiful flower!
Drop dead!	Me, guilty?
Drive carefully.	Halt!

10. Why do questions and exclamations not constitute claims? Are definitions claims? Why or why not?

11. Find the claim in each of the following arguments and label it as to type (simple declarative, qualified, evaluative, etc.).

   a. Because the older and more experienced members of the faculty have a better understanding of the aims of education and a clearer grasp of student needs than do the younger faculty members, they probably should be given the dominant voice in planning the curriculum and setting degree requirements. Not to recognize the value of long experience would be like refusing to buy a product of proven worth and selecting one that has just come on the market.

b. The great masses' receptive ability is only very limited, their understanding is small, but their forgetfulness is great. As a consequence of these facts, all effective propaganda has to limit itself only to a very few points and use them like slogans until even the very last man is able to imagine what is intended by such a word. *Adolf Hitler,* Mein Kampf.

c. It may seem strange to some man, that has not well weighed these things, that Nature should thus dissociate, and render man apt to invade, and destroy one another; and he may therefore, not trusting to this Inference made from the Passions, desire perhaps to have the same confirmed by Experience. Let him therefore consider with himselfe, when taking a journey, he armes himselfe, and seeks to go well accompanied; when going to sleep, he locks his dores; when even in his house he locks his chests; and this when he knows there bee Lawes, and publike Officers, armed, to revenge all injuries [that] shall bee done him; what opinion he has of his fellow subjects, when he rides armed; of his fellow Citizens, when he locks his dores; and of his children, and servants, when he locks his chests. Does he not there as much accuse mankind by his actions, as I do by my words? *Thomas Hobbes,* Leviathan.

d. A man who employs rhetoric to induce consent [on philosophical issues] and pretends to be defending his conclusions by philosophical reasoning is either a rogue or a fool. He is a fool if he believes his words have philosophical value, and he is a rogue if, knowing his methods are irrelevant to rational inquiry, he parades his silvery words in the role of serious argument. *James W. Cornman and Keith Lehrer,* Philosophical Problems and Arguments: An Introduction, *pp. 36–37.*

e. Bankruptcy is defined as the state of being at the end of one's resources. What are the intellectual values or resources offered to us by the present guardians of our culture? In philosophy, we are taught that man's mind is impotent, that reality is unknowable, that knowledge is an illusion, and reason a superstition. In psychology, we are told that man is a helpless automaton, determined by forces beyond his control, motivated by innate depravity. In literature, we are shown a line-up of murderers, dipsomaniacs, drug addicts, neurotics, and psychotics as representatives of man's soul. . . . In politics, we are told that America, the greatest, noblest, freest country on earth, is politically and morally inferior to Soviet Russia, the bloodiest dictatorship in history. . . . If we look at modern intellectuals, we are confronted with the grotesque spectacle of such characteristics as militant uncertainty, crusading cynicism, dogmatic agnosticism, boastful self-abasement and self-righteous depravity—in an atmosphere of guilt, of panic, of despair, of boredom and of all-pervasive evasion. If this is not the state of being at the end of one's resources, there is no further place to go. *Ayn Rand,* For the New Intellectual, *p. 4.*

12. It is sometimes difficult to decide whether a given claim is evaluative or actuative. List some simple tests which may be applied to a claim to determine into which category it properly falls.

13. Find in newspapers, magazines, textbooks, or other likely sources arguments containing at least three of the types of claims discussed in this chapter.

For Additional Reading

Cicero. *Topica.* Trans. H. M. Hubbell. Cambridge, Mass.: Harvard University Press (Loeb Classical Library), 1949. Pp. 443–47.

Cohen, Morris R., and **Ernest Nagel.** *An Introduction to Logic and Scientific Method.* New York: Harcourt Brace Jovanovich, Inc., 1934. Chapter 2, "The Analysis of Propositions."

Ehninger, Douglas, and **Wayne Brockriede.** *Decision by Debate.* New York: Dodd, Mead & Co., 1963. Chapter 14, "Analyzing the Proposition."

Evans, D. Luther, and **Walter S. Gamertsfelder.** *Logic: Theoretical and Applied.* Garden City, N.Y.: Doubleday & Co., Inc., 1937. Chapter 6, "The Logical Structure of Propositions"; Chapter 7, "The Interpretation of Propositions and the Process of Immediate Inference."

Kruger, Arthur N. *Modern Debate.* New York: McGraw-Hill Book Co., 1960. Chapter 2, "The Debate Proposition."

Leonard, Henry S. *Principles of Right Reason.* New York: Holt, Rinehart & Winston, Inc., 1957. Unit 16, "Statements and Propositions."

Mills, Glenn. *Reason in Controversy: An Introduction to General Argumentation.* Boston: Allyn & Bacon, Inc., 1964. Chapter 3, "The Basis of Controversy."

Terris, Walter F. "The Classification of the Argumentative Proposition." *Quarterly Journal of Speech,* 49 (October 1963), 266–73.

Wagner, Russell. *Handbook of Argumentation.* New York: The Ronald Press Co., 1936. Pp. 12–16.

Chapter IV.
Definition

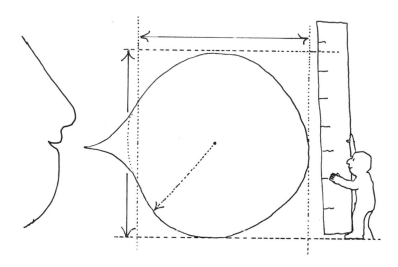

In the preceding chapter it was pointed out that the linguistic units comprising the subject and object (or predicate adjective or noun) of a three-part claim are known as its *terms.*

Sometimes the meaning of these terms is self-evident. At other times, however, their meaning is, for one reason or another, obscure or elusive. Suppose, for example, that the claim in question reads, "In a good society equality of educational opportunity is paramount." Immediately a host of questions arise. What does the person advancing the claim mean by a "good society"? Is it simply a society that is peaceful and prosperous, or also one in which justice prevails and the arts and sciences flourish? Is it a society in which every person has an assigned status to which he is by law confined, or one in which he may through his own efforts rise to the highest positions of power and influence? And how are we to interpret the words "equality of educational opportunity"? Do they mean that the colleges as well as the elementary and secondary schools are open to all, irrespective of educational background and demonstrated ability? Is a system of free, publicly supported higher education implied? And finally, what of the term "paramount," which in its strict signification means "highest in rank or jurisdiction; preeminent, supreme"?[1] Does the person advancing the claim really mean that providing equal educational opportunity is the most important of all of the responsibilities resting upon the state? That it should take precedence over such matters as national defense, economic stability, and the control of crime?

---

[1] *Webster's New Collegiate Dictionary* (Springfield, Mass.: G. & C. Merriam Co., 1949).

As this example suggests, one of the principal obligations resting on the author of a claim that is in any way obscure or indefinite is to make clear to the reader or listener exactly what he means by the terms he employs. By the same token, when a reader or listener acting in the role of critic encounters a claim of this sort, one of his first tasks should be to determine how the vague or confused terms are to be understood. Until this is done, not only will the precise sense or intent of the claim remain in question, but it will be impossible to judge with any degree of accuracy the appropriateness of the evidence and reasoning offered in its support.

What sorts of terms tend to be obscure, and hence to require definitions? What are some of the ways in which the meanings of obscure terms may be clarified? What standards or criteria should a satisfactory definition meet? Let us consider these questions in order.

Terms Requiring Definition

Four sorts of terms tend to be obscure or elusive, and hence to require definition.

Vague Terms

Vague terms denote areas or ranges of meaning that lack precise boundaries. As a result, it is difficult to determine what they include or exclude, and each person is free to interpret them in the light of his own preferences and prejudices.

Let us, for example, suppose that a candidate for public office announces as a major plank in his platform the securing of *social justice* for all. The rich man, when he hears this phrase, may understand by it the right to retain the gains of his labors free of a confiscatory level of taxation. To the poor man, on the other hand, it may mean the guarantee of a minimum standard of living for himself and his family. For members of minority races, *social justice* will imply full equality in all areas of education and employment. Schoolteachers and other public employees will interpret it as including the right to bargain collectively for better wages and working conditions. Because the meaning of the term is not clearly delimited, all of these readings, as well as countless others, are possible.

Equivocal Terms

Equivocal terms, unlike vague ones, have precise enough boundaries. The problem is that their boundaries are drawn so as to include two or more quite different meanings.

A classic instance of an equivocal term is the word *fast.* We speak of a *fast* horse, a *fast* woman, of going on a *fast,* making a boat *fast* at the dock, etc., in each case using the word in a distinctly different sense.

Fortunately, so far as the word *fast* is concerned, the intended meaning is in each case made reasonably clear by the context. This, however, is not always the case. To the English visitor in America for whom the word *subway* means *underpass* and not *underground train,* the direction "Ride the subway as far as the next stop" may be bewildering rather than helpful.

Similarly, if someone says of a poem, "It has no *meaning* for me," we are unsure whether he fails to grasp the author's ideas cognitively or whether the poem leaves him unmoved emotionally.

Many words commonly used in claims are both vague and equivocal. A case in point is *democracy*. *Democracy* is equivocal because it sometimes denotes any form of government in which public officials are selected by means of the elective process, while at other times it is used in a more restricted sense to refer only to a government in which all citizens participate directly in the making of laws and decisions. *Democracy,* however, is also vague, since when it is used in the first of the senses mentioned above, it leaves unspecified precisely how general the franchise must be or what form it must take if the term is to be applicable. If, because of property qualifications or other restrictions, only 5 percent of the citizens in a country are allowed to vote, we would hardly call the government of that country democratic. On the other hand, total or universal suffrage, regardless of age, length of residence in a given voting district, and the like, clearly is not an essential requirement. At what point, then, will the necessary condition be met? When 70 percent of all citizens have the franchise? When that number is increased to 85 or 90 percent? It is like the old question of how many hairs make a beard or what height a man must attain before he is to be considered tall.

New and Coined Terms

New terms are words and expressions that have only recently come into the language, and have yet, therefore, to gain wide currency. Many of the terms connected with space travel—*command module, lunar buggy, reentry belt,* etc.—fall into this category.

Coined terms are words or phrases invented by a speaker or writer in order to convey an idea for which he can find no existing label. Under this head also fall the many terms used by private and public agencies to describe developments of current interest. *Nixonomics, agribusiness, Phase IV,* and *SALT Talks* are examples common at this writing.

Technical Terms

Technical terms are terms given a restricted or specialized meaning by persons working in a given field or following a given line of endeavor. The logician, for instance, designates as *particular* any proposition that does not make an assertion about all of the members of a class, even though the assertion may cover hundreds or thousands of items. When the printer says *widows* are to be avoided, he is referring not to women whose husbands are deceased, but to short lines of type at the beginning of a new page. Clearly, if terms which thus have a limited or specialized meaning are allowed to go undefined, a reader or listener will become confused or will mistakenly assume that they carry their usual significance.

Kinds of Definitions

Two different kinds of definitions are commonly employed by the authors of arguments to clarify the meaning of obscure or indefinite terms.

Reportive Definitions

As their name implies, reportive definitions report the conventional meaning of a term. They tell how that term customarily is used, what people in general understand it to signify. The definitions found in a dictionary are reportive; that is, they describe what a given term is characteristically taken to mean, rather than prescribe what it should or must mean.

Stipulative Definitions

Stipulative definitions announce a speaker's or writer's intention to use a term in a certain way, to give it a particular range or focus of meaning. Thus, defining stipulatively, one might say, "For purposes of this discussion, I mean by 'good student' any undergraduate whose cumulative GPA is 3.0 or higher."

Because stipulative definitions are announcements or declarations concerning the meaning that will arbitrarily be assigned to a term, they can in no sense be regarded as true or false, but are always to be judged solely in terms of their effectiveness in communicating a clear idea of the phenomenon in question. Reportive definitions, on the other hand, may be regarded as true or false depending on whether or not they accurately report what a given term is generally understood to mean. Because they possess this property of truth or falseness, reportive definitions sometimes are viewed as constituting a special class of propositions known as *definitional propositions.*

Methods of Definition

From a strictly logical point of view, the preferred sort of definition consists of a declarative sentence—a sentence that names that property or quality which distinguishes the item being defined from all the other members of its class, and which, therefore, makes it stand forth as a unique aspect of the world.

Since what ultimately distinguishes a triangle from such other plane-closed figures as the square or parallelogram is the fact that it has three and only three sides, three-sidedness is taken to be the defining characteristic of this sort of figure, and, therefore, to furnish the predicate noun by which the definitional statement is completed ("A triangle is a closed plane surrounded by three straight lines"). Similarly, if it is decided that what, in the final analysis, distinguishes man from all other animals is his ability to reason abstractly, a definition based on this essential or defining characteristic would read, "Man is the animal who reasons abstractly."

But while in theory definitions framed on the unique-property principle possess a high degree of precision and stability, they are often difficult to formulate and are not always the best way to clarify the meaning of a term.

There are at least two reasons why this is so. First, when the object or concept being defined has many properties, it is not always clear which of these is, in fact, the crucial one. Why, for example, should we declare that man differs from all other creatures by virtue of his ability to engage in abstract thought, rather than by his ability to learn a foreign language or to write a novel or poem? At bottom, is not such a decision always a matter of subjective choice or judgment? Does it not depend on how the person framing the definition views the matter? And if this is so, are we not merely expressing a personal preference?

Second, as has already been noted, many of the terms that require definition do so because they lack precise boundaries. What, if we use this method of definition, are we to select as the defining characteristic of mental illness? Since such illness takes many forms, some of which are mild and temporary while others are severe and prolonged, we would need to select a trait not only common to a wide range of species, but also capable of discriminating mentally ill persons from those who are for the moment depressed or distraught.

Third, definitions based on an essential or crucial characteristic are difficult to frame because in some instances no single element can be pointed to as absolutely essential to a thing's being; no characteristic can be found which the phenomenon being defined could not do without and yet merit the label assigned to it. Most humans walk, talk, reason abstractly, and stand erect. Yet if we encountered a person who could do none of these things, we would still be apt to refer to him as a human—a crippled or abnormal human, perhaps, but a human nonetheless.

Finally, even if we do succeed in framing a sound definition based on the essential characteristic of the object or concept in question, the result may be of little use in conveying to other persons what is important for them to know about it. A definition of gold stated in terms of its atomic weight may, for example, name the defining characteristic by which that substance differs from all others. Yet for most persons this knowledge is not nearly so useful as an understanding of what gold looks like, what it is used for, or what its current value is in the international money markets.

Because formal or logical definitions of the sort just described are difficult to frame and often of limited usefulness, the authors of arguments frequently employ other methods to clarify the meanings of terms. As a rule, these alternative methods lack the precision and compulsiveness of definitions based on an essential quality. They may, however, be much more effective in communicating to others the sense a term generally carries, or in explaining how in the case at hand it is being employed.

Of these nonformal or logically imperfect methods of definition, the following are, perhaps, most commonly used in argumentative discourse.

Behavioral Definitions

The meaning of a theoretical concept or of a phenomenon that cannot be experienced directly may sometimes be clarified by describing the sort of observable behavior that is associated with it. *Intelligence,* for example, may be defined in terms of a certain level of performance on standard intelligence tests, or the meaning of *obstreperous* may be made clear by recounting some of the ways in which an obstreperous person acts.

Definition by Analysis

Definition by analysis is an attempt to clarify the meaning of a term by naming the subclasses into which it may be divided. "A *definition,*" one might say, "is either a report of what a term is generally understood to mean or an announcement of the meaning assigned to the term by the person using it." Or the meaning of *social science* might be conveyed by saying, "When one studies a *social science*, one studies either history, sociology, anthropology, political science, or economics."

Definition by analysis obviously bears a close resemblance to the logically preferred type of definition described earlier. Here, however, the predicate noun, instead of naming a single crucial or defining characteristic of the subject, merely lists the various sorts of things to which the subject term may be applied.

Definition by Example

Definition by example consists of pointing out or naming a concrete instance of the term being defined. "That [pointing to the object] is a hackberry tree," or "The tree near the Jones' front door is a hackberry."

When the meaning of the term to be clarified is obscure or the difference between it and another term is slight, a number of instances may be mentioned. For example, "A good idea of what I mean by English Gothic architecture may be gained by driving past the Methodist, Baptist, and Episcopal churches on Front Street."

Contextual Definitions

Under some circumstances the most efficient way to clarify the meaning of a term is to use it in a phrase or sentence. This is especially the case when dealing with a foreign or relational expression, or when trying to suggest the emotional tone a word carries. Consider these examples.

The repulsive *stench* of the garbage filled his nostrils.

By standing on his toes, the *taller* of the two men was able to grasp a branch that was beyond the reach of the other.

Take off your old dress and *change* into your new one before going to school.

Thanks to the excellent *esprit de corps,* each of the members considered only the welfare of the group as a whole.

Operational Definitions

Operational definitions seek to clarify the meaning of a term by citing the results that will follow from carrying out a given operation or series of operations. Like contextual definitions, definitions by operation are particularly useful in making clear the meaning of relational terms.

If you rub two stones together, the *harder* of the two will scratch the *softer.*

If Surface B reflects less light than Surface A, then it is *darker* than A.

If you take the total amount of income derived from an investment and deduct the amount paid in taxes and brokerage fees, the resulting figure will be the *net income* the investment yields.

Definition by Negation

Definition by negation proceeds by pointing out what a term does *not* denote or imply. Some words can, as a practical matter, only be defined negatively. An *orphan* is a child who does *not* have parents. *Homeless* means to have *no* home. An insolvent is someone who is *not* able to meet his financial obligations. In other cases definition by negation is employed not out of necessity, but because it is judged to be the best way to explain a term.

By *open classroom,* I do not mean a situation in which each child is allowed to do exactly as he pleases.

Socialists, who believe in the public ownership of basic industries, are not to be confused with communists, who believe in the common ownership of all property.

Although it may, and indeed sometimes does, stand alone, definition by negation is more commonly combined with one or more of the other methods here described. Under these circumstances, it normally constitutes the first or opening phrase of the defining process.

A *good teacher* is not one whose lectures are uniformly entertaining, but one who presents sound and pertinent materials in an objective and organized manner.

Definition by Synonym

A new or unfamiliar term may frequently be clarified by mentioning one or more synonymous terms with which the reader or listener is already familiar.

To be *candid* means to be honest, frank, straightforward.

When this method is used, however, care must be taken to select synonyms which preserve the connotative, or emotional, meaning of the original term, as well as its denotative significance. Thus if, without offering additional explanation or qualification, one were to choose *jalopy* as a synonym for *automobile,* or *booze* as a synonym for *spiritous liquor,* one would be placing quite different emotive meanings on terms that share a common denotative base.

Definition by Etymology

Closely related to definition by synonym is definition by etymology. When defining etymologically, however, instead of mentioning another term which carries essentially the same meaning as the term being defined, we explain the historical roots from which the term in question is derived. The word *anthropology,* for example, comes from the Greek words *anthropo,* a combining form meaning *human being* or *man,* and *logy,* another combining form meaning *science of.* Thus we have anthropology, the science of man. Another well-known word which might be defined etymologically is *republic,* derived from the Latin *res* meaning *thing* and *publicus* meaning *public* or *people,* so that a republic is in literal terms a thing of the people. Yet another word is *convert,* which comes from the Latin *con* meaning *toward* and *vertere* meaning *turn,* so that to convert someone is to turn him to your way of thinking.

Not all terms can profitably be defined by etymology, and usually the method works best when a reader or listener is acquainted with the language from which the term is derived. However, when this condition is met—and especially when the term to be defined is polysyllabic—definition by etymology may be especially helpful.

Definition by Function

When the term to be defined denotes an object or instrument that performs a function, its meaning may often be best clarified by telling what that function is. Thus one might say, "An *actuarial table* is a statistical compilation used by insurance companies to estimate life expectancy," or, "A *barometer* is an instrument which helps us predict the weather by recording changes in atmospheric pressure."

Definition by Authority

When the meaning of a term is uncertain or in dispute, it is sometimes helpful to cite the definition advanced by a reputable authority. "As explained by Professor Henry Smith, chairman of our economics department, *cost pull inflation* is a situation in which prices are being forced upward by the increasing cost of labor and raw materials."

Rules for Definition

Stated broadly, a good definition is one that enables a reader or listener to grasp quickly and accurately the meaning of the term being defined. If, however, a definition is to achieve this purpose, a number of more specific rules need to be observed.

1. *A definition must be framed so as to include all of the items that properly fall under the term being defined.* To define a *motor vehicle* as "a gasoline-powered contrivance designed to transport people from place to place" would be defective both because it fails to include trucks as motor vehicles that carry freight rather than people and also because some motor vehicles use diesel fuel or electricity as a source of power. Similarly, pointing to a dress or shirt would not accurately convey the meaning of *clothing* because it would leave unrecognized the many other sorts of garments this term comprehends.

2. *A definition must be framed so as to exclude all items that do not properly fall under the term being defined.* Because four-footed mammals other than dogs are known to howl at night, one could not properly define a *dog* as "a four-footed, night-howling mammal." Nor could one say that a *microscope* is "an instrument used to enlarge small objects," since this statement would not draw a proper distinction between a microscope and a magnifying glass.

3. *A definition should be adapted to the purpose for which it is intended.* When writing an examination in zoology, it is appropriate to define a *cat* as "a mammal of the genus Felis libyca domestica." Such a definition would,

however, be of little use in telling a person who knew nothing about cats how to recognize that animal if he saw one, or what sort of behavior to expect from it. Or suppose one defined *strychnine* in terms of its chemical composition ($C_{21}H_{22}N_2O_2$). While technically this definition would meet the tests of inclusion and exclusion just described, it would be of little use in making clear to the average individual what he needs to know about the substance. For this purpose it would be more appropriate to define *strychnine* as "a poisonous liquid which, if consumed in more than minute quantities, will cause death."

4. *A definition should not be circular.* Neither the term being defined nor any word derived from that term should be included in the definition. To define *manly* as "acting like a man" or *objectivity* as "the quality of looking at things objectively" does little to clarify the meaning of the words in question. To define the *sun* as "the star that shines by day" would also be circular because *day* itself is defined in terms of the shining of the sun. For the same reason it would be improper to define *health* by saying, "Since disease is the absence of health, *health* may be defined as the absence of disease."

5. *A definition should be expressed in words that are clearer and more readily understood than the term being defined.* To define a *post hoc fallacy* as "a special form of nonsequitur," or an *enthymeme* as "a truncated syllogism," would in both cases be technically correct. Persons inexpert in the fields of logic and rhetoric, however, would find the definitions as unclear and mysterious as the terms being defined. Nor does the average individual find much help in Samuel Johnson's famous definition of a *net* as "a reticulated fabric decussated at regular intervals, with interstices at the intersections."

So far as argument is concerned, figurative or "pictorial" language is also to be avoided when framing definitions. To speak of *Gothic architecture* as "frozen music," or the *heart* as "the motor that keeps the machinery of the body running," may be acceptable in poetry, but it furnishes an insecure basis for reasoning and proof.

6. *A definition should be free of loaded or question-begging language.* A definition of a *liberal* is "a muddleheaded idealist who rejects time-honored values for the sake of remedying temporary social ills" tells more about the prejudices of the person offering the definition than it does about the meaning of the term *liberal.* And when the English logician Richard Whately defined *woman* as "that irrational creature who stirs the fire from the top," he obviously was expressing an attitude rather than attempting an objective description.

Exercises

1. Which items in the following list are definitions and which are merely statements of belief or opinion? Defend your choices.

   Religion is the opiate of the masses.

   Anger is when you get red in the face and shout at a person.

Brevity is the soul of wit.
An optimist is not a realist.
Bread is the staff of life.
Carrots are yellow vegetables.
Beauty is truth; truth, beauty.
Man is the symbol-using animal.
Poverty is the absence of wealth.
A child is an immature adult.
To err is human; to forgive, divine.
A circle is a round line.
Based on your analysis of the foregoing, what do you conclude about the relationship between a definition and a statement of belief or opinion?

2. Refer back to those statements which you decided were definitions. In each case tell (1) what method was used in developing the definition, and (2) whether the criteria of a good definition were met.

3. Distinguish between a stipulative and a reportive definition, and give several examples of each.

4. Spend some time getting acquainted with the following reference books:
Oxford English Dictionary (OED)
Dictionary of American English (DAE)
Webster's Third New International Dictionary
Funk and Wagnalls New Standard Dictionary
American College Dictionary
Cobb's English Synonyms
Roget's International Thesaurus
An Etymological Dictionary of the English Language
   How do these books differ in scope and purpose? What are the strong points and limitations of each? Under what conditions might a student or critic of argument need to refer to each? (In answering these questions, consult the introductory matter supplied by the books' editors.)

5. Look up the meanings of the following words in the *Oxford English Dictionary* and either *Webster's Third New International* or *Funk and Wagnalls New Standard Dictionary.*

premise	enthymeme	belief	claim	refutation
inference	fallacy	persuasion	sorites	rebuttal
syllogism	argument	induction	evidence	deduction

6. Define at least three of the terms in List A and three in List B using one of the methods of definition discussed in this chapter. Then define the same terms again using another method of definition.

List A	*List B*
democracy	neoclassicism
balance of payments	phenomenology
bull market	impressionism
regressive tax	ode
censorship	literature
appellate jurisdiction	new music

7. Criticize the following definitions:

Antimetabolites are such substances as alphatocopheral quinone and pantoyltaurine which attack amino acids and vitamins. *Daniel S. Robinson,* Principles of Reasoning, *p. 71.*

Communism is that form of government which believes in the viability of a communistically organized social structure.

Money is the compensation we receive for the work we do.

The wolf is not a member of the cat family.

Acid is a substance that turns litmus paper red.

Life is a puppet show in which unseen forces pull the strings.

8. React critically to each of the following statements:

Any definition that consists of other words is simply circular, and therefore tells us nothing.

Words such as *sweet, beautiful, yellow,* etc., cannot be defined by other words.

You say a good definition must be intelligible to the receiver? In that case the definitions used in higher algebra are terrible—because I can't understand them. *Max Black,* Critical Thinking: An Introduction to Logic and Scientific Method *(2nd. ed.), p. 227.*

9. Name the method or methods of definition employed in each of the following passages.

a. There are three kinds of wrongdoing: *premeditated wrongdoing,* or the calculated harming of another; *impulsive wrongdoing,* or a harm committed on the spur of the moment; and *accidental wrongdoing,* or a harm done unintentionally.

b. According to the most correct use of the term, a "Presumption" in favour of any supposition, means, not (as has been sometimes erroneously imagined) a preponderance of probability in its favour, but, such a *pre-occupation* of the ground, as implies that it must stand good till some sufficient reason is adduced against it; in short, that the *Burden of proof* lies on the side of him who would dispute it. *Richard Whately,* Elements of Rhetoric, *i.iii.2.*

c. . . . the true use of the celebrated precept "to do as we would be done by," is often overlooked; and it is spoken of as if it were a rule designed to supersede all other moral maxims, and to teach us the intrinsic character of Right and Wrong. This absurd mistake may be one cause why the precept is so much more talked of than attempted to be applied. . . . The true meaning of the precept plainly is, that you should do to another not necessarily what you would *wish,* but what you would expect as *fair and reasonable,* if you were in his place. *Richard Whately,* Elements of Rhetoric, *i.iii.3.*

d. Liberal education means two things essentially. On the side of the liberal arts, it means all the basic skills of the mind—the skills of reading and writing and speaking and listening, observing, measuring, and calculating; skills essential to all forms of learning; the skills required for all forms of communication. And on the side of substance, liberal education means the humanities, which centuries ago would have been called "humane letters." By that, one does not just mean poetry or history, but even more philosophy and theology, and even the natural and social sciences when these are studied with a humane rather than a mere technical interest. *From an address by Mortimer Adler, reprinted in* Town and Gown, *January 1963.*[2]

e. There are two kinds of theories—general and special.

A general theory is a proposition which, if true, is universally true. It covers all things or all events—all, always, everywhere—of the class referred to. A generalization is a simple type of general theory. An explanation also is "general" if it applies to all things, or all events, of the sort that are being explained. . . .

A special theory refers to one particular set or selection of facts. It is an attempt to explain them in their relations to one another. The theory must fit all the "known" facts to which it refers; but it reveals also the identity of some other fact or facts, hitherto unknown. *A. E. Mander,* Logic for the Millions, *pp. 138–139.*

f. "Anomie" literally means normlessness. The term can be and has been applied to the state of mind of individuals regardless of the state of society. . . . We shall use the term, however, to refer solely to a certain condition in a social system, large or small. Quite adequate and less recondite terms already exist to refer to the personality states for which the term "anomie" has been used. Anomie, then, is a condition in which many persons in a social system have a weakened respect for some social norm or norms, and this loss of legitimacy is traceable in part to something about the social structure itself. *Harry M. Johnson,* Sociology: A Systematic Introduction, *p. 557.*

g. "Pure experience" is the name which I gave to the immediate flux of life which furnishes the material to our later reflection with its conceptual categories. Only new-born babes, or men in semi-coma from sleep, drugs, illnesses, or blows, may be assumed to have an experience pure in the literal sense of a *that* which is not yet any definite *what,* tho' ready to be all sorts of whats; full both of oneness and of manyness, but in respects that don't appear; changing throughout, yet so confusedly that its phases interpenetrate and no points, either of distinction or of identity, can be caught. Pure experience in this state is but another name for feeling or sensation. But the flux of it no sooner comes than it tends to fill itself with emphases, and these salient parts become identified and fixed and abstracted; so that experience now flows as if shot through with adjectives and nouns and prepositions and conjunctions. Its purity is only a relative term, meaning the proportional

[2]Reprinted by permission from an address by Mortimer Adler to the University of Portland on the occasion of the inauguration of its fifteenth president, the Rev. Paul E. Waldschmidt, January 13, 1963.

amount of unverbalized sensation which it still embodies. *William James, "The Thing and Its Relations,"* The Journal of Philosophy, Psychology, and Scientific Method, *II (January 19, 1905).*

h. That which it is good to be rid of is evil; and that which it is evil to be rid of is good. *Francis Bacon,* Colours of Good and Evil.

Writing or Speaking Assignment

Prepare a short speech or essay designed to clarify the meaning of some term that is not widely or correctly understood. Begin by stating the term to be clarified, and if necessary show why an understanding of it is important to the reader or listener. Then clarify the term by using at least two of the methods of definition described in this chapter—more if possible. Close with a summarizing sentence that states in a concise way the meaning of the term in question.

Suggested Subjects

Wishbone T	No-fault insurance
Theatre of the Absurd	Marxism
Open classroom	Suicide squeeze
Closed shop	Baroque
Neoclassicism	Existentialism

Before delivering your speech or turning in your essay, test it by asking the following questions:

1. Have I dealt with a term that is of interest or importance to my readers or listeners?
2. Are the methods of definition I have used appropriate to my subject and audience?
3. Could other and better methods be used?
4. Is my speech or essay interesting as well as informative?

For Additional Reading

Beardsley, Monroe. *Thinking Straight.* 3rd ed. Englewood Cliffs, N.J.: Prentice-Hall, Inc., 1966. Chapter VI, "Definition and Control of Meaning."

Black, Max. *Critical Thinking: An Introduction to Logic and Scientific Method.* 2nd ed. Englewood Cliffs, N.J.: Prentice-Hall, Inc., 1952. Chapter XI, "Definition."

Copi, Irving M. *Introduction to Logic.* 3rd ed. New York: The Macmillan Co., 1968. Chapter IV, "Definition."

Enhinger, Douglas, and **Wayne Brockriede.** *Decision by Debate.* New York: Dodd, Mead & Co., 1963. Chapter XIV, "Analyzing the Proposition."

Leonard, Henry S. *Principles of Right Reason.* New York: Holt, Rinehart & Winston, Inc., 1957. Part IV, "The Theory of Definition."

Olson, Robert. *Meaning and Argument: Elements of Logic.* New York: Harcourt Brace Jovanovich, Inc., 1969. Chapter VI, "Reportive Definitions," and Chapter VII, "Stipulative and Recommendatory Definitions."

Ruby, Lionel. *The Art of Making Sense.* Philadelphia: J. B. Lippincott Co., 1954. Chapter IV, "Define Your Terms."

Chapter V.
The Foundation of Argument: Evidence

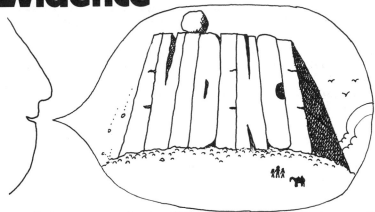

In Chapter II, evidence was defined as the foundation on which an argument rests, that part of the argument the person addressed is willing to take at face value, to accept or endorse in the absence of proof. But what sorts of materials elicit such endorsement and, therefore, furnish the foundation for arguments? And what standards must these materials meet if they are to constitute sound evidence—evidence that not only is accepted by a reader or listener, but also merits the confidence placed in it?

The first of these questions is essentially a psychological one, involving an inquiry into the primary grounds or sources of belief. The second question, on the other hand, is essentially logical and calls for an examination of the conditions under which the ready endorsement of an assertion is warranted. In this chapter we shall examine the two questions in order, first surveying the various sorts of materials that, as a rule, are accepted without proof, and then turning to a consideration of the conditions under which such action is justified.

Types of Evidence

The types of evidence most commonly encountered in arguments may conveniently be classified under the heads of *fact* and *opinion*.

Factual Evidence
Facts are not easy to define. For our purposes, however, they may be thought of as those things men believe to be the case, either because they have

experienced them at firsthand or because they are regarded as the truthfully reported experiences of others.

Because facts are grounded in experience, they are in theory, if not always in practice, verifiable empirically. That is, one can either put them to the test of personal observation, or at least imagine how, if the appropriate means or resources were available, he might go about doing so. Thus we hold it as a fact that sugar is sweet because we ourselves have tasted it; and if in the future doubt about the correctness of this belief should arise, we know that we can again proceed to verify it by tasting a bit of sugar. On the other hand, though we ourselves may never have tasted breadfruit, we also hold it as a fact that breadfruit is not sweet because one or more persons whose reliability we respect have reported this to us. And the reported taste of breadfruit, no less than the experienced taste of sugar, we take to be a fact, not only because it is rooted in someone else's firsthand observation, but also because we can, in theory at least, verify it for ourselves by going to a South Sea island and eating some breadfruit.

Facts introduced into arguments as evidence customarily take the form of reports of specific occurrences or states of affairs, statistics, exhibits, or presumptions.

Reports of Specific Occurrences or States of Affairs. Reports of specific occurrences or states of affairs are commonly referred to as *examples* or *illustrations*. They may make only passing reference to the event or situation in question or they may describe it at some length. Compare the following passages:

> Actually, applying the term "good" or "bad" to dissent is nonsense.
>
> It is the *purpose* and the *form* that determines the goodness or badness of the process of dissent.
>
> I think this becomes quite evident when we take a look at some of the most famous dissenters of history.
>
> Immediately some names come to mind.
>
> Socrates dissented with piercing questions.
>
> Thomas Paine . . . dissented with a powerful pen.
>
> Wendell Phillips dissented with agitation and oratory.
>
> John Peter Altgeld dissented by statesmanship.
>
> Mahatma Gandhi dissented with nonviolent disobedience.
>
> Think of those names and recall the acts of moral and physical courage, the wisdom and the rightness of those dissenters.[1]

> The 1968 G[un] C[ontrol] A[ct] is a moderately good means of checking gun ownership *after* somebody gets shot. But the wounding of Governor Wallace . . . is a prime demonstration of the Federal law's inability to prevent the criminally unhinged from wrapping their mitts around a deadly weapon.
>
> When Wallace's accused assailant, Arthur Bremer, bought his first Charter Arms snubnosed .38, a gun that fits neatly inside the palm of the hand, he satisfied Milwaukee and Washington law by filling out Form 4473. After Bremer was arrested by Milwaukee police last N:vember for illegally

[1]Lawrence F. O'Brien, "The Dissenter," *Vital Speeches of the Day,* February 1, 1968, p. 232.

carrying the $80 revolver concealed—a possible felony—the charge was reduced to a misdemeanor and Bremer was released despite a patrolman's testimony he had been "incoherent" at the time of arrest.

When Bremer bought his second revolver, technically he was still within state and Federal law in signing another Form 4473 with its stipulation that the purchaser not be a felon. In a superstrict control area like New York City, where even supersolid citizens need pull to get a gun permit for their home or business, this could not happen. But in a majority of municipalities, it could happen again tomorrow.[2]

Statistics.   Statistics are numerical expressions of a factual nature about a given population or a sample drawn from that population. The population or sample in question may consist of people, animals, physical objects, institutions, concepts, or any imaginable body of phenomena.

Statistics may, as in the first of the instances cited below, take the form of raw data; or they may, as in the second instance, be stated as medians, percentages, and the like.

The Omnibus Crime Control and Safe Streets Act of 1968 that authorized expanded bugging and tapping also required full government reports to Congress detailing the annual costs, results, and number of wiretaps conducted. The reports have now been issued for the years 1968 to 1971, and they prove conclusively that wiretapping is at best of very little value.

Here are the facts:

In 1968, when there was no federal eavesdropping, state officials listened in on 66,716 conversations.

In 1969, when both federal and state officials eavesdropped, 173,711 conversations were overheard.

In 1970, the amount of eavesdropping doubled to 381,865 conversations.

In 1971, at least 498,325 conversations were overheard, a jump of 30 percent over 1970.

What were the results?

In 1968, out of 66,716 overheard conversations, *no* convictions were reported.

In 1969, out of 173,711 conversations, 294 convictions resulted.

In 1970, out of 381,865 conversations, 538 convictions resulted.

In 1971, out of at least 498,325 conversations, 322 convictions have resulted so far.

In the four years since the bill was passed, 93,080 people have been spied upon, and thus far, only 1,154 have been reportedly convicted—*barely more than 1 percent.*[3]

Indications are that the economic position of the working woman is inherently unequal relative to her working companion, a man. In 1969 a fulltime woman worker earned a median income of $5,077, while a man

[2]Paul Good, "Blam! Blam! Blam! Not Gun Nuts, but Pistol Enthusiasts," *New York Times Magazine,* September 17, 1972, p. 34.

[3]Ira Glasser and Herman Schwartz, "Your Phone Is a Party Line," *Harper's Magazine,* October 1972, pp. 108, 111.

earned $8,668. A black woman earned the least of all fulltime workers, $4,126. The distribution level reveals that 51 percent of the women but only 16 percent of the men earned less than $5,000, while at the other end of the scale, only 5 percent of the women but 35 percent of the men had incomes of $10,000 or more.[4]

Exhibits.   In addition to employing verbal reports in the form of examples or statistics, the author of an argument that is being presented in a face-to-face situation sometimes introduces as factual evidence artifacts, photographs, tape recordings, samples of handwriting, and the like—things that can actually be seen, heard, touched, or tasted by his listeners. In the courtroom, exhibits of this sort are termed *real* evidence, and are distinguished from *personal* evidence as given by word of mouth. Outside of the courtroom, the usefulness of exhibits as evidence depends largely upon the nature of the subject being discussed and the conditions under which the argument is presented.

Presumptions.   Presumptions are predictions or projections based upon uniform patterns of past experience, and judged so probable that they are accepted without demanding proof. Thus, while no one has ever experienced directly tomorrow morning's sunrise, the fact that the sun has risen without fail on millions of mornings in the past makes us willing to endorse the claim that, when tomorrow morning comes, the sun will rise. Using the same reasoning, in the law of evidence a person absent and unheard of for a period of seven years is presumed dead, and a child born in wedlock is presumed legitimate. Over many years, in thousands upon thousands of cases, these conditions have so often and with such a high degree of regularity been found to obtain that the presentation of positive proof on their behalf is not required.

Because presumptions are predictions or projections based upon things experienced in the past, they, like facts, can in theory at least always be verified empirically. Thus we could, if we wished, withhold assent until tomorrow's sunrise actually has been observed or until direct proof of the person's death or the child's legitimacy has been set forth. In the interest of conserving time and energy, however, the matters are regarded as established and proof judged superfluous.

Opinion Evidence

Whereas facts are beliefs held on the basis of experience, opinions are judgments concerning the meaning or significance of facts. They indicate how, in the estimation of the person or persons advancing the opinion, a certain event or state of affairs is to be understood, evaluated, or dealt with.

Because opinions in their role as evidence interpret or evaluate facts or make recommendations concerning facts, they resemble the classificatory, evaluative, and actuative claims described in Chapter II. Despite this resemblance, however, they differ from such claims in an important respect. Rather than requiring proof or support as a condition of their acceptance, they themselves supply an essential part of the support on which a claim rests. Either because of the prestige of the source from which they come or because

[4]Jacqueline St. John, "Women's Legislative Issues," *Vital Speeches of the Day,* June 15, 1972, p. 529.

they accord with beliefs already entertained by the persons to whom they are addressed, they are endorsed at face value. In the following passage, for example, the quoted statement is derived from a study that most persons would regard as authoritative. Therefore, it provides the evidential base for the speaker's claim that the root causes of crime are economic and social.

Why has our crime problem reached such proportions? The public does not always understand that the amelioration of social and economic injustice is a battle which must be fought together with the battle against crime.

There can be no war on crime without a war on poverty, a war on racial discrimination, a war on inadequate housing, a war on underemployment. The National Crime Commission 1967 report relates crime to the general environment of society.

The Commission finds, first, that America must translate its well-founded alarm about crime into social action that will prevent crime. It has no doubt whatever that the most significant action that can be taken against crime is action designed to eliminate slums and ghettos, to improve education, to provide jobs, to make sure that every American is given the opportunities and the freedoms that will enable him to assume his responsibilities. We will not have dealt effectively with crime until we have alleviated the conditions that stimulate it. To speak of controlling crime only in terms of the work of the police, the courts, and the correctional apparatus is to refuse to face the fact that widespread crime implies a widespread failure by society as a whole.[5]

Evaluating Evidence

Now that the types of materials which most commonly serve as the evidential bases for arguments have been catalogued and described, let us turn to the second of the major questions raised at the beginning of this chapter, and inquire into the tests which these materials must meet if they are to constitute a sound foundation for proof. In so doing we shall, as was suggested earlier, pass from what is essentially a psychological question concerning the sources of belief to the logical question of what conditions must obtain if belief is to be justified on objective or rational grounds.

Tests of Factual Evidence

Tests of factual evidence probe the accuracy of the observation upon which the evidence is based and the faithfulness with which the results of that observation are reported.

Tests of Reports of Specific Occurrences or States of Affairs. When the evidence consists of a report based on the firsthand observation of the reporter, the following tests are pertinent:

1. *Was the person making the observation qualified to do so physically and mentally?* Was he sane, in full possession of his senses, sleepy or awake, drunk or sober, ill or in good health, etc.? The ability to observe a situation fully and

---

[5]Patrick V. Murphy, "The Criminal Justice System," *Vital Speeches of the Day,* August 15, 1972, p. 663. Reprinted by permission of the publisher.

accurately varies not only from person to person, but also depending on the physical and mental state of the reporter at the time the observation was made.

2. *Was the person making the observation qualified to do so by training and experience?* So far as many of the occurrences of everyday life are concerned, one person's powers of observation are as good as another's. Thus it takes no special training or experience to observe that the street upon which an accident occurred was wet or that the dress of today's college students is quite different from what it was twenty or thirty years ago. On the other hand, experience has shown that most untrained people are not very accurate in judging the size of a crowd or estimating the speed at which an automobile is traveling down a busy highway. Accurate judgments concerning matters of this second sort call for special training or experience.

3. *Under what conditions was the observation made?* Was the event or state of affairs being reported observed in daylight or darkness? Was the visibility good or poor? Was the reporter's view free of obstructions? Is the report based on a fleeting glimpse or a prolonged examination? If the report concerns conditions in a given region of the country or area of the world, was the reporter in that place for a day, a month, or a year?

The angle or perspective from which an event is viewed also makes a difference. As the old story about the blind men and the elephant illustrates, it is impossible to witness any phenomenon from all points of view at once. Either we must see it from the right or the left, the top or the bottom, the inside or the outside, etc. If we do wish to view it from more than a single position, we must stand first at one point and then at another, thus extending our observation over a period of time during which the phenomenon itself may change.

Finally, it makes a difference whether the observation was prearranged or casual—whether the observer acted intentionally and approached his task with a carefully thought-out plan or procedure, or whether he encountered the event or situation by accident and without previous preparation for recording or evaluating what he saw. For obvious reasons, prearranged observations are to be preferred over casual ones in most cases. There is, however, always the danger that if one has a preconceived notion of what he is looking for, his perception will be biased and he will find what he expects.

4. *Is the situation still essentially the same as it was when the observation was made?* While some situations or states of affairs remain relatively stable over a period of time, most are subject to fluctuation or change. A report on the unemployment rate in a given city or on the price of processed food products based on data gathered in January may not be valid in February or March. An estimate of a person's character or personality made when he was in his twenties can hardly be taken as an accurate evaluation of the sort of individual he is at sixty.

5. *May the observer's attitude toward the event or situation have colored his perception?* To a surprising extent, the average person's perception of an event or situation is colored by his desires or prejudices, so that he sees what he wishes to see and hears what he wishes to hear. The home fan sees his team's base runner as safe; the supporter of the visiting team sees him as out. The mother whose small son breaks a neighbor's window sees the occurrence as an accident; to the neighbor it is a clear case of malicious destructiveness.

6. *May the observer's attitude toward the person or persons receiving the report have influenced his description or account?* People not only tend to see what they want to see, but all too often they tend to report what they think their readers or listeners would like to hear. In an attempt to gain favor for themselves or avoid injuring the feelings of the persons addressed, they omit some details and give unwarranted interpretations or emphasis to others. It has, for example, been frequently pointed out that during the closing months of World War II Hitler did not have an accurate appreciation of the seriously deteriorating military situation on the Western Front because his generals were reluctant to confront him with the facts as they knew them to be. In the area of interpersonal relations, people usually try to find something complimentary to say to a student who has obviously made a poor speech or in some other way failed to measure up to expectations.

7. *Were the actions, events, or conditions described in the report actually witnessed by the observer, or did he infer them from other actions, events, or conditions he did witness?* One may actually see Car A hit Car B or, coming upon the scene just after the accident has occurred, may infer from the skid marks on the pavement, the dents in Car B's fender, and the position of Car A relative to a stop sign that Car A was responsible for the collision. Similarly, one may be told by the leader of a certain nation that his government intends to normalize relations with a neighboring country to which it previously has been hostile, or may infer this intention from the discontinuance of unfriendly acts, the opening of cultural exchanges, the tone of press comment, and the like.

Reports based on actual observations are said to constitute *direct* evidence; reports based on inferences of the sort just described give rise to evidence that is *circumstantial.*

Although in many cases where direct evidence in unavailable, circumstantial evidence may be made to serve as the foundation for an argument, it always must be viewed with an appropriate degree of suspicion. Outward marks or indications are never a completely reliable indication of a condition or state of affairs, and they may often lead to a conclusion that is completely contrary to fact. Thus the individual caught with stolen goods in his possession may be the unwitting victim of another's cunning; or the man whose fine clothes, expensive car, and large home mark him as wealthy may actually be only one step ahead of his creditors.

8. *Was the report made orally or in writing?* While it is by no means the case that oral reports are always uttered hastily or framed carelessly, it is still true that when a person reduces a statement to writing he generally pays closer attention to the words he employs and to the way in which various facts and ideas are presented. Moreover, while an oral report may vary somewhat in tone or content each time it is repeated, a written statement remains the same, subject only to varying interpretations by the reader or listener.

9. *Was the report based on the testimony of another?* As has already been remarked, the report of an event or condition, instead of being based on the firsthand observation of the reporter, may be based on information communicated to him by another person. In such cases, all of the tests just described apply to the observation as originally carried out. Was the observer competent? Did he observe accurately and report objectively? Under what conditions was the observation made? Is the situation still essentially

the same? In addition, however, under these circumstances still another test should be applied. This consists of inquiring into the accuracy with which the results of the observation have been transmitted. Even when the greatest care is exercised, reports tend to become altered in both tone and substance as they pass from person to person, a fact which has led to the rule that *hearsay* evidence is inadmissible in a trial at law. In the absence of such care, the facts of a situation as told by a person who hears them at fourth- or fifthhand may bear little resemblance to the event or situation they profess to describe.

Tests of Statistical Evidence.   While statistics furnish a useful form of evidence on a wide range of subjects, they are also particularly prone to errors and misinterpretations, and must, therefore, be subjected to careful scrutiny both by the person who employs them and by the person to whom the argument is addressed. At a minimum, the following tests should be applied before accepting statistical data as valid.

1. *Do the statistics come from a reliable source?* The gathering and analysis of statistical data is a highly complicated task which calls for special knowledge and training. The nature and number of the samples surveyed, the measuring instrument employed, and the language in which the results are reported are all important if an accurate picture of a given situation is to be conveyed. Therefore, data gathered by such experts in polling and statistical techniques as the Gallup Poll, the Brookings Institute, and the United States Bureau of the Census are to be preferred over studies undertaken by the campus newspaper or surveys conducted by a group of students interviewing customers at a local supermarket.

2. *Do the statistics cover a sufficiently long period of time?* When developing or evaluating statistical data, care must be taken to distinguish between momentary fluctuations and major trends of a permanent or significant nature. The fact that the cost of living index shows a drop for a period of one or two months does not mean that a long-term inflationary trend has finally been reversed and that prices will now stabilize. Nor does the fact that Henry studied for nine hours a day during the two weeks prior to final examinations mean that he will continue to do so throughout the coming semester.

The exact period of time which the data must cover before they can be said to reveal a significant trend will vary, depending on the nature of the phenomenon under study. Always, however, this period must be long enough so that momentary fluctuations are not mistaken for permanent states of affairs.

3. *Are the units comparable?* When statistics draw a comparison among two or more phenomena it is important that these phenomena be defined or conceived of in the same way. If Valley College counts as members of its student body only persons enrolled on a full-time basis, while Hills College includes in this figure persons attending short courses and conferences, data comparing the enrollments of the two institutions will obviously be misleading. Similarly, in order to make a comparison of the number of indigent persons in England, the United States, and Germany, we would first need to know whether the information-gathering agencies in each of these countries define *indigent* in the same way.

4. *Does the method of reporting the data hide significant variations within them?* Statistical reports expressed in terms of means, modes, or medians often

hide or suppress significant variations within the data they summarize. A mean is a quotient obtained by dividing the sum total of a set of figures by the number of those figures. As such, it tells us nothing about the individual items from which the quotient was derived.

Suppose a multimillionaire were suddenly to walk into a room where you and a friend were sitting. The mean wealth of the persons in that room immediately would increase enormously. Yet neither you nor your friend would have a cent more in your pockets than you had before. In the same way, a report that over the past few years the average income of the American family has increased 10 percent, while perhaps entirely true, leaves unrepresented the plight of the worker in a marginal industry whose income may actually have decreased during this period.

The *median,* a figure midway between the extremes, or the *mode,* that figure within a body of statistical data which occurs most frequently, likewise may leave significant variations or exceptions unrepresented. This does not mean that such measures are useless and should be abandoned. It does mean, however, that they always are to be used with caution and approached with a full awareness of the limitations inherent within them.

Tests of Exhibits. So far as factual evidence in the form of exhibits is concerned, two tests are pertinent.

1. *Is the exhibit genuine?* Is the document offered as evidence authentic or forged? Has the photograph been altered in some way? Is the voice heard on the recording actually that of the person in question? Was the object or artifact found where it is alleged to have been found? Is it real or synthetic?

Because an exhibit can actually be seen, heard, touched, or tasted, its genuineness all too often goes unquestioned. Here, as in the case of oral evidence, however, a measure of skepticism is often healthy.

2. *Is the item offered in evidence typical of the class of phenomena it is alleged to represent?* If the exhibit is presented as representative of a given class of phenomena—the quality of themes written by college freshmen, vegetables grown by the organic method, tires that have traveled forty thousand miles, etc.—is it indeed a typical member of that class? Has it been selected completely at random, or with a view to demonstrating certain properties which the author of the argument wishes it to show? The large and luscious apples, pears, and peaches on display at the county fair must always be recognized for what they are—the best that a given farmer has been able to produce, and not randomly selected samples from his crop as a whole.

Tests of Presumptions. Presumptions as predictions or projections based upon patterns of experience that have proved uniform in the past are to be tested by asking a single crucial question: *Are there any reasons to believe that in the case at hand things will turn out differently than they have in the past?*

New factors or elements introduced into a situation may disturb the normal course of events so that the uniformity of occurrence displayed by a phenomenon in the past no longer obtains. Thus, while experience may dictate that at least some students enrolled in beginning calculus during the current school year will fail the course, the introduction of a new teaching method, the adoption of a "no-flunk policy" by the mathematics department, or a much more rigid admissions policy on the part of the college may operate to invalidate the presumption on which this judgment rests.

Tests of Opinion Evidence

Earlier in this chapter, *opinions* were distinguished from *facts* by saying that, while facts are beliefs held on the basis of experience, opinions are judgments which interpret or evaluate facts or recommend courses of action that should be pursued relative to them.

This distinction is important to keep in mind as the tests of opinion evidence are considered, for it reminds us that, while facts are in practice or principle verifiable empirically, this is not the case with opinions. Because opinions are inferences drawn from facts, they cannot be put to the test of direct experience, and hence cannot be proved true or false in any final or definitive sense. Instead, they can at best be shown to be probable or improbable, reasonable or unreasonable, pertinent or irrelevant. With this limitation in mind, however, the following tests may serve as guides to the reliability of opinion evidence.

1. *Does the person offering the opinion possess the background of knowledge and information upon which a sound judgment must rest?* The amount of knowledge and information required to make a sound judgment varies, depending on the nature and complexity of the matter under consideration. While on some subjects the opinion of one man may be as good as that of another, on other subjects only the opinion of an expert can be relied on. For this reason, the law makes a distinction between what it terms *ordinary* and *expert* witnesses, and allows only the latter to express opinions on the stand.

Although in the arguments of everyday life so sharp a distinction between ordinary and expert testimony need not always be preserved, opinions advanced as evidence must as a basic condition be accepted as authoritative by the reader or listener. Where this quality is lacking, rather than serving as the evidential basis for an argument, the opinion itself requires support by means of argument.

2. *Is the person offering the opinion reasonably unbiased?* Someone may be an acknowledged expert on a given subject or state of affairs, but for personal or public reasons may be highly partisan concerning it. Football coaches who make predictions concerning the outcome of a crucial game or political candidates who issue statements assessing their chances in a coming election can hardly be regarded as detached or objective observers. What they say often is not so much intended to describe or evaluate the situation as to offer hope to their partisans or discourage their opponents.

No one can be completely impartial and objective all of the time, and on some matters impartiality is not even expected. In general, however, sound opinion evidence comes from sources that are reasonably unbiased, or if it does not, it is at least presented in such a way that whatever biases are present are made evident to the person addressed.

3. *Was the person offering the opinion in a position to observe at firsthand the facts upon which his judgment bears?* Even the best expert cannot offer a sound opinion concerning an event or situation if he has been denied access to certain facts or if he has been obliged to gather his data from the observations of others rather than from firsthand experience or the study of primary source materials. The best judge of the nature and significance of a new archeological find is a trained archeologist who examines at the site of the digging the various artifacts unearthed. The best judge of the social conditions in a given country is a trained sociologist who has repeatedly visited that country for

extended periods of time. In short, besides expertness and objectivity, first-hand access to the necessary facts is a third desideratum of good opinion evidence.

General Tests of Evidence

In the preceding sections we examined under separate heads some of the major tests which facts and opinions must meet if they are to furnish sound evidence for the claims advanced in arguments. Let us now take a broader view of the problem and consider four tests that are applicable to all evidence, factual and judgmental.

1. *Is the evidence consistent with other evidence?* Because nature is not completely uniform and because people's actions often are unexpected or unpredictable, the fact that a given piece of evidence differs in form or content from other evidence bearing on the same point does not necessarily mean that it is false or inaccurate. Such deviation from the norm is, however, a justifiable cause for suspicion. If three persons who visit a city all report that the public transportation system is inadequate while a fourth reports that it is excellent in every respect, it is only natural to regard the fourth person's report with some skepticism. Similarly, a judgment that runs counter to all other estimates concerning the character of a man, the worth of an institution, or the likelihood of an event, though it alone may, in fact, be the correct one, ordinarily invites something less than immediate and unqualified endorsement.

2. *Is the statement consistent with itself?* Not only does the report of an event or situation or the expression of an opinion arouse suspicion when it is inconsistent with other known evidence; it also invites suspicion when it contains apparent inconsistencies or contradictions within itself. If, for example, one set of figures in the report of an investigating committee shows that the use of drugs among students in large metropolitan high schools is increasing while another table in the same report indicates that drug use in these schools is decreasing, the reliability not only of these data but of the report as a whole is thrown into question. Or if early in the course of an argument an authority is cited as favoring a certain course of action and later in the same argument is cited as opposing it, we are at the very least moved to inquire into the reason for this apparent discrepancy.

3. *Is the evidence consistent with human nature?* Human behavior, as was remarked earlier, is not always predictable. Yet it is true that, by and large, people tend to respond to certain sorts of situations in standard and foreseeable ways. When threatened, they act to protect their persons or possessions. They defend those they love, imitate those they admire, strive to improve their positions socially and economically, seek love and companionship, and the like. Because these are the usual patterns of human behavior, when by word or action an individual or group behaves otherwise, this fact in and of itself tends to arouse suspicion. Hence a report that a mother has testified against her son, that a known miser has suddenly given away his wealth, or that a worker has voluntarily requested a cut in salary bears more than ordinary investigation before being accepted as true.

4. *Is the evidence clearly and objectively presented?* In Chapter I it was pointed out that the arguer addresses the understanding of the reader or listener directly in an effort to cause him to see for himself the validity of the

claim advanced. Since this aim can be achieved only when the facts and opinions upon which an argument rests are fully comprehended and accurately evaluated, clarity and objectivity are essential qualities for all good evidence.

Is the evidence, as presented, adapted to the person or persons for whom it is intended? Are their fixed attitudes and values, their knowledge of the subject, their educational level and habits of thought taken into account? Is the evidence presented fully and slowly enough so that its full significance can be grasped? Are needless details omitted and obscure or technical language translated into more immediately understandable terms? Are sources cited and their credibility established? Are statistics made meaningful through the use of comparisons and contrasts? In short, is everything possible done to put the reader or listener in full possession of those data upon which an informed judgment necessarily must rest?

Besides being presented clearly, is the evidence presented objectively, free of the colorings which the preferences and prejudices of the arguer may consciously or unconsciously impose upon it? Are the facts allowed to speak for themselves? Is testimony cited without undue comment or distortion? Are overstatement and understatement carefully avoided? Unless all the pertinent evidence bearing upon a point is given exactly the weight it deserves—neither more nor less—judgment is impaired and faulty beliefs or unwise actions result.

Checklist

I. Types of Evidence
  A. Factual evidence
   1. Reports of specific occurrences or states of affairs
   2. Statistics
   3. Exhibits
   4. Presumptions
  B. Opinion evidence

II. Evaluating Evidence
  A. Tests of factual evidence
   1. Tests of reports of specific occurrences or states of affairs
     a. Was the person making the observation qualified to do so physically and mentally?
     b. Was the person making the observation qualified to do so by training and experience?
     c. Under what conditions was the observation made?
     d. Is the situation still essentially the same as it was when the observation was made?
     e. May the observer's attitude toward the event or situation have colored his perception?
     f. May the observer's attitude toward the person or persons receiving the report have influenced his description or account?

   g. Were the actions, events, or conditions described in the report
      actually witnessed by the observer, or did he infer them from
      other actions, events, or conditions he did witness?
   h. Was the report made orally or in writing?
   i. If the occurrence or condition was witnessed by someone other
      than the reporter, did that person transmit to the reporter a
      full and accurate account of what he saw?
2. Tests of statistical evidence
   a. Do the statistics come from a reliable source?
   b. Do the statistics cover a sufficiently long period of time?
   c. Are the units comparable?
   d. Does the method of reporting the data hide significant varia-
      tions within them?
3. Tests of exhibits
   a. Is the exhibit genuine?
   b. Is the item offered in evidence typical of the class of phe-
      nomena it is alleged to represent?
4. Tests of presumptions
   a. Are there any reasons to believe that in the case at hand
      things will turn out differently than they have in the past?
B. Tests of opinion evidence
   1. Does the person offering the opinion possess the background of
      knowledge and information upon which a sound judgment must
      rest?
   2. Is the person offering the opinion reasonably unbiased?
   3. Was the person offering the opinion in a position to observe at
      firsthand the facts on which his judgment bears?
C. General tests of evidence
   1. Is the evidence consistent with other evidence?
   2. Is the evidence consistent with itself?
   3. Is the evidence consistent with human nature?
   4. Is the evidence clearly and objectively presented?

Exercises

1. Clip five magazine advertisements in which two or more of the types of
   evidence discussed in this chapter are used to support the advertiser's
   claim. In each case, evaluate the appropriateness and adequacy of the
   evidence employed. Was the evidence well chosen? Was it sufficient in
   amount? Was it fairly presented? Report your findings orally or in
   writing, using the advertisements as exhibits to support your analysis.

2. Collect from newspapers, magazines, textbooks, or other likely sources
   two or three examples of statistics used to explain or prove a point. Were
   the statistics clear and easily understood? Were they free of fallacies?
   Can you think of ways in which the presentation of these data might
   have been improved?

3. Listen to some of the claims advanced by your friends and classmates in classes and in informal conversations. How many of these claims are backed up by evidence of some sort and how many are merely assertions offered without proof? What sorts of facts and opinions are used as evidence? Is real evidence ever introduced?

4. In his First Inaugural Address, Lincoln offered as evidence of his attitude toward slavery a passage quoted from a speech he had given on a previous occasion. Does such a quotation, in your opinion, constitute sound and acceptable evidence? Why or why not?

5. As a general rule, hearsay evidence is not admissible in courts of law, nor is an ordinary witness allowed to express opinions or to draw inferences from the facts he reports. Do you think these rules are justified, or are they too restrictive? Support your answer.

6. Distinguish between circumstantial evidence and presumptions used as evidence. How are they similar? In what ways do they differ?

7. Keeping in mind the definitions of "fact" and "opinion" presented in this chapter, decide which of the following statements are facts and which are opinions:

In the United States, any sort of discrimination on the basis of race or sex is unconstitutional.

According to Professor Jones, a prominent art historian, Rubens was a more accomplished painter than Rembrandt.

During the coming winter the citizens of Minneapolis will experience at least a few days of subzero weather.

With proper training, women can perform many manual tasks more efficiently than men.

The reason many students drop out of college is that they regard what they are learning as irrelevant.

Men are descended from monkeys.

Hockey is rougher than football.

It is wrong to tell lies.

8. React to the following: Opinion evidence, no matter how good the source, is never as strong as factual evidence.

9. Which of the following statements would you be willing to accept on the word of an ordinary witness and for which would you demand the word of an expert? Defend your choice.

Johnny has the measles.

The Reds lost the series primarily because of poor pitching.

Smoking is injurious to the health.

This gun has not been fired for some days.

The food at Hamburg Heaven is excellent.

Professor Smith's tests are hard but fair.

The cost of living rose steadily between 1969 and 1972.

Paris is the most beautiful city in the world.

We can gather all the data we need about the moon without landing men on the lunar surface.

10. Is the evidence offered in support of these claims direct or circumstantial? Explain your answers.

    It must have begun to rain. I see people with their umbrellas raised.

    Jones told my wife only last week that he had made another killing in the market.

    You are driving over the speed limit. The speedometer registers nearly eighty.

    Old Mr. Brown is drunk again. See how he staggers down the street.

    According to this letter from my son, soldiers on foreign duty have a great deal of free time.

    If Congress really wished to reform itself, it could do so. Any body of intelligent men and women can always find a way to accomplish what they want to accomplish.

11. What questions would you like to have answered before accepting the following claims as true or probable?

    In a letter to the local paper, Anna White predicts that the Democrats will elect at least three aldermen in the next election.

    Citizens of Plain View like movies better than do citizens of Star City. In fact, last year the theater in Plain View had over 25,000 paid admissions, while the Star City Theater had less than 9,000.

    Samples taken from five different packing houses show that many meat products do not measure up to required standards of fat content.

12. As was pointed out in this chapter, in most instances good evidence should be consistent with itself, with other evidence, and with human nature. Can you think of cases in which evidence that violates one or more of these rules may actually be stronger than evidence that does not?

13. It is sometimes said that "the evidence of the senses"—that knowledge which comes to us through our own sight, taste, hearing, or touch—is not to be questioned or disputed. Do you think such a position is justified? Why or why not?

Writing or Speaking Assignment

Prepare a short speech or essay in which you make a simple declarative claim, and support that claim by using statistics, examples, and testimony. Begin with a categorical statement of the claim you wish to establish, present your evidence in a clear and orderly fashion, and close with a summary.

The claim itself should be narrow enough so that it can be adequately dealt with in a short speech or essay. If the authorities you cite are not well known, be sure to tell why they are experts on the matter in question, what special opportunity they have had to study the facts, and why they are unbiased. Examples should meet the basic tests of sufficiency and random selection. Statistics should be used as sparingly as possible, stated (when practical) in round numbers, illustrated by means of striking comparisons, and derived from authoritative sources. Check in particular to make sure they are free of the fallacies discussed in this chapter.

Suggested Subjects
Moon landings are worth the cost.
You are safer in an airplane than on the highway.
The price of new cars will continue to rise.
Intelligence can be increased.
It pays to advertise.
Television programs have an undesirable effect on children.
The streets of our large cities are unsafe at night.
Francis Bacon wrote some of the plays attributed to Shakespeare.

For Additional Reading

Brandes, Paul D. "Evidence." In *Argumentation and Debate: Principles and Practices,* ed. James McBath. 2nd ed. New York: Holt, Rinehart & Winston, 1963.

Ewbank, Henry Lee, and **J. Jeffery Auer.** *Discussion and Debate: Tools of a Democracy.* 2nd ed. New York: Appleton-Century-Crofts, 1951. Chapter VII, "Exploring the Problem: Evidence."

Miller, Gerald R. "Evidence and Argument." In *Perspectives on Argumentation,* ed. Gerald R. Miller and Thomas R. Nilsen. Glenview, Ill.: Scott, Foresman and Company, 1966.

Mills, Glen E. *Reason in Controversy.* Boston: Allyn & Bacon, Inc., 1964. Chapter VI, "Evidence."

Monroe, Alan H., and **Douglas Ehninger.** *Principles of Speech Communication.* 6th ed. Glenview, Ill.: Scott, Foresman and Company, 1969. Chapter VI, "Supporting One Point."

Newman, Robert P., and **Dale R. Newman.** *Evidence.* Boston: Houghton Mifflin Company, 1969.

Chapter VI.
Relating the Evidence to the Claim: Warrant

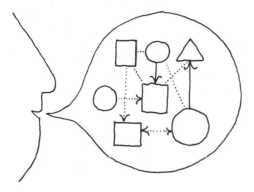

With the evidence on which an argument is based clarified and set forth, the next step is to show why the evidence warrants or justifies the claim. In this chapter, we shall consider five basic methods for accomplishing this task. In the chapter that follows, a number of more specific types or lines of argument will be discussed.

At the outset, however, it is important to remind ourselves of a fact pointed out in Chapter II: while in many cases all three parts of an argument—evidence, warrant, and claim—are present, at other times one of these parts may be omitted as unnecessary. This, you will find, is especially true of the warrant, the part of the argument we are now to consider. Because the relation of the evidence to the claim is often apparent at a glance, the warrant is either skipped or stated in an abbreviated form. For this reason, the examples presented in the following pages should be viewed as model arguments rather than actual working ones. In order to illustrate as clearly as possible how in each case the evidence is brought to bear on the claim, the warrant is explicitly stated. In practice, however, it probably would, in a number of instances, be omitted.

The five basic sorts of relationship which may be established between evidence and claim are based, respectively, on techniques of comparison, generalization, classification, division, and connection.

Techniques of Comparison

Techniques of comparison assert that what is known or believed to be true of one thing will likewise be true of something else which is in all essential respects like the first. Such comparisons take two basic forms: direct comparisons, in which the evidence consists of one or more instances or cases that are themselves similar to the case in question, and indirect comparisons, in which, though the cases being compared are not themselves similar, each stands in the same relationship to an additional item of knowledge. The first of these forms constitutes what we shall call *argument from parallel case;* the second, *argument from analogy.*

Argument from Parallel Case

In argument from parallel case, the evidence, as we have said, consists of one or more instances or cases which are in some essential respect similar to the case under consideration. The warrant in turn asserts, and if necessary proves through the use of one or more properly backed supporting statements, that the case or cases described in the evidence and the case represented in the claim are indeed closely parallel.

With the relationship between evidence and claim thus established, the claim statement draws the conclusion that what is true of the case or cases constituting the evidence will also be true of the case referred to in the claim. Here is an example:

Evidence   As statements by both faculty members and student leaders show, the introduction of the honor system has significantly reduced cheating on examinations at College X.

Warrant   Since College Y is very similar to College X in size, curriculum, composition of student body, examination system, etc.,

Claim   We may expect that the introduction of the honor system would likewise significantly reduce cheating on examinations at College Y.

Sometimes more than one instance or case of a parallel nature may be drawn upon as evidence.

Evidence   The introduction of the honor system has significantly reduced cheating on examinations at College V, as well as at College W and College X.

Warrant   Since each of these colleges is very similar to College Y in size, curriculum, composition of student body, examination system, etc.,

Claim   We may expect that the introduction of the honor system would significantly reduce cheating on examinations at College Y.

Tests of Parallel Case

Obviously, the strength of an argument from parallel case depends on how closely the case named in the claim resembles the case or cases set forth as evidence. To the extent that these items are similar, the argument gains force; insofar as they are different, the strength of the argument is impaired.

More specifically, it is important that the cases brought into comparison be similar in those particular respects that are most relevant to the claim in question. The fact that Colleges V, W, and X, which are used as evidence, are modernistic in architecture, while College Y is Williamsburg Colonial, or the fact that Colleges V, W, and X are located in mountainous regions, while College Y is on the seashore, clearly would have little or no bearing upon a claim concerning the effects of the honor system on reducing cheating during examinations. The specific factors named in the example, however— composition of the student body, nature of the examination system, and the like—would presumably affect the degree of confidence the claim elicits. So also might such other factors as whether the schools being compared all have strong systems of student government, how much a student's final grade is determined by his score on examinations, and whether the examinations are, as a rule, of the objective or essay type.

Matters which thus bear directly upon the relationship assumed to exist between evidence and claim are said to be *crucial* to the argument. Therefore, the basic test which is always to be applied to an argument from parallel case is this: Do the crucial points of similarity between the case or cases brought forth as evidence and the case embodied in the claim outweigh the crucial points of difference? To the degree that similarities prevail over differences, the argument yields a probable conclusion; to the degree that differences outweigh similarities, the likelihood of the claim is weakened.

Argument from Analogy

In argument from analogy, the relationship between the case or cases used as evidence and the case named in the claim, instead of being direct and explicit, is indirect and implicit.

Suppose, for example, that someone were to advance as a claim this statement: "Just as the free and unimpaired circulation of the blood is essential to the health of the body, so is the free and unimpaired flow of information essential to the well-being of society."

Observe that in this argument it is not contended that the free flow of information through society is in one or more crucial respects similar to the flow of the blood through the body, that the circulation of information and the circulation of the blood are, for all practical purposes, one and the same. Instead, the argument proceeds indirectly by comparing two independent or autonomous relationships: that between the circulation of the blood and bodily health on the one hand, and that between the free flow of information and the well-being of society on the other. These relationships, it is contended, while not in themselves similar, are parallel or isomorphic in the sense that they call for the same sort of response from a listener or reader.

If we were to label the first of these relationships AB and the second CD, the entire argument might be stated by declaring, "As A is to B, so C is to D" (A:B:C:D). Or expressed in terms of the three basic constituents of evidence, warrant, and claim, we would have:

Evidence The free and unimpaired circulation of the blood, as everyone knows, is essential to the health of the body.

Warrant   Since the news media as carriers of information stand in the same relationship to the body politic as the blood as a carrier of nourishment and oxygen stands to the human body,

Claim   Therefore, the free flow of information is essential to the well-being of society.

Because it rests upon a resemblance of relationships rather than upon a comparison of phenomena that are themselves intrinsically similar, and in this sense is indirect or figurative rather than direct or literal, analogy has frequently been called the weakest form of argument. Indeed, many persons would hold that it is not a form of argument at all, but merely a device for clarifying or illustrating a subject, or for presenting a point of view in a particularly striking or memorable way.

The position one takes on this question obviously depends in large part on how he defines an argument, and on the level or degree of probability he expects an alleged relationship to produce before he is willing to regard it as a proof rather than merely an illustration.

If one confines his definition of an argument to those thought movements from evidence to claim which produce conclusions that are clear and conclusive or have a relatively high degree of likelihood, analogies would hardly qualify as arguments. If, however, one includes within his definition of an argument all instances in which a claim purports to be based on an accepted fact or value, analogies must be regarded as arguments; for, using as evidence a relationship that a reader or listener is willing to endorse in the absence of proof, an analogy asserts the existence of a second relationship that the reader or listener disbelieves or doubts.

In this connection, however, it is important to remember that in the form in which they commonly appear in argumentative discourse, arguments from analogy seldom contain an explicit warrant. Instead, the fact that a comparison is being drawn between evidence and claim is conveyed either by the syntax ("Just as the free and unimpaired circulation of the blood is essential to the health of the body, so is the free and unimpaired flow of information essential to the well-being of society.") or by the presence of such words as "like" or "comparable."

Tests of Analogy

Because analogies depend on the recognition of a similarity between two separate and autonomous relationships, rigid tests of reliability are not applicable to this mode of argument. In general, however, the probative value of an analogy increases in proportion as the similarity between the relationship cited as evidence and the relationship asserted in the claim is clearly and readily apparent, and in proportion as the parallels adduced as evidence for the claim increase in number.

Under the first of these criteria an analogy which reads, "As food is to the body, so ideas are to the mind," would be stronger than one reading, "As food is to the body, so dreams are to the spirit." Under the second criterion, the fact that three parallels rather than only one are cited as evidence adds force to the following argument: "As the axe is an extension of the arm, the wheel of the foot, and the radio of the ear, so is the book an extension of the eye."

Techniques of Generalization

Whereas techniques of comparison establish a claim about a single item of knowledge or experience by showing its similarity to one or more items of the same sort, techniques of generalization assert that what is true of a number of the members of a given class, taken as a representative sample, will also be true of additional members of the same class.

On some occasions the generalization is limited and stops short of asserting that what is true of the sample will also be true of each and every member of the class from which the sample is drawn. On other occasions the claim is extended so as to make a blanket assertion concerning all class members, without exception. In the first instance we have what may be termed an *argument from some to more;* in the second we have an *argument from some to all.*

Basically, the requirements an argument from generalization must meet if it is to yield an acceptable conclusion are the same whether the inference is from some to more or from some to all. In the latter case, however, an additional requirement must be satisfied—that it be applicable to all. The basic criteria any argument from generalization, irrespective of the scope of its claim, must meet are three.

Class Requirement

First, the sample which serves as evidence, and upon which, therefore, the argument is grounded, must consist entirely of items drawn from the same class or category, and this class must be the one concerning which the claim makes an assertion. A sample consisting partly of apples, partly of potatoes, and partly of grains or cereals obviously cannot yield a valid conclusion concerning the nutritive value of fruit.

In many instances, however, the fact that the items comprising the sample do not belong to the same class or to the class generalized about in the claim is not so readily apparent. In examining a generalization concerning the attitudes of college students toward language requirements, shall we admit as evidence students who are attending two-year colleges, people who take an occasional evening course with no thought of pursuing a degree, teachers who return for summer refresher work, and the like? Who, in short, for the purposes of this generalization is to be regarded as a college student, and who is to be excluded from this category?

We also must be sure that the items surveyed in the sample are the same as the items concerning which the claim generalizes. If our sample concerning college students' attitudes toward language requirements is taken exclusively from full-time undergraduates enrolled in four-year colleges, our claim cannot validly be extended to the two-year, part-time, or summer-session students mentioned above.

As a first requirement, then, all of the items comprising the sample must belong to the same class, and this class must be the same as the one concerning which the claim makes a generalized statement.

Random Selection Requirement

Second, besides coming from the same class, the items used as evidence must also be typical or, as we say, randomly selected members of that class. A sample limited to or heavily loaded with students who are majoring in a foreign language will hardly yield a reliable generalization concerning the attitudes of college students toward language requirements. Nor, for that matter, would a sample that excluded language majors entirely produce a sound claim. If the generalized claim or conclusion the argument seeks to establish is to command confidence, the sample upon which that claim is based must be a random one, reflecting all segments of the student body.

Sufficient Number Requirement

Third, as common sense tells us, the items used as evidence must be sufficient in number to warrant the generalization they are designed to support. One swallow does not make a spring, nor do the actions of a small number of radicals seeking to disrupt the normal processes of education prove that the majority of college students are bent on such disruption.

But just as it is not always easy to determine whether a given item does or does not belong within a certain class, so it is not always easy to determine how large an evidential sample must be in order to warrant the generalization in question.

For one thing, the size of the sample clearly will need to vary, depending on the nature of the subject under discussion. Insofar as the subject presents a regular or uniform character and consists of processes or events that occur in predictable patterns, the size of the sample may be reduced. On the other hand, if the subject matter is irregular or consists of things that occur in unusual and highly unpredictable ways, the size of the sample must be enlarged. Thus a claim concerning the behavior of animals, since they are guided largely by instinct, might be adequately supported by a relatively small number of instances, while a claim concerning the behavior of human beings, whose actions are the result of a more complex set of factors, would require a proportionately larger sample.

In addition, the amount of evidence required as a sample depends on the audience to whom an argument is addressed and, more specifically, on the attitude that audience holds toward the claim being advanced. If the audience is disposed to look on the claim with favor, fewer rather than more items in the evidential sample will be regarded as sufficient; if the claim is in some way repugnant to the audience's interests or runs counter to its goals and desires, a larger number of items is required.

Both when constructing an argument of one's own and when evaluating the argument of another, it is therefore important that the known or likely attitudes of the recipients, as well as the subject matter of the argument itself, be borne in mind. To dismiss or condemn an argument because the evidential sample seems abnormally small may be to charge unfairly a proof which, because it is addressed to persons who already are well disposed toward the claim, requires relatively little in the way of an evidential base. On the other hand, to endorse an argument without knowing the degree of hostility its claim is likely to arouse in the persons addressed can lead to an equally improper evaluation.

As has been repeatedly emphasized, the purpose of arguments is to establish claims; and claims, while they follow from the evidence and justification offered on their behalf, are more than just inferences or conclusions based on reasoning. As the term *claim* implies, they also have a distinctly persuasive or hortatory quality in that they are demands made upon the belief or behavior of another; in addition to asserting something, they ask that what is asserted be approved or acted upon. It is because claims do have this hortatory quality that the evaluation of any argument, but especially an argument from generalization, must include a consideration of the audience addressed.

In sum, then, a sound argument from generalization, whether it entails a movement from some to more or from some to all, must meet the three requirements just described: (1) The sample brought forth as evidence must consist entirely of items belonging to the same class, and this class must be the one concerning which the claim generalizes. (2) The sample must be made up of items or instances chosen entirely at random. And (3) the sample must be sufficient in size or scope to support the claim advanced.

Explanation of Exceptions Requirement

When, however, an argument from generalization, instead of merely claiming something about many or most of the members of a class, extends its claim to encompass that class as a whole—when, in other words, the movement of the argument, instead of being from some to more, is from some to all—an additional requirement must be met. This is that instances which appear to run counter to the rule must be explained or accounted for by showing either that they do not, in fact, belong to the class about which the generalization is being made, or, if they do, that they are abnormal or atypical. Thus, for example, if one makes the blanket statement "In all the residential areas of our town the established speed limit is twenty-five miles an hour," he must be prepared to protect this generalization by showing either that areas in which this speed limit does not apply are not classified as residential or that the speed limit has been raised or lowered by special action of the city council. Unless such explanation is offered, the generalization remains subject to question in the mind of the reader or listener, and therefore fails to merit his acceptance.

Techniques of Classification

Thus far, in our discussion of comparison and generalization, we have been considering types of arguments in which the evidence consists of one or more instances or relationships that are taken as constituting a representative sample of a given class of phenomena. Then, upon the basis of that sample, a claim is advanced concerning one or more additional members of the same class.

In the techniques of classification we are now to consider the evidence consists not of one or a number of items taken as a sample, but rather of some trait or characteristic acknowledged to belong to all or most of the known members of a class. With this as the foundation of his proof, the arguer then advances a claim concerning one or more new or previously unknown or unexamined instances which are alleged to fall within the class in question, and therefore to partake of the characteristics of the class as a whole.

Here, then, the inference, instead of proceeding (as in the argument from parallel case) from *one to one* or (as in the argument from generalization) from *some to more*, proceeds in the opposite direction, from *all to one* or from *more to some.* The process, in short, is one of establishing the characteristics of the items in question by showing that they are to be classified with a group of other items, the properties or traits of which are already known or admitted.

Broken down into the three major steps of evidence, warrant, and claim, an argument from classification may be described as follows: The *evidence* states one or more known or assumed characteristics of a given class of phenomena. The *warrant* asserts that one or more previously unknown or unexamined items fall within the class thus characterized. The *claim* alleges that what is known or assumed to be true of the class as a whole is also true of the item or items named in the warrant.

Argument from classification, as the preceding paragraphs suggest, takes two basic forms. In the first form, one or more prevailing characteristics of a given class of phenomena are used as evidence for a claim concerning a single item of knowledge or experience. In the second, one or more prevailing class characteristics furnish the evidential basis for a claim concerning a number of such items.

Form 1

Evidence   Persons who are overprotected in childhood often find it difficult to adjust to the demands of adult life.

Warrant   If ever a child was overprotected, Mrs. Jones' little Johnnie is.

Claim   Therefore, Mrs. Jones' Johnnie probably will find it difficult to adjust to the demands of adult life.

Form 2

Evidence   Persons who are overprotected in childhood often find it difficult to adjust to the demands of adult life.

Warrant   Children raised by widowed mothers tend to be overprotected.

Claim   Therefore, children raised by widowed mothers often find it difficult to adjust to the demands of adult life.

Regardless of whether the claim in question belongs to the first or the second of the categories just described—that is, regardless of whether it makes an assertion concerning a single item or a group of items—the same basic conditions must be met if the argument is to be sound.

First, the statements offered as evidence and warrant must be true, must report what actually is the case. Second, the item or items named in the warrant must fall within the class generalized about in the evidence. Only if it is indeed the case that persons who are overprotected as children find it difficult to adjust to the demands of adult life will any assertion concerning Johnnie or the children of widowed mothers merit credence. Moreover, unless it is true that Johnnie as an individual and the children of widowed mothers as a group are overprotected—unless, that is, they may properly be put into the class of overprotected children—we can draw no conclusion concerning the difficulties they may encounter in later life.

Therefore, the two crucial questions to be asked about any argument from classification are these: (1) Are the statements advanced as evidence and justification for the claim true? (2) Does the item (or items) named in the warrant actually fall within the class generalized about in the evidence?

In addition to these basic questions which obtain whenever an argument by classification is advanced, another important consideration arises when the evidence makes an assertion concerning only some of the members of a given class—when it alleges something to be true of many or most of the members of that class.

Under these circumstances, as one can readily see, any claim concerning one or more previously unexamined items immediately becomes suspect. If most, but not necessarily all, children who are overprotected face adjustment difficulties, into which of these two categories will Johnnie and the children of widowed mothers fall—into the class of those with adjustment difficulties or those without? From the information we are given as evidence, we have no way of knowing for sure.

Because of the uncertainty which inevitably arises when the evidence statement of an argument from classification encompasses something less than all of the members of a class, assertions containing or implying the limiting terms "some," "most," "usually," etc., are not regarded by the logician as acceptable premises for proofs. In the practical arguments and reasonings of everyday life, however, we need not hold to so rigid a standard, provided we do not forget to place the proper qualifications upon our claims. Indeed, were we to reject premises of this sort, argument by classification would be of little use since most of the subjects about which arguments are framed—the behavior of men, the worth of institutions, the soundness of policies, and the like—defy generalization.

What is important is to avoid advancing in the claim of an argument from classification more than is warranted by the evidence at hand, to avoid concluding as certain something the evidence describes as only probable or likely. If the evidence shows that 98 percent of all persons who are overprotected as children develop adjustment problems in adult life, we may say that "Johnnie almost certainly will do so." If the evidence shows that only a majority of such children are maladjusted as adults, our claim can contend no more than that "Johnnie may" or "is likely to" experience problems of this sort. In no case, however, must the claim exceed the evidence either in scope or in force.

Techniques of Division

Closely related to the techniques of classification are those of division. But whereas in the argument by classification we depend on the principle of inclusion, in the argument by division we employ a process of exclusion or elimination.

Suppose that, after a careful study of the alternatives, we come to believe that unless the government imposes a permanent system of wage and price controls, the cost of living over the years will continue to rise steadily. And suppose further that, as a result of our study of the situation, we come to the conclusion that the government will not take this action. In communicating this judgment to others, we might build the following argument:

Evidence   Either the government must impose a permanent system
of wage and price controls on the economy or the cost of
living will continue to rise year by year.

Warrant   But as the President and other responsible officials in the
Administration have made clear, they will not ask for the
imposition of controls of this sort.

Claim   Therefore, with this one possible check on prices eliminated, we may expect that the cost of living will continue
to rise year by year.

In the foregoing example, the argument by division is based on a single pair
of alternatives. Sometimes, however, a number of possibilities are presented in
the evidence, and the argument proceeds by a process of elimination to show
that only one of these is tenable.

Evidence   The only likely candidates for the nomination are Jones,
Smith, Brown, and Williams.

Warrant   But Jones is too liberal, Smith too conservative, and
Brown completely inexperienced in government.

Claim   Therefore, you should vote for Williams.

Regardless of the number of alternatives named in the evidence, the
conditions an argument by division must meet if it is to yield a sound
conclusion remain the same.

First, the items mentioned as alternatives must include all reasonable
possibilities—must constitute an exhaustive list of all the likely choices for
belief or action. Second, the alternatives must, for all practical purposes, be
mutually exclusive or capable of being divided into independent and self-
contained units. Unless all reasonable alternatives are included in the
evidence, one cannot be sure that the situation described or the action called
for in the claim is preferable to another possibility that has gone unnoticed.
Unless the possibilities named in the evidence are distinct and separate, they
are incapable of being divided in such a way that the elimination of one or
several of them leaves the remaining items intact.

Techniques of Connection

The last of the five basic techniques for relating evidence to claim asserts
that two phenomena are connected or conjoined in such a way that from the
existence of the first we may infer the existence of the second.

Techniques of connection are of two sorts: argument from cause and
argument from sign.

Argument from Cause

In argument from cause the phenomena in question are connected along a
time line, the one which occurs first acting as a productive or generative agent
which brings the second into being. Since it is possible to travel along a time

line both forward and backward, one may either connect a present cause with a future effect or connect a present effect with a preceding cause.

Here are two examples of arguments that move forward in time from cause to effect. In the first, the movement yields a categorical claim; in the second, the claim is qualified because the evidence on which the argument rests reports what is usually rather than invariably the case.

Evidence With the coming of spring, the heavy winter snow cover is beginning to melt rapidly.

Warrant Since the runoff from rapidly melting snow causes rivers and streams to overflow their banks,

Claim Low-lying areas along these waterways will be flooded.

Evidence Increased expenditures for advertising usually result in more sales.

Warrant The Ideal Corporation has just increased its advertising budget by 20 percent.

Claim Therefore, other things being equal, its volume of sales will rise.

In the next two examples, the argument follows the opposite path and moves backward in time from effect to cause, yielding in the first case a categorical claim and in the second case a qualified or restricted one.

Evidence During the past month, ridership on our city buses has more than doubled.

Warrant Since, except for a ten-cent reduction in fare, the service is exactly the same as it was earlier,

Claim This reduction is the cause of the increased ridership.

Evidence Last semester John received the highest grades he has had since entering college.

Warrant Since at the beginning of the semester John moved from his fraternity house to an apartment,

Claim It is likely that this move to a quieter and less distracting atmosphere is responsible for his improved performance academically.

Tests of Cause

Before arguments from cause are accepted as sound, they should be tested by asking the following questions:

Is it true that the phenomena in question are causally connected? Is the first really responsible for the existence of the second, or do they just happen to occur one after the other? The fact that Event or Condition B follows Event or Condition A does not in itself prove that A caused B.

Few of us, for example, believe that if we did poorly on a quiz, it was because a black cat crossed our path earlier in the day or because we happened to walk under a ladder on the way to class. Old wives' tales to the contrary, we recognize that in neither case could the first of these events have caused the second.

In other circumstances, however, the temptation to name a prior event or condition as the cause of a subsequent one is less easy to resist. A candidate for public office, let us say, is endorsed by a newspaper known for its ultraconservative views, and a month later a public opinion poll shows that his popularity has dropped 5 percent. Was the endorsement the cause of the decline? Or, after losing three games in a row, the coach of a basketball team decides that his players are stale and gives them a four-day holiday from practice. The team wins its next game by a large margin. Was the rest the cause of the victory?

Although in both cases we may suspect that the factor named was responsible for the observed result, we cannot be at all certain. In matters as complicated as a political candidate's popularity rating or the winning of basketball games many factors are operative, any one of which individually or all of which collectively could be responsible for the result noted.

While it may, for our purposes, be taken as a truism that nothing happens without a cause, in the practical affairs of everyday life few actions or states of affairs are the result of a single factor. For this reason—and especially when dealing with matters of personal or social behavior—determining causes is at best a complicated business. Certainly it is dangerous to leap to the conclusion that just because one phenomenon occurs prior to another, the first is the cause of the second.

Is the factor pointed to as a cause capable of producing the alleged effect? Suppose someone were to assert that a drastic drop in enrollment at Springville Academy is due to the fact that the dates of spring recess have been changed from early April to the middle of March. Although this change may well have been the cause of some student dissatisfaction or may even have led one or two individuals to transfer, it is improbable that a relatively minor alteration in schedule could be responsible for a marked decrease in enrollment.

When considering the ability of a cause to produce an effect, it is often helpful to distinguish between what the logicians call *necessary* and *sufficient causes.* A *necessary cause* is one in whose absence a given result cannot occur, but which in itself is not capable of bringing that result about. A *sufficient cause*, as its name implies, can lead to the result named.

Thus, a necessary cause or condition for a fire's burning is that oxygen be present. Yet the presence of oxygen alone will not result in fire. For a flame to be produced, combustible material must be ignited by the striking of a match, the rubbing of sticks together, etc. Similarly, though moisture and sunshine must be present in appropriate amounts if one is to have a vegetable garden, they are not in themselves sufficient causes for the garden's existence. In addition, obviously, one must plant the right sorts of seeds.

Are there factors in the situation which impede or negate the alleged cause? In the area of human affairs, most actions and conditions are not only the result of a number of causes operating in concert; they are also, more often than not, the product of a competition between conflicting or counteracting causes. Consider these examples:

Each year for the past five years, two selected members of the River City police force have attended the summer Traffic Institute conducted by North-western University. There they have learned the most modern methods of accident prevention, and upon returning home have put these methods into effect. Over the same five-year period, however, the volume of traffic in River City has increased approximately 40 percent. Hence, despite the introduction of improved methods of traffic control, the accident rate has dropped only slightly.

A small manufacturer of hand tools hires an efficiency expert to find ways of cutting production costs. At the same time that cost-cutting machinery is being installed, however, wages and the cost of raw materials continue to rise. As a result, the efforts of the efficiency expert do not result in significant savings.

Though obviously hypothetical, these examples are typical of the way in which a cause that in itself might produce a given effect often comes into conflict with one or more other causes that run counter to it. Under these circumstances, the outcome will be quite different than if a single cause had operated alone and unimpeded.

Argument from Sign

The argument from sign, instead of connecting phenomena on the basis of cause and effect, connects them on the basis of symptom and condition. It asserts that some observable mark or indication is evidence of the existence of a past, present, or future state of affairs.

In the examples that follow, the first shows how an argument from sign may be used to establish the claim that a certain state of affairs existed in the past; the second concerns a state of affairs existing at present; and the third makes a prediction about the future.

Evidence   John wears a Veterans of Foreign Wars button in his lapel.

Warrant   Since a requirement for membership in the Veterans of Foreign Wars is that one has served in the armed forces overseas,

Claim   We may assume that John at one time served in the armed forces overseas.

Evidence   The state flag is flying over the capitol. *effect*

Warrant   Since the state flag flies over the capitol only on those days on which the legislature is in session,

Claim   The legislature is in session today. *cause*

Evidence   Buds are forming on the rose bushes.

Warrant   Since rose bushes usually burst into bloom shortly after the buds appear,

Claim   We will have roses soon.

The distinction between argument from cause and argument from sign is sometimes a source of confusion. The point to keep in mind, however, is that while argument from sign tells *what* is the case by alleging that a given condition has existed, is existing, or will exist, argument from cause explains *why* this is the case—accounts for the existence of the phenomenon in question.

All of us know many things to be so without knowing *why* they are so—without being able to account for them. In the first of the examples given above, we know from John's VFW button that he has served in the armed services overseas. On the basis of this indication alone, however, we are unable to say why he did so. Did he volunteer for overseas service? Was he sent abroad because men with his military speciality were needed in a certain country? Likewise, although we know on the basis of experience that roses usually bloom so many days after the buds appear, we may not be able to explain in either technical or ordinary language the reason for this particular time span.

Complicating the problem still further is the fact that occasionally the argument from sign and the argument from cause coincide. Thus a rash of a certain sort may be both a sign (a way of our knowing) that a child has measles and also an effect of his having contracted the disease. Despite this occasional coincidence, however, the arguments remain separate and distinct in purpose, the aim of sign being to tell us *what* is the case and of cause to explain *why* it is so.

Tests of Sign

Obviously, not all signs merit the same degree of confidence. The fact that a young man is seen entering a voting booth on election day may be taken as strong assurance that he is at least eighteen years of age. The fact that two weeks earlier he and some of his friends went to hear the Republican candidate speak is by no means a certain indication that he voted a straight Republican ticket.

In evaluating arguments from sign, therefore, one should always ask: How reliable is the sign in question? Can it be taken as a certain or infallible indication of the action or condition named in the claim, or does it merely suggest a possibility or likelihood? In the latter case, before drawing a conclusion one way or the other, one should look for corroborating signs. To the extent that these are present, endorsement of the claim to which they point is justified. If they are absent, the claim frequently needs to be qualified or restricted.

Checklist

I. Techniques of Comparison
    A. Argument from parallel case
        1. Do the crucial points of similarity between the case or cases brought as evidence and the case embodied in the claim outweigh the crucial points of difference?
    B. Argument from analogy
        1. Is the similarity between the relationship cited as evidence and

the relationship asserted in the claim clearly and readily apparent?

2. Can additional relationships be cited as evidence for the claim?

II. Techniques of Generalization

A. Argument from some to more

1. Do all of the items in the sample used as evidence belong to the same class?
2. Are the items in the sample used as evidence typical members of that class?
3. Is the sample used as evidence large enough to support the generalization advanced in the claim?

B. Argument from some to all

1. All three of the foregoing tests.
2. Are negative instances satisfactorily accounted for?

III. Techniques of Classification

A. Argument from all to one or from all to some

1. Are the statements offered as evidence and justification true to fact?
2. Do the item or items named in the warrant fall within the class generalized about in the evidence step?

B. Argument from some to one or from some to some

1. Both of the foregoing tests.
2. Is the claim statement appropriately qualified or restricted?

IV. Techniques of Division

A. Do the items mentioned as alternatives include all reasonable alternatives?

B. Are the items mentioned as alternatives mutually exclusive?

V. Techniques of Connection

A. Argument from cause

1. Is the alleged cause the true cause?
2. Is the factor pointed as a cause capable of producing the alleged effect?
3. Are there factors in the situation which impede or negate the alleged cause?

B. Argument from sign

1. Is the alleged sign a reliable indication of the presence of the condition it is said to represent?

Exercises

Classify each of the following arguments as to type and explain why you believe it to be sound or unsound.

1. (First traveler to second traveler:) I see a Howard Johnson sign ahead.

Let's stop there for lunch. Howard Johnson restaurants always have clean restrooms and decent food.

2. The merchants out at the new shopping center must be getting rich. The big parking lot is filled with cars from morning to night.

3. If we continue to sell wheat to Russia, the cost of bread in this country will continue to rise.

4. I'm afraid that Mrs. Green's Johnny will come to no good end. The old saying "Spare the rod and spoil the child" is just as true today as it ever was.

5. Any football team that lacks a solid defense cannot hope to win all of its games. Look at the Falcons and Eagles this year and at the Rangers and Braves last season.

6. Plato must have been happy; for the wise alone are happy, and Plato certainly was a wise man.

7. A man may be both learned and a fool. Haven't you heard it said of James I, "He never said a foolish thing and never did a wise one"?

8. Impatience is not always a bad thing. Consider the person who is dissatisfied with our progress in eliminating discrimination against minority groups. He is impatient, but quite justifiably so.

9. If, as some people claim, legal abortions should be available to every woman who wants one, why should we not also legalize homicides of all sorts, thus placing in the hands of any individual power over the life of another?

10. Is it so bad, then, to be misunderstood? Pythagoras was misunderstood, and Socrates, and Jesus, and Luther, and Copernicus, and Galileo, and Newton, and every pure and wise spirit that ever took flesh. To be great is to be misunderstood. *Emerson.*

11. No body can be healthful without exercise, neither natural body nor politic; and certainly to a kingdom or estate, a just and honorable war is the true exercise. A civil war indeed, is like the heat of a fever, but a foreign war is like the heat of exercise and serveth to keep the body in health. *Bacon, "Of the True Greatness of Kingdoms and Estates."*

12. The new family that moved in down the street certainly must be nice people. They have a lighted Christmas wreath in every window and a large, gaily decorated tree near the front door.

13. Alexander died after a drinking bout, Caesar was murdered, Mussolini was hanged, Hitler took poison, Napoleon wasted away on lonely St. Helena. Clearly, to live by the sword is to perish by it.

14. Only three persons knew the combination to the safe: Jones, the president of the company, Andrews, the treasurer, and Black, the general manager. But on the night of the robbery Jones was in New York and Andrews was sick in bed. Therefore, the culprit is Black.

15. The student activism that marked our campus during the years 1968–71 will not recur. After all, the draft has been abolished, the Vietnam War is over, parietal rules have been relaxed, and students have been given an effective voice in the governance of the university.

16. Movies today have lost all sense of decency. Only last week I saw a film so full of violence and nudity that I walked out in disgust.

17. If you speak the truth, men will hate you. If you do not, the gods will hate you. Therefore, it is best to remain silent.

18. (President of Acme Manufacturing Company to the company's stockholders:) During June and July we spent $80,000 for advertisements in newspapers and magazines. During August and September we spent the same amount, but in addition to newspaper and magazine advertisements we bought time on local television stations. Our August and September sales were a third larger than those for the preceding two months. Therefore, in the future we shall spend increasing amounts of our advertising budget for television advertising.

19. Whatever you do, don't go into farming if you want to make money. When crops are good, oversupply forces the price down; when, because of poor crops, prices are high, you have little or nothing to sell.

20. Prudence . . . will dictate that Governments long established should not be changed for light and transient causes; and accordingly all experience hath shown, that mankind are more disposed to suffer, while evils are sufferable, than to right themselves by abolishing the forms to which they are accustomed. But when a long train of abuses and usurpations, pursuing invariably the same Object evinces a design to reduce them under absolute Despotism, it is their right, it is their duty, to throw off such Government, and to provide new Guards for their future security.—Such has been the patient sufferance of these Colonies; and such is now the necessity which constrains them to alter their former Systems of Government. The history of the present King of Great Britian is a history of repeated injuries and usurpations, all having in direct object the establishment of an absolute Tyranny over these States. *The Declaration of Independence.*

21. Mercury, the planet nearest the Sun, is certainly too hot to support life. The side of Mercury that is turned toward the Sun has an average temperature of 660°F. Since the orbit is rather eccentric this temperature becomes as high as 770°F, hot enough to melt lead, when Mercury is closest to the Sun. The opposite side is extremely cold, its temperature not being known. Gravity on Mercury is about one-fourth that on Earth. This fact combined with the high temperature makes it certain that Mercury has no atmosphere, which is consistent with observational data on this point. It is quite impossible that life as found on Earth could exist on Mercury. *Edward U. Condon,* Scientific Study of Unidentified Flying Objects, *p. 29.*

22. If you cut up a diamond into little bits, it will entirely lose the value it had as a whole; and an army divided up into small bodies of soldiers, loses all its strength. So a great intellect sinks to the level of an ordinary one, as soon as it is interrupted and disturbed, its attention distracted and drawn off from the matter in hand: for its superiority depends upon its power of concentration—of bringing all its strength to bear upon one theme, in the same way as a concave mirror collects into one point all the rays of light that strike upon it. *Schopenhauer, "On Noise."*

23. It is ironic that our present pot laws are upheld chiefly by the older generation, and flouted and condemned by the young; for it is the senior generation that should understand the issue most clearly, having lived through the era of alcohol prohibition. They saw with their own eyes that the entire nation—not just the drinkers and the sellers of liquor— suffered violent moral and mental harm from that particular outbreak of armed and rampant puritanism. They should certainly remember that attempts to legislate morality result only in widespread disrespect for law, new markets and new profits for gangsters, increased violence, and such wholesale bribery and corruption that the Government itself becomes a greater object of contempt than the criminal classes. Above all, they should be able to see the parallel between the lawless Twenties and the anarchic Sixties and realize that both were produced by bad laws—laws that had no right to exist in the first place. *From "Pot: A Rational Approach," by Dr. Joel Fort,* Playboy *Magazine, October 1969, p. 131.*[1]

24. *Socrates.* And now, Laches, do you try and tell me in like manner, What is that common quality which is called courage . . . ?

Laches. I should say that courage is a sort of endurance of the soul, if I am to speak of the universal nature which pervades [all cases of courage].

Soc. But that is what we must do if we are to answer the question. And yet I cannot say that every kind of endurance is, in my opinion, to be deemed courage. Hear my reason: I am sure, Laches, that you would consider courage to be a very noble quality.

La. Most noble, certainly.

Soc. And you would say that a wise endurance is also good and noble?

La. Very noble.

Soc. But what would you say of a foolish endurance? Is not that, on the other hand, to be regarded as evil and hurtful?

La. True.

Soc. And is anything noble which is evil and hurtful?

La. It would be wrong, Socrates, to say so.

---

[1]Reprinted by permission of *Playboy* Magazine and by Joel Fort, M.D., founder-leader, National Center for Solving Special Social and Health Problems—FORT HELP, San Francisco; author, *Alcohol: Our Biggest Drug Problem* and *The Pleasure Seekers;* and lecturer, School of Criminology, University of California at Berkeley.

Soc. Then you would not admit that sort of endurance to be courage—for it is not noble, but courage is noble?

La. You are right. *Plato, "Laches,"* The Dialogues of Plato.

25. If the world had no beginning in time, then an eternity must have elapsed up to every given point of time, and therefore an infinite series of successive states of things must have passed in the world. The infinity of a series, however, consists in this, that it never can be completed by means of a successive synthesis. Hence an infinite past series of worlds is impossible, and the beginning of the world is a necessary condition of its existence. *Emanuel Kant.*

26. The prevalence of the different forms of Christianity after the Reformation shows a coincidence with Race that chance would not account for. The Greek church was propagated principally in the Slavonic race; the Roman Catholic church coincides largely with the Celtic race; and the Protestant church has found very little footing out of the Teutonic races. From this coincidence must be presumed a positive affinity between the several forms and the mental peculiarities of the races. *Alexander Bain*, Logic.

27. "Looky here, Jim; does a cat talk like we do?"

"No, a cat don't."

"Well, does a cow?"

"No, a cow don't, nuther."

"Does a cat talk like a cow, or a cow talk like a cat?"

"No, day don't."

"It's natural and right for 'em to talk different from each other, ain't it?"

"Course."

"And ain't it natural and right for a cat and a cow to talk different from us? You answer me that."

"Is a cat a man, Huck?"

"No."

"Well, den, dey ain't no sense in a cat talkin' like a man. Is a cow a man?—or is a cow a cat?"

"No, she ain't neither of them."

"Well, den, she ain't got no business to talk like either one er the yuther of 'em. Is a Frenchman a man?"

"Yes."

"Well, den! Dad blame it, why doan' he talk like a man? You answer me dat!" *Mark Twain,* Huckleberry Finn.

28. The more minutely psychology studies human nature, the more clearly it finds there traces of secondary affections, relating the impressions of the environment with one another and with our impulses in quite different ways from those mere associations of coexistence and succession which are practically all that pure empiricism can admit. Take the love of drunkenness; take bashfulness, the terror of high places, the tendency to seasickness, to faint at the sight of blood, the susceptibility to musical sounds; take the emotion of the comical, the passion for poetry, for mathematics, or for metaphysics—no one of these things can be wholly explained by either association or utility. They *go with* other things that can be so explained, no doubt; and some of them are prophetic of future utilities, since there is nothing in us for which some use may not be found. But their origin is in incidental complications to our cerebral structure. . . . *William James, "The Moral Philosopher and the Moral Life."*

29. I had a couple of friends who were in the habit of losing their tempers, and when they lost their tempers they were in the habit of using very unparliamentary language. Some of their friends induced them to make a promise that they never would swear inside the town limits. When the impulse next came upon them, they took a street car to go out of town to swear, and by the time they got out of town they did not want to swear. . . . Now, illustrating the great by the small, that is true of the passions of nations. *Woodrow Wilson, "Address at Pueblo, Colorado, September 25, 1919."*

30. In maintaining a friendship, as in a footrace, you must train yourself not only so that you succeed in running as far as is required, but so that . . . you easily run beyond that point.   Rhetorica ad Herennium, *iv. 47.60.*

31. Again however solid things are thought to be, you may yet learn from this that they are of rare body: in rocks and caverns the moisture of water oozes through and all things weep with abundant drops; food distributes itself through the whole body of living things; trees grow and yield fruit in season, because food is diffused through the whole from the very roots over the stem and all the boughs. Voices pass through walls and fly through houses shut, stiffening frost pierces to the bones. Now if there are no void parts, by what way can the bodies severally pass? You would see it to be quite impossible. Once more, why do we see one thing surpass another in weight though not larger in size? For if there is just as much body in a ball of wood as there is in a lump of lead, it is natural it should weigh the same, since the property of body is to weigh all things downwards, while on the contrary the nature of void is ever without weight. Therefore, when a thing is just as large, yet is found to be lighter, it proves sure enough that it has more of void in it; while on the other hand that which is heavier shows that there is in it more of body and that it contains within it much less of void. Therefore that which we are seeking with keen reason exists sure enough, mixed up in things; and we call it void. *Lucretius,* On the Nature of Things.

32. We may observe a very great similitude between this earth which we inhabit, and the other planets, Saturn, Jupiter, Mars, Venus, and Mercury. They all revolve around the sun, as the earth does, although at different distances and in different periods. They borrow all their light from the sun, as the earth does. Several of them are known to revolve round their axis like the earth, and, by that means, must have

a like succession of day and night. Some of them have moons, that serve to give them light in the absence of the sun, as our moon does to us. They are all, in their motions, subject to the same law of gravitation, as the earth is. From all this similitude, it is not unreasonable to think, that those planets may, like our earth, be the habitation of various order [sic] of living creatures. *Thomas Reid, Essay I,* Essays on the Intellectual Powers of Man.

33. Now if we survey the universe, so far as it falls under our knowledge, it bears a great resemblance to an animal or organized body, and seems actuated with a like principle of life and motion. A continual circulation of matter in it produces no disorder: a continual waste in every part is incessantly repaired; the closest sympathy is perceived throughout the entire system: and each part or member, in performing its proper offices, operates both to its own preservation, and to that of the whole. The world, therefore, I infer, is an animal, and the Deity is the *soul* of the world, actuating it, and actuated by it. *David Hume,* Dialogues Concerning Natural Religion.

34. Whatever is in motion is moved by another: and it is clear to the sense that something, the sun, for instance, is in motion. Therefore it is set in motion by something else moving it. Now that which moves it is itself either moved or not. If it be not moved, then the point is proved that we must needs postulate an immovable mover: and this we call God. If, however, it be moved, it is moved by another mover. Either, therefore, we must proceed to infinity, or we must come to an immovable mover. But it is not possible to proceed to infinity. Therefore, it is necessary to postulate an immovable mover. *St. Thomas Aquinas,* Summa contra Gentiles.

35. Two prominent Philadelphia psychiatrists recently declared: "The country has been terribly misled into believing that marijuana is a harmless substance. It ain't so harmless."

   After studying thirteen adults between the ages of twenty and forty-one who smoked pot three to ten times a week, they found in every one of them difficulty in remembering recent events and perceiving lapses of time, as well as such symptoms as apathy, fatigue, sluggishness, and lack of physical coordination. When the patients quit smoking marijuana the symptoms disappeared. *Based on a report in the* National Observer, *October 14, 1972, p. 3.*

36. To find the solution of a definite problem requires a greater effort of genius than to resolve one not specified; for in the latter case hazard, chance, may play the greater part, while in the former all is the work of reasoning and intelligent mind. Thus, we are certain that the Dutchman, the first inventor of the telescope, was a simple spectacle-maker, who, handling by chance different forms of glasses, looked, also by chance, through two of them, one convex and the other concave, held at different distances from the eye; saw and noted the unexpected result; and thus found the instrument. *John Joseph Fahie,* Galileo: His Life and Works, *p. 80.*

37. Theology teaches that the sun has been created to illuminate the earth. But one moves the torch in order to illuminate the house, and not the house in order to be illuminated by the torch. Hence it is the sun which revolves around the earth, and not the earth which revolves around the sun. *Besian Array, 1671.*

38. No man is allowed to be a judge in his own cause, because his interest would certainly bias his judgment, and, not improbably, corrupt his integrity. With equal, nay with greater reason, a body of men are unfit to be both judges and parties at the same time; yet what are many of the most important acts of legislation, but so many judicial determinations, not indeed concerning the rights of single citizens, but concerning the rights of large bodies of citizens? And what are the different classes of legislators but advocates and parties to the causes which they determine? Is a law passed concerning private debts? It is a question to which the creditors are parties on one side and the debtors on the other. *James Madison*, Federalist Papers.

39. My argument against God [when I used to be an atheist] was that the universe seemed so cruel and unjust. But how had I got this idea of *just* and *unjust?* A man doesn't call a line crooked unless he has some idea of a straight line. What was I comparing this universe with when I called it unjust? If the whole show was bad and senseless from A to Z, so to speak, why did I, who was supposed to be part of the show, find myself in such violent reaction against it? A man feels wet when he falls into water, because man isn't a water animal: a fish wouldn't feel wet. Of course, I could have given up my idea of justice by saying it was nothing but a private idea of my own. But if I did that then my argument against God collapsed too—for the argument depended on saying that the world was really unjust, not that it just didn't happen to please my private fancies. Thus in the very act of trying to prove that God didn't exist—in other words, that the whole of reality was senseless—I found I was forced to assume that one part of reality—namely my idea of justice was full of sense. Consequently, atheism turns out to be too simple. If the whole universe has no meaning, we should never have found out that it has no meaning; just as if there were no light in the universe and therefore no creatures with eyes we should never know it was dark. *Dark* would be a word without meaning. *C. S. Lewis*, The Case for Christianity, *pp. 34–35.*[2]

Writing or Speaking Assignment

Prepare a short speech or essay in which you support a claim using one of the basic types of arguments (comparison, generalization, classification, division, or connection).

Select a claim narrow or restricted enough so it can be supported by a single argument. Ground the warrant on a strong base of evidence. In reasoning from evidence to claim, observe the rules and suggestions set forth in this chapter.

When choosing a subject for your speech or essay, ask yourself the following questions: Is this something I am interested in and would like to learn more about? Would this topic be of interest to my readers or listeners? Can it be handled adequately in the time or space available? Is it worthwhile talking or writing about? Will a knowledge of it or right attitudes toward it be important to those who hear or read what I shall say?

For Additional Reading

Ehninger, Douglas. "The Logic of Argument." In *Argumentation: Principles and Practice*, ed. James McBath. 2nd ed. New York: Holt, Rinehart & Winston, 1963. Pp. 169–91.

Ehninger, Douglas, and **Wayne Brockriede.** *Decision by Debate.* New York: Dodd, Mead & Co., 1963. Chapter 10, "Substantive Proof."

Gautheir, David P. *Practical Reasoning: The Structure and Foundations of Prudential and Moral Arguments and Their Exemplification in Discourse.* London: Oxford University Press, 1963.

Olson, Robert G. *Meaning and Argument: Elements of Logic.* New York: Harcourt Brace Jovanovich, Inc., 1969. Chapter 13, "Generalization," and Chapter 14, "Confirmation."

Perelman, Chaim, and **L. Olbrechts-Tyteca.** *The New Rhetoric: A Treatise on Argument.* Notre Dame, Ind.: University of Notre Dame Press, 1969. Part III, "Techniques of Argumentation."

Ray, Jack, and **Harry Zavos.** "Reasoning and Argument: Deduction and Induction," and "Reasoning and Argument: Some Special Problems and Types." In *Perspectives on Argumentation*, ed. Gerald R. Miller and Thomas Nilsen. Glenview, Ill.: Scott, Foresman and Company, 1966. Pp. 50–109.

Toulmin, Stephen. *The Uses of Argument.* London: Cambridge University Press, 1958. Chapter 3, "The Layout of Arguments."

Chapter VII.
Patterns of Proof

The purpose of an argument, as we learned in Chapter I, is to win warrantable assent to a claim that is disbelieved or doubted. To this end the claim must, as a first requirement, be supported by sound evidence and cogent reasoning. Unless this requirement is met the argument will fail, for though assent may be gained, it will not be warranted. As an additional requirement, however, the evidence and reasoning contained in the argument must successfully put to rest those questions which are likely to occur to a reader or listener when the claim is advanced. Unless this requirement is met, assent will not only be unwarranted; it cannot even be gained.

An argument, in short, has both a logical and a rhetorical component—is both a self-contained unit of proof and a practical instrument for effecting persuasion. Logically, the purpose of an argument is to show that a claim deserves acceptance because it follows from or is implied by the evidence and reasoning offered on its behalf. Whether or not anyone endorses the claim is, from this point of view, irrelevant. Rhetorically, an argument succeeds only when a claim that has been shown to be relevant is actually endorsed by the person or persons for whom it is intended. No matter how strong the evidence or cogent the reasoning, unless such acceptance is gained rhetorically the argument fails.

Up to this point we have been concerned primarily with matters relating to the logical components of an argument—kinds and tests of evidence, criteria of valid reasoning, and the like. In this chapter we shall shift our focus and consider the rhetorical or persuasive components.

Because each individual who is exposed to an argument approaches the experience with a unique set of attitudes and expectancies, it is impossible to predict in advance exactly what he will require in the way of proof before acceding to the claim advanced. Through long experience, however, it has become possible to predict with a considerable degree of certainty the sorts of questions people in general tend to raise when confronted with each of the types of claims described in Chapter III. Using these questions as his guides, the arguer is able to direct his appeals into those broad channels which are most likely to lead him to the goal he seeks. Then, through a more detailed study of the individuals who comprise his immediate audience, he can further sharpen and refine his appeals.

For obvious reasons, the discussion that follows is limited to the first of these two steps in analysis. Specifically, it reviews the various sorts of assertions encompassed by declarative, classificatory, evaluative, and actuative claims. Then it considers the questions readers or listeners typically wish to have answered before these assertions are accepted.

Declarative Claims

Declarative claims, it will be recalled, assert either (1) that some act has/has not occurred in the past, is/is not occurring in the present, or will/will not occur in the future; or (2) that some condition or state of affairs has/has not existed in the past, does/does not exist at present, or will/will not exist in the future.

Here are some examples of declarative claims concerning acts:

Past.   Senator Jones secretly promised party leaders he would not run for reelection this year.

Present. Senator Jones now seems to be reconsidering this decision.

Future. Senator Jones will probably run for reelection this year.

The next three declarative claims make assertions concerning conditions or states of affairs:

Past.   Party leaders privately were pleased by Senator Jones' promise not to seek reelection.

Present. Party leaders are disturbed at the news that Senator Jones is reconsidering.

Future. Without the support of party leaders, Senator Jones' bid for reelection will probably fail.

In any of the six cases cited, before assenting to the claim advanced, readers or listeners customarily ask to be supplied with answers to some or all of the following questions:

1. *What SIGNS or SYMPTOMS suggest the likelihood of the alleged act or state of affairs?*
2. *What MOTIVES or CAUSES account for this state of affairs?*
3. *Were/are CIRCUMSTANCES favorable to the occurrence of the act or the existence of the state of affairs?*
4. *Does the TESTIMONY of qualified persons lend credibility to the claim?*

In the first of the sample proofs that follow, *sign* and *cause* are combined with *circumstance* and *testimony* to establish the probability of a past action. The second example illustrates how these same ingredients might support the claim that a given state of affairs will exist in the future.

Claim   There can, I think, be little doubt of the fact that Senator Jones secretly promised party leaders he would not run for reelection this year.

Evidence and Warrants.   Not only has he refused all invitations to speak and to participate in party councils (*Signs*), but it is well known that party leaders strongly urged him to withdraw from the race (*Cause*). Nor would such action on Senator Jones' part be at all surprising. For months, his potential opponents have been steadily gaining ground in the opinion polls, while he has been falling ever farther behind (*Circumstance*). Adding it all together, is it surprising that Tod Roberts, the well-known political analyst of the *Tribune*, should declare, "We can now almost certainly say that Senator Jones has secretly promised party leaders he will not seek reelection this year" (*Testimony*)?

Claim   Why do I believe that, if Senator Jones runs without the support of party leaders, his bid for reelection will probably fail?

Evidence and Warrants   Well, first, no one running in this state without the full support of his party has ever won a senatorial seat (*Sign*). Second, lacking the support of his party, he will lose the much-needed services of hundreds of precinct captains and party workers (*Cause*). Third, in a state changing as rapidly as ours, Senator Jones' policies are so out-of-date that they alone will not carry the day (*Circumstance*). And, fourth, the six best students of state politics I know all agree that he would have little or no chance (*Testimony*).

Although in the preceding examples all four elements of *sign, cause, circumstance,* and *testimony* are present, rhetorically effective arguments in support of declarative claims often consist of only one or two of these types of proof. The signs indicative of an act or condition may be so clear and numerous, the motives or causes so transparent, the circumstances so obviously favorable or unfavorable, or the testimony so authoritative that corroborating support is not required. At other times, two of these elements—for example, cause and sign or cause and circumstance—may combine to produce convincing proof.

The point to be borne in mind, however, is that when a declarative claim is advanced, all four of the questions stated above become relevant and represent potential points of doubt on which a reasonable reader or listener may seek assurance before acceding. For this reason they always need to be considered, both when advancing declarative claims of one's own and when evaluating the declarative claims advanced by others.

Classificatory Claims

While declarative claims are concerned with whether something was, is, or will be the case, classificatory claims are concerned with how something recognized to be the case should be defined or classified—with the category into which an acknowledged act or condition properly falls.

Although in most instances classificatory claims offer judgments relative to past or present actions or conditions, they may, when stated as hypothetical or "if-then" propositions, also advance judgments about future occurrences or states of affairs.

Consider these examples of classificatory claims bearing on past, present, and future actions:

Past.   The act of the protesters in entering the building to destroy files and records can only be described (classified) as criminal trespass.

Present. Entering a building to destroy the files and records housed therein is an act of (is classifiable as) criminal trespass.

Future. If the protesters enter the building to destroy the files and records, they will be guilty of (their act will be classifiable as) criminal trespass.

These classificatory claims advance assertions concerning past, present, and future conditions or states of affairs:

Past.   Prior to the revolution of 1905, Zorbia was (classifiable as) an autocracy.

Present. Today Zorbia is (classifiable as) communistic.

Future. If present trends continue, it is likely that in a few years Zorbia will be (classifiable as) a democracy.

Since the purpose of a classificatory claim is to designate the category into which a given item of knowledge or experience properly falls, a reader or listener may, as a condition of granting his endorsement, require information concerning (1) the properties a thing must possess in order to qualify for membership in a given class or (2) the nature of the item in question.

The questions that arise when a classificatory claim is advanced are, therefore, two:

1. *What specifications must an item of knowledge or experience meet in order to qualify for membership in the class named?*

2. *Does the item under consideration meet these specifications?*

Here are some sample proofs developed in support of two of the classificatory claims stated above. Observe how in each case the appropriate questions are dealt with.

>   ***Evidence and Warrants***   On the matter of criminal trespass the law is clear. I quote the definition of the term as given in Bouvier's *Law Dictionary:* "Any unauthorized entry upon the realty of another to the damage thereof" (*Specifications of an act of trespass set forth*).

And what did the protesters do? They forcibly entered the building by breaking down the locked doors. They not only tore the records from the file cabinets, but, as they themselves admit, they deliberately set fire to the records and watched them burn (*Act shown to meet specifications*).

Claim   If this does not constitute criminal trespass, then what in the world does?

Claim   If, as is generally conceded, an autocracy is a government ruled over by a single individual whose authority is unlimited and whose decisions are in all cases final, then prior to the revolution in 1905 Zorbia clearly was an autocracy (*Specifications of an autocracy set forth*).

Evidence and Warrants   Zorbia in those days had no legislature to make laws and no court system to interpret or enforce them. Elections were entirely unknown. The king was not only the political head of state, but also commander-in-chief of the armed forces and high priest of the only officially recognized religion. In one year alone he ordered more than five hundred persons put to death without trial and altered or abolished no fewer than eighty statutes which he deemed dangerous to his own position. In these and other ways he ruled alone and unchecked, just as his ancestors had done for centuries (*Conditions in Zorbia shown to meet specifications of an autocracy*).

In the sample proofs just presented, attention is paid to both of the questions indicated above. That is, the specifications an item must meet in order to qualify for membership in a given class are set forth, and the assignment of a particular act or condition to this class is justified. When one or the other of these considerations is acknowledged by the reader or listener, however, it need not receive attention in the proof pattern. Under these circumstances, a classificatory proof might take this form:

Evidence and Warrants   If present trends toward extension of the franchise, encouragement of private enterprise, toleration of artists and writers, and guaranteed civil liberties for all continue, within a few years Zorbia will be (classifiable as) a democracy (*Conditions that would justify classifying Zorbia as a democracy described; specifications which a country must meet in order to be thus classified omitted as understood by person addressed*).

Evaluative Claims

So far as their rhetorical component is concerned, evaluative claims bear a close resemblance to classificatory claims. When we declare that something is good, right, or desirable, what we are really doing is assigning it membership in the class of things which meet with our approval. In declaring something bad, wrong, or undesirable, we are assigning it to the class of things which in our judgment deserve censure.

Observe how in each of these examples evaluation proceeds by placing the subject of the claim in the class of things disapproved:

Past. Your decision to withhold information from the police was (fell into the class of things that are) wrong.

Present. Withholding information from the police is (falls into the class of things that are) wrong.

Future. If you withhold information from the police, you will be doing (your act will fall into the class of things that are) wrong.

Because evaluating is essentially a matter of categorizing, here, as in the case of classificatory claims, a reader or listener may legitimately require additional information concerning either the item under consideration or the characteristics of the class to which that item is being assigned. That is, he may properly ask one or both of the following questions:

1. *By what criteria are we to measure the goodness/badness, rightness/ wrongness, desirability/undesirability of an act or condition such as this?*

2. *Does the act or condition presently in question meet the specifications indicated? Does it qualify for membership in the class as delineated by the criteria mentioned?*

Following is an example of how answers to these two questions may combine to provide support for an evaluative claim:

Evidence   A well-established principle of human conduct recognized by men of all ages holds that any act which endangers the safety or security of another person is wrong (*Specification of a wrong act*).

Warrant   Clearly, withholding information from the police hampers the apprehension of criminals, and thus poses a threat to the community (*Explanation of why withholding information from the police qualifies for membership in the class previously described*).

Claim   Can there be any doubt that withholding such information is wrong?

Actuative Claims

Although actuative claims reflect an appraisive judgment on the part of the person proposing them, they differ from evaluative claims in two important respects.

First, rather than assessing the worth of something that is already the case, they recommend that something new be made the case. Thus they call not only for appraisal, but also for performance. They terminate not merely in belief, but in belief translated into action.

Second, whereas evaluative claims may concern things past or present as well as things future, actuative claims, as recommendations concerning behavior that should be undertaken, look only to the future. They set forth what, in the judgment of their author, the appropriate agent ought to do or effect.

Each of these characteristics may be observed in the sample actuative claims that follow. In the first instance, the proposed agent of change is the person to whom the claim is addressed. In the second, a third party is named as the change agent.

1. Next semester you ought to double the amount of time you devote to study.
2. Our state legislature should pass a law requiring that all automobiles more than two years old pass a rigid safety inspection every six months.

What, then, are the points on which a reader or listener might demand assurance before endorsing an actuative claim?

Although all four of these questions may not arise in every instance, it always is appropriate to inquire of the claim's author:

1. *Is the action you recommend needed? What problems or deficiencies exist in things as they now are?*

2. *Would the action you recommend remedy this situation? Would it solve the problems or repair the defects you point to?*

3. *Assuming the action you recommend is practicable, is it also desirable? Would it achieve the sought-after result without undue cost or danger, or without introducing new evils that are worse than the existing ones?*

4. *Is the action you recommend superior to all alternative methods of solving the problem or meeting the need?*

In the first of the following sample proofs, all four questions are dealt with. In the second, it is assumed that the persons addressed already recognize the existence of a need or problem. Therefore, only the last three questions are covered.

Claim   I think I need hardly remind you that over the course of the last three semesters your cumulative grade point average has fallen steadily until it is now dangerously close to the 1.5 figure at which students in this college are placed on academic probation (*Problem or need pointed out*).

In view of this situation, you must at least double the amount of time you devote to study each day.

Evidence and Warrant   As repeated investigations have shown, an extra hour a day spent at one's books raises an undergraduate's GPA half a point and three extra hours a day raise it nearly two points (*Proposed action shown to provide effective remedy*).

Since you obviously can no longer go on as you are, certainly this plan is preferable to being placed on probation and losing all social privileges (*Desirability of proposed action indicated*).

You can argue with instructors about grades until you are hoarse. You can change majors, or even transfer to another school. In the end, you will find that none of these things helps. Instructors will hold to their standards; other majors and other schools are just as tough. If you want to raise your GPA above the danger line, there is only one way to do it. And that is to double your study time (*Alternatives shown unfeasible*).

Claim   One effective way to reduce the slaughter on the streets and highways would be for our state legislature to pass a law requiring all automobiles that are more than two years old to pass a rigid inspection every six months.

Evidence and Warrant   I say this because figures gathered by the International Institute of Traffic Safety show that, in states where such an inspection law is in effect, traffic fatalities have been reduced by more than 5 percent (*Practicability of proposed solution established*).

Nor would such a requirement be burdensome to the average automobile owner. An inspection of the sort required takes only a few minutes and may be made at convenient neighborhood locations almost any hour of the day or night (*Desirability of proposal stated*).

Giving tickets for speeding and other traffic violations will not solve this part of the problem. As long as unsafe automobiles are on the road, an important cause of accidents will remain. Nor, as our state safety commissioner, Henry Black, has said, will the drivers of such cars have them repaired unless they are forced to do so (*Absence of feasible alternative established*).

We must urge the passage of a rigid inspection law.[1]

---

[1]In the examples here given, the actuative claims grow out of problem situations that strongly call for remedy. This, however, is not always the case. Sometimes actuative claims are advanced simply on the ground that the policies they embody represent desirable rather than necessary alterations in existing states of affairs. For example, an arguer may say, "I do not pretend that the two-way traffic now carried on Elm Street results in intolerable delays or that the accident rate is appreciably higher there than elsewhere in the city. I do submit, however, that traffic could flow still more smoothly and pedestrian crossings could be made safer if all westbound traffic were routed on Pine Street and if Elm were made a one-way artery for cars going east." In cases of this sort, besides showing that conditions are less perfect than they might be, an arguer generally is expected to show that the proposal he offers is feasible and that it would bring the advantages he claims. His remarks, however, tend to be cast in comparative rather than categorical terms and the weight of his argument usually falls on the advantages to be gained.

Mutually Supportive Logical and Rhetorical Components

In an argument that achieves its purpose of winning warrantable assent to a claim that is disbelieved or doubted, the logical and rhetorical components interact and are mutually supportive. Appropriate attention to rhetorical considerations directs evidence and reasoning into the proper channels, and thus assures that they will exert the maximum persuasive impact. Sound evidence and reasoning, in turn, provide convincing answers to the questions that naturally arise when the claim is advanced, and therefore effectively put to rest the doubts and hesitations that prevent belief or block action.[2]

Exercises

Be prepared to discuss in class what sort of claim (declarative, classificatory, evaluative, or actuative) each of the following passages seeks to support. (There may be room for some differences of opinion here.) Then undertake to evaluate how effective the passage is rhetorically—that is, how strong and persuasive a case it makes out for the claim advanced. (Here almost certainly opinions will differ.)

1. Against Plastic Milk Containers

To the Editor:

I am hoping to awaken Cedar Rapids citizens and other Iowans to an environmental problem of which they may otherwise be unaware. The problem is the now popular use of plastic containers for packaging milk . . . . I think it is the duty of the citizens who are concerned with our environment to discourage the manufacture and use of containers of this type.

Plastics now constitute over 3 percent of total collected household, commercial and industrial waste. About two-thirds of this share is plastic packaging. More use of plastic packaging will cause this percentage to rise, thus causing more problems with disposal. Plastic containers are not returnable, thus they are disposed of by the normal process of trash disposal. The only known method for the final disposition of plastics is incineration or sanitary landfill. I feel that both these methods are impractical and ecologically unsound. . . .

Finally, because of the nonreturnability of plastic containers, consumers must pay increased prices for milk. I think the solution . . . is merely a return to glass bottles for milk. . . .

Glass containers are returnable, and milk in glass containers is cheaper for the consumer. Glass, if disposed of, can be recycled easier and for many

[2]Although in the preceding examples each step in the argument is supported by a single unit of proof, obviously chains or clusters of proofs are often needed to win a reader's or listener's adherence.

more uses than plastic. . . . Recycled glass has already been substituted for limestone components in asphalt street material. Also, when properly used, glass particles can serve as an effective soil conditioner. Furthermore, when glass is ground, it returns to the soil in virtually the same forms from which it came . . . .

I strongly urge citizens of Iowa to . . . return to purchasing milk packaged in glass.—James Brenner, 1200 First Ave., N.E., Cedar Rapids, Ia. 52402.   Des Moines Register, *Sunday, April 30, 1972, p. 9C.*[3]

2. Legal Heroin: An Escape From Plague

By Dean R. Spencer

The President has recently begun to mount another one of a long series of assaults on heroin traffic entering this country in an attempt to end the drug and the related crime problems. By attempting to stop the flow of drugs, he feels that these problems can be solved. This approach to the solution is wrong, for it is not possible to completely stop the flow of drugs into this country. The most that they could hope for would be a significant reduction in drug traffic.

Assuming that they are able to accomplish this, let us take a look at what would happen. First, the demand for drugs would not diminish. Because the supply is now more limited, the price would climb. This would mean that people who are on addictive drugs would now have to come up with more money to support their habit. For all too many of them that means turning to crime, for that is the only way they can get the needed money. The first result, then, is that the crime rates will go up. The second is that more people will enter the trade. With the increased profits that are now possible, more and more people will be willing to take the risks necessary in this business. In addition to the rising crime rate, we now have more people trading in drugs, which is just the opposite result from that which was desired.

A much more economically rational plan would be to legalize the distribution of heroin or a substitute from centers such as those found in England. This would have several effects. First, the users of drugs would not need nearly the money to support their habits that they now do. This should result in a dramatic fall in the crime rate. Most addicts are able to lead fairly normal lives as long as they have their daily dose. They could now become productive members of society instead of being the economic leeches that so many of them now are. And finally, the drug trade would be destroyed, for if there is no demand for a product that can only be supplied at a high cost and a high risk, then there will soon be no supply.

This is a workable policy, but as long as the feeling persists that the only way to meet this problem is with force and by paying Turkish farmers not to grow flowers, we are going to have to continue living with our present problem on an increasing scale. Daily Iowan, *September 8, 1972, p. 4.*[4]

[3]Reprinted by permission of James Brenner and the *Des Moines Register.*

[4]Reprinted by permission of the *Daily Iowan.*

3. Electronic Ignition

What's Behind the Expression "Extra Care in Engineering"

Chrysler Corporation's engineering excellence began with its first car in 1924. Through the years, Chrysler Corporation engineers have pioneered many important breakthroughs. Always, the objective has been to contribute to a more carefree, troublefree car. Plainly stated, the goal is to create a car that takes care of itself.

Electronic ignition is a typical case in point. This engineering advance was introduced in 1972 as a V-8 engine option, and it is standard on all 1973 engines built in North America. To owners, electronic ignition offers several vital benefits:

• There are no ignition breaker points to wear and need replacement. Ever. There is no condenser to be replaced either.

• Original engine timing is good for 50,000 miles, or longer.

• No ignition tuneups except a spark plug change at 18,000 miles, or longer.

• Delivers up to 35% higher ignition voltage at starting than a conventional system. Climatic extremes have no effect on electronic ignition.

• Eliminates major cause of engine misfiring.

• Reduces emissions caused by engine misfiring.

These direct benefits are measurable to the environmentalists properly concerned with ecology. And to the economy-minded owners properly concerned with operating and maintenance expenses, electronic ignition reduces the cost of ignition tuneups and parts replacement.

To appreciate electronic ignition, one must first understand the limitations of a conventional ignition system. The weak link in the conventional system is the distributor breaker points. At 4000 R.P.M.—top highway speed—the points open and close 16,000 times per minute in a V-8 engine. At idle, points open and close approximately 2,800 times per minute. That's a lot of action! Understandably, breaker points wear and need replacement.

Further, electrical current feeds back to the points from the coil. This adds deterioration by pitting and corrosion—both reduce the efficiency of the ignition system. The electrical voltage output varies and this, in turn, impairs the performance of the spark plugs.

It all goes back to the breaker points: by the standards of today's space-age technology, mechanically operated breaker points are an inefficient way of switching electrical circuits.

The electronic ignition system has no breaker points. No condenser is needed to reduce electrical feedback from the coil. The switch that turns the low-voltage circuit off and on is transistorized; it functions electronically, with no moving parts. There really is only one major moving part, the reluctor, and it doesn't touch anything! With no friction, there is nothing to wear and need adjustment or replacement. The result is consistently high voltage delivered to the spark plugs, and thus, consistent ignition. Combustion is initiated more evenly, more consistently; and this reduces the likelihood of engine misfiring, and the emissions caused by misfiring.

Above everything, electronic ignition is reliable. And consistent. It maintains performance for thousand and thousands of miles; there is no slow, day-by-day deterioration of the ignition system as we know it in a conventional system.

This, then, is an ideal example of the philosophy, "Extra Care in Engineering." Dodge Adventurer, *September 1972, p. 21 (Box 916 Detroit, 48231).*[5]

4. *Wisconsin* v. *Yoder,* 1972

Respondents Jonas Yoder and Adin Yutzy are members of the Old Order Amish Religion, and respondent Wallace Miller is a member of the Conservative Amish Mennonite Church. They and their families are residents of Green County, Wisconsin. Wisconsin's compulsory school attendance law required them to cause their children to attend public or private school until reaching age sixteen, but the respondents declined to send their children, ages fourteen and fifteen, to public school after completing the eighth grade. The children were not enrolled in any private school, or within any recognized exception to the compulsory attendance law, and they are conceded to be subject to the Wisconsin statue.

Amish objection to formal education beyond the eighth grade is firmly grounded in . . . central religious concepts. They object to the high school and higher education generally because the values it teaches are in marked variance with Amish values and the Amish way of life; they view secondary school education as an impermissible exposure of their children to a "worldly" influence in conflict with their beliefs. The high school tends to emphasize intellectual and scientific accomplishments, self-distinction, competitiveness, worldly success, and social life with other students. Amish society emphasizes informal learning-through-doing, a life of "goodness" rather than a life of intellect, wisdom rather than technical knowledge, community welfare rather than competition, and separation rather than integration with contemporary worldly society.

. . . in order for Wisconsin to compel school attendance beyond the eighth grade against a claim that such attendance interferes with the practice of the legitimate religious belief, it must appear either that the State does not deny the free exercise of religious belief by its requirement, or that there is a state interest of sufficient magnitude to override the interest claiming protection under the Free Exercise Clause.

The essence of all that has been said and written on the subject is that only those interests of the highest order and those not otherwise served can overbalance legitimate claims to the free exercise of religion. We can accept it as settled, therefore, that however strong the State's interest in universal compulsory education, it is by no means absolute to the exclusion or subordination of all other interests.

We come then to the quality of the claims of the respondents concerning the alleged encroachment of Wisconsin's compulsory school attendance statute on their rights and the rights of their children to the free exercise of the religious beliefs they and their forebears have adhered to for almost three centuries.

As the society around the Amish has become more populous, urban, industrialized, and complex, particularly in this century, government regulation of human affairs has correspondingly become more detailed and pervasive. The Amish mode of life has thus come into conflict increasingly with requirements of contemporary society exerting a hydraulic insistence on conformity to majoritarian standards. So long as compulsory education laws were confined to eight grades of elementary basic education imparted in a nearby rural schoolhouse, with a large proportion of students of the Amish faith, the Old Order Amish had little basis to fear that school attendance would expose their children to the worldly influence they reject. But modern compulsory secondary education in rural areas is now largely carried on in a consolidated school, often remote from the student's home and alien to his daily home life. As the record so strongly shows, the values and programs of the modern secondary school are in sharp conflict with the fundamental mode of life mandated by the Amish religion; modern laws requiring compulsory secondary education have accordingly engendered great concern and conflict. The conclusion is inescapable that secondary schooling, by exposing Amish children to worldly influences in terms of attitudes, goals, and values contrary to beliefs, and by substantially interfering with the religious development of the Amish child and his integration into the way of life of the Amish faith community at the crucial adolescent state of development, contravenes [their] basic religious tenets and practices. . . .

Insofar as the State's claim rests on the view that a brief additional period of formal education is imperative to enable the Amish to participate effectively and intelligently in our democratic process, it must fall.

The independence and successful social functioning of the Amish community for a period approaching almost three centuries and more than two hundred years in this country is strong evidence that there is at best a speculative gain, in terms of meeting the duties of citizenship, from an additional one or two years of compulsory formal education. Against this background it would require a more particularized showing from the State on this point to justify the severe interference with religious freedom such additional compulsory attendance would entail.

For the reasons stated we hold, with the Supreme Court of Wisconsin, that the First and Fourteenth Amendments prevent the State from compelling respondents to cause their children to attend formal high school to age sixteen. . . . *From United States Supreme Court decision on* Wisconsin *v.* Yoder.

5. Three Ways to Reform the Booby Prize

1

By Sterling D. Spero

CANAAN, Conn.—In recent years, with the absurdities of the balanced ticket becoming apparent, a new method of choosing the Vice Presidential candidate has come into being. The Presidential nominee designates his choice of a running mate for *pro forma* approval of the convention. This practice in effect amounts in case of a vacancy to selecting a President of the

United States by appointment, a procedure flagrantly at odds with the republican spirit of the Constitution.

In view of the present tendencies toward enhancement of executive power with diminishing popular accountability, the Vice President, especially when the personally designated successor to a vacant Presidency, poses a danger which should no longer be tolerated. New procedures to reform the process of the selection are of little avail.

The problem is the Vice Presidency itself. The best way to reform it is to abolish it. Provision should be made by legislation, or a Constitutional amendment, if necessary, for filling of vacancies in the Presidential office. Such legislation should provide for an interim acting President to serve for a limited time, perhaps three months, until a new President can be elected. The tortuous process to which the country is subjected in choosing candidates for the Presidency contrasts with the cavalier and unrepublican manner in which vacancies for that office are filled by nonelected persons.

The United States recommends elections as the *sine qua non* of the political democratic process for practically every country in the world.

Why do we shy away from applying our own teaching to ourselves in filling vacancies in our highest office?

Why must we be wedded to the idea of elections bound to a quadrennial calendar instead of resorting to them when they are actually needed—the practice of other democratic countries? Does not the filling of a vacancy in the highest office of the land present a situation sufficiently critical to require the widest participation of the people?

Sterling D. Spero is professor emeritus of public administration at New York University.

2

By Dudley C. Lunt

SMALL POINT, Me.—What about this solution? The President should choose his successor after and not before his election. Let the Constitution be amended to require that the elected President shall choose as his successor that one of his Cabinet whom he deems best qualified to carry on the aims and aspirations of his office.

This would do away with the low political bargaining that in every campaign stains the access to the offices of President and Vice President. Also—and this is of cardinal importance—the choice by the elected President would be motivated by considerations calculated to provide the country with the best man and not one who could bring votes to an elective ticket.

There is good precedent for this. For years a statute governed the succession in the event of the demise of both the President and the Vice President. In such a circumstance the succession was in a list of the members of the President's Cabinet, starting with Secretary of State.

A few years ago this line of succession was unwisely abandoned in favor of the present arrangement, which starts with the Speaker of the House. Suffice it to say that a recent incumbent was, until the election of the present Speaker, a man in his eighties and totally unfit to be President.

There could be coupled with this alteration of the procedure for choosing a Vice President the long mooted and badly needed repair of the electoral system by requiring the electors to cast their votes for the candidate who received in the popular election the largest popular vote.

Dudley C. Lunt is a newspaperman and author of "Thousand Acre Marsh."

3

By Volney Righter

BEDFORD HILLS, N. Y.—I tried out the following idea in a letter to The New York Times after the 1968 election, but it was not printed. It's very simple in principle, but it takes some thought to realize all its implications.

Every voter pulls down two levers, one for President and the other for Vice President. He can split his ticket if he wishes. But only one party wins, President and Vice President being in the same party. For example

1968 Election
(000,000 omitted)

Nixon	21	Humphrey	18
Agnew	16	Muskie	20
	37		38

Democrats win.

Nixon	21	Humphrey	16
Agnew	16	Muskie	18
	37		34

Republicans win.

In this way, the Vice Presidents count for something and can make or break the election.

Likewise, when he arrives in Washington, the Vice President would also count for something because he actually ran and contributed something.

Volney Righter is a businessman.

The New York Times, *Saturday, September 9, 1972, p. C23.*[6]

6. Fines Are Unjust

There are many forms of inequity in our present judicial system. Many of them occur because the effect that the same punishment may have on different people is very diverse and this is not taken into account by the judges who administer the laws. One good example of this is the present method of giving out fines for traffic violations. Many judges have a fixed set of standard fines they hand out for certain offenses. For example, a judge may give the average person who comes before him a standard fine of ten dollars plus court costs for running a stop sign. On the surface this may seem to be a fair method of doing things because everyone is treated equally. If we look closely at the matter, however, we see that this is not what actually occurs.

For example, a single person with a ten-thousand-dollar-a-year income will suffer no real harm if he has to pay the ten-dollar fine. He will be unhappy that he couldn't spend it on something else, but the punishment is relatively minor. This same ten-dollar fine on a male student with a three-thousand-dollar-a-year income who is trying to support a wife and a child would suffer a tremendous financial loss by paying the same fine. The value of the ten dollars to the student is obviously much greater than to the single person, and therefore the punishment is much harsher.

A much more equitable method of doing it would be to base the fines on some percentage of income of the person or as a percentage of the value of the car. The judge would still have the power to vary the fine as he saw fit, but for the average case this method of fixing the standard fine would be much fairer. Extending the example that I gave above, if the standard fine was set at 0.1 percent, then the single person will still have to pay the ten-dollar fine. The student would only have to pay a three-dollar fine. The amount of punishment would be the same in both cases, only the units that it is measured in would be different.

For people with no current income, the amount of the fine could be based on the value of their car. Here I am assuming that if they can afford to run a more expensive car, then they probably have more money to spend than someone with a ten-year-old VW.

This is just one area in which our methods of punishing wrongdoers [are] going to have to change if we are going to achieve a truly equitable method of dispensing justice.   Daily Iowan, *October 19, 1972, p. 4.*[7]

7. A branch office computer that makes your main computer far more efficient.
Ask your data processing manager and he'll tell you: what robs a big computer of efficiency is using it for little jobs.

Using it to format and balance data coming in from branch offices, for instance.

Using it to verify data that should have been verified before it entered your computer, for instance.

And most of all, using it for branch office billing, accounting, sales reports, and inventory control that should be handled in the branch offices.

Up till now, there wasn't an efficient system that could handle branch office paperwork in the branches, and still report summary data accurately and instantly to your home office main computer.

Now there is: SYSTEM TEN* business computer, by Singer. It's a computer. It's a computer terminal. Two functions in one machine. At a remarkable price/performance ratio.
Everything you need in a stand-alone terminal system.
SYSTEM TEN computer offers you multi-programming capabilities. It can perform up to 20 functions simultaneously. A person can be checking credit

---

[7]Reprinted by permission of the *Daily Iowan.*

while another person writes a sales order. Both at the same time.

The amount of data that a SYSTEM TEN computer can store is prodigious. Direct access storage from 10 million to 100 million characters is available. Core storage is in increments of 10K, from 10K to 110K.

But more than numbers is involved in making the SYSTEM TEN computer a perfect branch office computer.

As far as your people are concerned, the biggest asset is basic operating simplicity.

Since this is not a punched card system, you have none of those operational headaches to contend with.

People who are used to working with electric typewriters can learn to use SYSTEM TEN terminals in a day. No mumbo-jumbo.

It is so simple, in fact, that technical management is not needed to operate or even oversee it. So there is no wasteful staffing of technical people in your remote locations. A blessing that both your data processing manager and your comptroller will appreciate.

The SYSTEM TEN computer can process all those jobs that now seem to strangle your keypunch-to-mainframe computer. It can edit, balance, format, and summarize data: on the spot. It can perform many day-to-day operations without using your central mainframe at all: billing, accounting, payroll, sales reports, and inventory control.

Everything you need in an intelligent terminal.

No other mini-system works so easily, so completely, with your mainframe computer.

SYSTEM TEN computer can handle any peripheral equipment you need: line printers, CRTs, paper tape and typewriter input/output, point of sale, and data collection devices; as well as disc drives, card readers, and punches—and they can be 2000 feet from the CPU, connected via simple two-wire connections. It can also interface with the 4300 Magnetic Data Recording System by Singer.

No matter what peripherals you are using now, SYSTEM TEN computer can take over with a minimum of fuss.

Your data processing manager will be interested in knowing that the SYSTEM TEN computer operates in synchronous mode, from 2000 to 9600 bps.

It can operate in OS, DOS, and HASP environments.

It operates in asynchronous mode from 110 to 1800 bps.

You can have it with automatic dial, too.

All this means that whatever works best for your big computer, when it comes to receiving and transmitting data, works best for the SYSTEM TEN computer, too.

It will also act as a point of sale data collection system with MDTS* computerized cash registers by Singer.

As you can see, this is far more than a simple input/output device.

Now, the best news of all: the cost of a SYSTEM TEN business computer.

All we ask of you is this:

Add up what you are now paying for "semi-intelligent" terminals and keypunching machines.

Add up what you are now paying in mainframe computer time to edit, format, and balance data.

With those figures in mind, call your nearest Singer Business Machines office and ask for the cost of a SYSTEM TEN computer installation.

You'll be amazed. Happily amazed. And you'll understand why more than 300 SYSTEM TEN computers are now installed.

For complete information, call your local Singer Business Machines office. Or write: Singer Business Machines, San Leandro, California 94577.

System Ten by SINGER

*A Trademark of THE SINGER COMPANY.

Advertisement in Fortune, *July 1972, p. 101.*[8]

8. *Socrates.* Well, there is another question: By friends and enemies do we mean those who are so really, or only in seeming?

Polemarchus. Surely, he said, a man may be expected to love those whom he thinks good, and to hate those whom he thinks evil.

Soc. Yes, but do not persons often err about good and evil: many who are not good seem to be so, and conversely?

Pol. That is true.

Soc. Then to them the good will be enemies and the evil will be their friends?

Pol. True.

Soc. And in that case they will be right in doing good to the evil and evil to the good?

Pol. Clearly.

Soc. But the good are just and would not do an injustice?

Pol. True.

Soc. Then according to your argument it is just to injure those who do no wrong?

Pol. Nay, Socrates; the doctrine is immoral.

Soc. Then I suppose that we ought to do good to the just and harm to the unjust?

Pol. I like that better.

Soc. But see the consequence:—Many a man who is ignorant of human nature has friends who are bad friends, and in that case he ought to do harm to them; and he has good enemies whom he ought to benefit; but, if so, we shall be saying the very opposite of that which we affirmed to be the meaning of Simonides.

Pol. Very true, he said; and I think that we had better correct an error into which we seem to have fallen in the use of the words "friend" and "enemy."

Soc. What was the error, Polemarchus? I asked.

Pol. We assumed that he is a friend who seems to be or who is thought good.

Soc. And how is the error to be corrected?

Pol. We should rather say that he is a friend who is, as well as seems, good; and that he who seems only, and is not good, only seems to be and is not a friend; and of an enemy the same may be said.

Soc. You would argue that the good are our friends and the bad our enemies?

Pol. Yes.

Soc. And instead of saying simply as we did at first, that it is just to do good to our friends and harm to our enemies, we should further say: It is just to do good to our friends when they are good and harm to our enemies when they are evil?

Pol. Yes, that appears to me to be the truth.

Soc. But ought the just to injure any one at all?

Pol. Undoubtedly he ought to injure those who are both wicked and his enemies.

Soc. When horses are injured, are they improved or deteriorated?

Pol. The latter.

Soc. Deteriorated, that is to say, in the good qualities of horses, not of dogs?

Pol. Yes, of horses.

Soc. And dogs are deteriorated in the good qualities of dogs and not of horses?

Pol. Of course.

Soc. And will not men who are injured be deteriorated in that which is the proper virtue of man?

Pol. Certainly.

Soc. And that human virtue is justice?

Pol. To be sure.

Soc. Then men who are injured are of necessity made unjust?

Pol. That is the result.

Soc. But can the musician by his art make men unmusical?

Pol. Certainly not.

Soc. Or the horseman by his art make them bad horsemen?

Pol. Impossible.

Soc. And can the just by justice make men unjust, or speaking generally, can the good by virtue make them bad?

Pol. Assuredly not.

Soc. Any more than heat can produce cold?

Pol. It cannot.

Soc. Or drought moisture?

Pol. Clearly not.

Soc. Nor can the good harm any one?

Pol. Impossible.

Soc. And the just is the good?

Pol. Certainly. *Plato*, The Republic.

9. The Great APE Complex

Editor's note: Today's Soapbox Soundoff is by Randy McVey, a senior in Education.

References are often made to the "Military-Industrial Complex." This implies that there is a certain amount of mutual cooperation and direction between the military and industrial establishments. This is not to say that all military men are in conspiracy with all industrialists, but this does imply the word substantial.

In this sense, a case can be made for the APE Complex, that is, the Athlete, Politician, and Entertainer Complex. Athletes are very much in vogue these days, and, of course, politicians and entertainers are very much in the public eye, oftentimes by their own necessity. Many of these APEs revel in the public limelight, foisting upon a celebrity status which brings at least notoriety and at most great personal and financial power.

Television is at the same time the great catalyst and the great medium—Catalyst in the sense that it makes possible the celebrity status of APEs and medium in the sense that it is a medium of power. Without TV a great APE would just be an ordinary APE. Thus television is the power that makes or breaks the APEs, and he who controls television, i.e., the programming, substantially controls the APE complex.

Is there mutual cooperation and direction between athletes, politicians, and entertainers? There appear to be coalitions or groups, either liberal or conservative. Certain entertainers and athletes publicly endorse political candidates. Some politicians, notable of whom are the President and the Vice President, are often publicly seen with famous athletes and entertainers. Entertainers sometimes become politicians, and athletes often become entertainers. Entertainers and politicians are seen as athletes, and athletes have been known to enter the political arena. Of course, this occupational movement is possible only because of the phenomenon of notoriety. Without publicity in the one field, APEs are not likely to enter the other field. How would Mark Spitz have gotten on the various television shows otherwise? Certainly there are plenty of talented entertainers who never make the TV screen, but nonentertainers are on entertainment programs.

Those people or organizations who have control of television programming have some means of control over who appears on the screen, and thus they determine who America's TV heroes are. The advertisers are not going to sponsor shows which reflect adversely upon capitalism, the American corporate structure, or the American government; therefore heroes will be Americana heroes. No "long hair, commie pinko" will be seen as a hero on American TV (until the day it will be pop). Real radicals would be screened out.

Although the media operators make APEs through the medium of television, the power itself is the lure and feel of personal wealth and celebrity status. Great wealth insures that APEs won't become radicals. We see $100,000 and $1,000,000 athletic contracts become commonplace. We see substantial investment and interest in American wealth by entertainers and politicians. Many of the great APEs are thus intimately tied to the American corporate structure.

Could it be that beyond a certain financial security one becomes intensely insecure and will thus vie to get all he can? There must be a large number of such people all dancing to the tune of Bigtime. Of course, the great APEs include some dancers within their ranks even if just by chance. Perhaps they could be called The Great Dancing APEs (refrain: Money: **What** I'd do for you!)

Three networks and PBS don't seem to bring much variety. Perhaps half primetime is law-n-order programs. How many cool private-eye detective lawmen are there? Look at the lineup of big actor names. All the biggies to paint a law-n-order picture of America. Look at the specials. Here is America!

The great performance is about to begin! Cast your eyes on the television stage! What you are seeing is the Great Dancing APEs performing in vivid color! Watch them giggle and guffaw, act tough and grimace! It's unabashedly defying towards your sensibilities. It's quite an act. (Remember Sammy?)   Daily Iowan, *April 5, 1973, p. 4.*[9]

10. Appreciate Foreign Languages
Editor's note: Today's Soapbox Soundoff is by George Knighton, who is presently a T.A. in the Spanish Department.

I have read with interest the articles both pro and con concerning the language requirement. Lately, however, I [have] read with ever-increasing consternation the growing trend to degrade and to discredit the language requirement at this institution. I feel concerned by this trend, because I feel that it but serves to foment ignorance, which is purported to be the enemy we are striving to overcome by our efforts at this University. "Down with the language requirement, and let ignorance prevail!" seems to be the standard of these articles.

I have personally been involved in the study of Spanish for over six years, and can say in all honesty and sincerity that I am a better, more productive citizen because of its influence in my life.

We, as Americans, tend to be egocentric enough to think that if there is anything innovative, original, or worthwhile in this world, we thought of it first; and consequently we say, "What need have I to study the language, culture, or philosophical or technological thought of another nation? These elements are obviously secondary in importance to American counterparts. Besides, if there were any developments in these areas that were worthwhile, I would be able to get an English translation at the library." To these statements I say: Who translated these works? Who went to these countries and could get to know and understand the people and their thought well enough to translate it, without foreign language? Let us not be unaware of the tragic and staggering losses that are caused by loss of the original thought in the translation of these works, because English as a language may lack the flexibility to encompass and communicate these ideas.

Too many people in this life are going around searching for excuses to take the course of easiest passage, and I personally decry this practice. Our time may be wasted in foreign language study if, and only if, we permit it be wasted, and only if we fail to realize the tremendous unifying power that foreign language study can be between people worldwide. We decry prejudice, discrimination, and misunderstanding which lead to abuse, yet we all write letters to our *Daily Iowan* to support a movement to help destroy the most effective tool we have: foreign language!

You may never understand the "Ugly American image" until you are in a marketplace and someone sticks a cigar in your face and says, "These

[9]Reprinted by permission of the *Daily Iowan*.

damned Mexicans! Why can't they learn to speak English like any civilized human being?" May we all realize the value for personal benefit and interhuman understanding which can come through the study of foreign languages.

Let us not relegate this controversy to people who are only searching for opportunities to publicly demonstrate their brilliant wit, nor to those who have through their own practices allowed these opportunities for growth and development to pass them by, nor to those who are bitter about the foreign languages because they have allowed themselves to fail. Let us encourage our representatives to seek a means so that we may appreciate these languages for what they are—keys to enlightenment and personal development, which are the goals we are supposedly striving for here at this University.   Daily Iowan, *March 5, 1973, p. 4.*[10]

Writing or Speaking Assignment

Frame an actuative claim drawn from a subject of current interest, and, either orally or in writing, develop an argument to support it.

In the course of your argument, be sure to show (if it is not already clear) why the action you propose is needed and to prove its practicability and desirability. Compare your proposal with alternative courses of action and demonstrate its superiority.

Base each step in your argument on solid evidence, and when you are done, test to see that your warrants meet the tests set forth in Chapter VI.

Suggested Subjects
Students should be given a direct voice in the hiring and promotion of faculty members.
Movies and books should be censored by local licensing boards.
The bachelor's degree should be awarded for three rather than four years of study.
The use of automobiles in a city's business district should be severely restricted.
Intercollegiate sports should be abolished.
The President of the United States should be restricted to a single six-year term.
The American jury system should be significantly changed.

[10]Reprinted by permission of the *Daily Iowan.*

For Additional Reading

Brandt, William J. *The Rhetoric of Argumentation.* Indianapolis: The Bobbs-Merrill Co., Inc., 1970. Part I, "Structural Rhetoric."

Bryant, Donald C., and **Karl R. Wallace.** *Fundamentals of Public Speaking.* 4th ed. New York: Appleton-Century-Crofts, 1969. Chapter 18, "Basic Materials of the Persuasive Situation"; Chapter 19, "Materials from the Audience"; Chapter 20, "Selection of Materials and Strategies."

Cicero. *De Inventione.* Translated by H. M. Hubbell. Cambridge, Mass.: Harvard University Press, 1949. I. viii–xi.

Ehninger, Douglas, and **Wayne Brockriede.** *Decision by Debate.* New York: Dodd, Mead & Co., 1963. Chapter 15, "Building the Case."

Eubank, Wayne C. "Building the Case." In *Argumentation and Debate: Principles and Practice*, ed. James McBath. 2nd ed. New York: Holt, Rinehart & Winston, Inc., 1963.

Monroe, Alan H. and **Douglas Ehninger.** *Principles of Speech Communication.* 6th ed. Glenview, Ill.: Scott, Foresman and Co., 1969. Chapter 11, "The Speech to Persuade."

Chapter VIII.
Sham or Counterfeit Proofs

A sound claim, as we have seen, is grounded on solid evidence and cogent reasoning. Some claims, however, which to the uncritical observer may seem sound, actually rest on sham or counterfeit proofs in the form of vague, unfair, or irrelevant appeals.

Pseudoproofs of this sort, known technically as *stratagems*, are many, and they have over the centuries been classified in a variety of ways. The stratagems discussed here are those most commonly encountered in the argumentative interchanges of everyday life. They are arranged in terms of the major constituents of oral and written discourse: language, thought, and the tone or manner of presentation.

Stratagems in Language

Four stratagems in language are of particular pertinence to the student of argument. The first three operate, in one way or another, to make the meaning of an assertion imprecise or uncertain. The fourth impairs the objectivity all sound judgments should possess.

Equivocation
As was pointed out in Chapter IV, equivocation is the use of the same word or phrase to mean two different things. When, during the course of an argument, there is a blatant or radical shift in the meaning of one or more key terms, its effect in rendering the claim suspect is easy enough to detect.

Consider the following example: "Whatever is immaterial is unimportant; whatever is spiritual is immaterial; therefore, whatever is spiritual is unimportant." Here we immediately recognize that the claim does not follow from the premise; and after a moment's reflection we realize this is because the word "immaterial," instead of holding a fixed meaning, is used in two quite different senses.

Sometimes, however, as in the following instances, the shift is more subtle: "Although all angles in a triangle equal two right angles, all of the angles in a triangle are less than two right angles." "An elephant is an animal; therefore, a small elephant is a small animal." "All metals are elements; brass is a metal; therefore, brass is an element."

When the argument in question is an extended one, stretching over a period of many minutes or the space of several pages, shifts in the meaning of key words become especially difficult to detect. Are the principal terms on which the argument depends clearly defined at the outset? Are these definitions honored as the discourse proceeds? Unless both of these questions can be answered affirmatively, the claim does not deserve our endorsement.

Ambiguity

Whereas equivocation is a matter of giving two different meanings to the same word or phrase, ambiguity arises when an entire sentence is constructed so as to be open to two or more interpretations. Here again the stratagem is sometimes obvious and sometimes extremely subtle and difficult to detect. The World War II slogan "Save soap and waste paper" clearly carries two different and contradictory meanings. So does the frequently quoted pronouncement of the Delphic Oracle: "The god Apollo says that the Greeks the Persians shall subdue."

Compare with these statements, however, the scriptural admonition "Drink ye all of it"; the paragraph in a will which reads, "I give and bequeath the sum of $50,000 to my wife and my son Thomas"; and the note from editor to author which says, "I shall lose no time in reading your manuscript."

In the statements of candidates for public office, ambiguities are common and often calculated. One candidate declares, "I stand for revenue sharing, or an equalization of the tax burden," leaving unclear whether the phrase following "or" restates the preceding phrase or names an acceptable alternative. Another announces, "I favor appropriations adequate to insure our national defense, but which do not place an undue burden on the taxpayer."

Even when a writer or speaker exercises the greatest care, some ambiguity may creep into his language. Unless this ambiguity is spotted and the speaker's or writer's actual position on the matter ascertained, it is impossible to judge the worth of his appeal.

Vagueness

As was pointed out in Chapter IV, a vague expression lacks definiteness or precision of meaning. Instead of specifying sharply the idea the speaker or writer wishes to convey, it opens up a broad and ill-defined spectrum of meanings, among which one may choose at will.

Sometimes vagueness arises because an arguer's vocabulary does not contain the words needed to make his ideas clear. More often, perhaps, it arises because he does not himself fully understand the data or concepts he is discussing. As a result, he substitutes broad or general terms for narrower and more precise ones, or he speaks in abstractions rather than concrete terms, hoping to catch in this way at least some of the meaning he is unable to express more exactly.

Vagueness, like ambiguity, is frequently found in the statements of public figures; and like ambiguity, it may be calculated rather than accidental. The political platform that announces a party's concern for "stability and progress," "peace with honor," or "a return to the American way" may be deliberately designed to invite a wide range of responses. These and similar uses of language, however, instead of contributing to the construction of solid proofs, are actually attempts to avoid or circumvent the proof process. Their purpose is to win a response to ideas quickly and automatically, and without a careful examination of the evidence and reasoning which might be offered on their behalf.

Emotionally Loaded Language

In addition to its usefulness in denoting ideas, language is a powerful instrument for expressing attitudes and feelings. By means of the words we choose to describe an object or concept, we can in a direct and unmistakable way indicate whether we view it objectively or with bias.

In recent decades the use of emotionally loaded language to implant attitudes and work persuasion has been developed into a fine art by advertisers, publicists, and spokesmen for pressure groups. Compare, for example, the following triads of terms commonly encountered in conversation or the press: pig–policeman–peace officer; dummy–slow learner–exceptional child; bra-burner–feminist–liberated woman. In each case the first term, in addition to denoting the referent, places it in a derogatory light; the second describes the referent in a basically objective or neutral fashion; the third gives it a favorable connotation. Similarly, a person of whom we approve might be characterized as pious, cautious, brave, or provident, while one of whom we disapprove might be considered bigoted, cowardly, foolhardy, or stingy.

In various forms of imaginative or creative discourse, language expressive of feeling or attitude is highly desirable. Indeed, if language did not possess the power to express and elicit feeling, most of the world's great literature would not exist. In arguments, on the other hand, loaded language, once it exceeds the natural warmth that always marks sincerity of belief and earnestness of purpose, is not to be tolerated. By operating in subtle ways, it, like vague language, avoids or circumvents proof and induces automatic, trigger reactions to claims.

Stratagems in Thought

Stratagems in thought, as their name implies, lie not in the words by which an argument is expressed, but rather in the ideas it contains or the inference patterns it employs. We shall consider four sorts of stratagems in thought: *extensions*, *diversions*, *silencers*, and *deceivers*.

Extensions

Extensions are so called because they project or extend a claim beyond the evidence and reasoning adduced on its behalf. They are designed to make a reader or listener believe that more has been proved than is actually the case.

Overstatement. A commonly encountered form of extension is simple overstatement, or asserting a stronger or more inclusive claim than the supporting evidence and reasoning warrant. If the facts justify at best a qualified or restricted assertion, the arguer, ignoring this limitation, makes a categorical one; if the evidence extends to only some of the members of a class, he pretends that it covers the class as a whole. By thus projecting his claim beyond the material available for its support, he seeks to gain an unfair advantage over a careless reader or listener.

Transfers. A second class of extensions are known collectively as transfers. There are four kinds of transfers.

1. *Simple Transfer.* A simple transfer is an attempt to make a reader or listener believe that because proof has been brought forth to establish one claim, another claim of a similar nature also has been proved.

If, for example, it is proved that Jones is unfaithful to his wife, it is also assumed without proof that he neglects his children. Or because Brown is a known drug addict, it is also alleged that he is a thief. In each of these instances, the second claim may, of course, be true; on the other hand, it may not be. Simply to assert it on the basis of the evidence adduced in support of the first claim constitutes an unwarranted transfer of proof.

2. *Transfer from the Parts to the Whole.* A second form of transfer asserts without warrant that what is true of the parts of something considered individually is also true of the whole which these parts comprise. An unwarranted transfer of this sort is known in traditional logic as "the fallacy of composition."

In some cases, obviously, the character of the whole *is* determined by the character of the parts. If every brick in a wall is red, the wall as a whole will be red; if every member of the fifth grade at Washington School reads at above the fifth-grade level, the class as a whole reads at above the fifth-grade level.

By way of contrast, however, consider these arguments: "Each child in the class is light in weight; therefore the class as a whole is light in weight and can safely be transported in a small airplane." "Three and two are odd and even; five is three and two. Therefore five is odd and even."

Sometimes an asserted relationship between the parts and the whole, instead of being clearly true or false, is uncertain and in doubt. "Each part of the machine works well; therefore the machine as a whole works well." "Every member of the city staff does his job efficiently; therefore our city government is efficient." When confronted with claims such as these, we cannot, in the absence of further explanation, tell whether assent is or is not warranted.

Because in some instances what is true of the parts is not true of the whole, while in other instances the relationship is uncertain and in doubt, claims resting on this base must always be examined carefully before they are accepted as true.

3. *Transfer from the Whole to the Parts.* Just as the character of the parts may not always determine the character of the whole, so, conversely, what is true of the whole may not automatically be assumed as true of the parts.

One cannot, for example, validly argue, "The American eagle is disappearing; this bird is an American eagle. Therefore, this bird is disappearing." "A large computer is an expensive machine; this is a part of a large computer. Therefore, we may assume that replacing this part will be expensive." Here, as in the case of inferences from the parts to the whole, each argument must be examined with care. For while in some instances we may, by reasoning from the whole to its parts, arrive at a warranted claim, at other times conclusions reached by this route will not be justified.

4. *Transfer from a Discredited Proof to an Undiscredited Claim.* A fourth sort of transfer is especially apt to lead the unwary astray. It consists of successfully refuting a weak or irrelevant proof and then, on this basis, alleging that a valid claim has been negated. The effect of the refutation is subtly transferred from the proof to the claim the proof is designed to support, and because the proof has been exposed as deficient, the claim is assumed to be false.

Proofs vary greatly in quality, depending on both the competence of their authors and the availability of the data necessary to develop them. For this reason, to assume automatically that, because a proof is easily refuted, the claim it supports is invalid is to overlook important variables in every argumentative situation.

Reducing a Claim to Absurdity.   By extending a claim analogically to a different but related set of circumstances, a critic may subject it to unwarranted ridicule and in this way cause it to be rejected on grounds other than its true merits. An extension of this sort is known as reducing the claim to absurdity.

Suppose, for example, it is claimed that students should have no hand in the governance of a college or university because they have no experience in such matters. An opponent of this view, instead of attempting to meet the contention fairly, might respond, "Then I suppose, in the light of your argument, you would never allow a child to go into the water until he had already learned how to swim."

What the opponent is, of course, saying is that one of the best ways—indeed, the only really good way—for a person to learn something is actually to do or practice it. And this, everyone would admit, is a perfectly legitimate response. Instead of presenting his point in a fair and objective manner, however, he attempts to discredit the claim by drawing a comparison between it and a second situation which, though allegedly parallel, is actually quite different. Here, as in the other forms of transfer, the effect is gained by an unwarranted extension of the original claim.

Diversions

Whereas extensions seek to project a claim in an unfair or unwarranted fashion, diversions have for their purpose turning attention away from the point at issue and fastening it on some matter of doubtful relevance. Diversions take many forms, the ones discussed here being only a few of the more common.

Diversions from Claim to Author.   One class of diversions attempts to direct attention away from the merits of a claim and to fasten it on the claim's author.

1. *Attack on the Character or Competence of the Person Advancing the Claim.* A claim must always be advanced by some person or group of persons,

and who these persons are makes a great deal of difference in how it is received. As was pointed out in the chapter on evidence (Chapter V), for example, claims advanced by persons with acknowledged reputations for expertness, veracity, and good judgment exert a stronger impact on a reader or listener than do claims authored by individuals lacking in these qualities.

As long as attention to the reputation or character of a claim's author serves only as a tentative guide to its worth, no harm is done. Indeed, a concern for these matters may improve the accuracy and reliability of judgment. When, however, the source of the claim ceases to serve simply as an indication and is taken as the sole criterion of judgment, attention is diverted from the central consideration to a secondary one, and the response of the reader or listener is unfairly influenced.

Diversions of this sort are frequently encountered in discussions of both public and private affairs. Robinson, it is claimed, would make a good sheriff because he is a faithful husband, a kind father, and a member of a certain lodge or civic club. Jones' opinions on practical matters are to be accepted because he is a graduate engineer; Green's opinions on the same matters are to be disregarded because he is a professor.

Clearly, if sound arguments are to be advanced and wise judgments result, it is essential that the worth of the idea or proposal in question be given primary consideration and that the personal qualities of its spokesman be kept subordinate.

2. *The Charge of Inconsistency.* A second sort of diversion from claim to author consists of an unwarranted charge of inconsistency—an attempt to dismiss a claim out of hand simply because it is in some respect inconsistent with a statement its author made on a previous occasion.

Within the frame of any given discussion or inquiry, consistency is admittedly an important ingredient. To demand perfect consistency in a person's views over a period of time or across a wide range of subjects, however, is to set an unfair and unrealistic standard. Given the complexity of many contemporary problems and the rapid pace of social and technological change, the summary rejection of a claim simply on the ground that it is inconsistent with an earlier one, while it may make for a dramatic rhetorical ploy, is often an unjustifiable procedure.

Here again, as in cases involving the character or competence of a claim's author, the final decision must be made on the merits of the idea itself, considered in the context of the facts and conditions that surround it. If a claim is obviously inconsistent with something its author said earlier, one should, of course, examine both his present statement and his previous one with care. To use inconsistency as the sole ground of rejection, however, may be an unfair and unproductive procedure.

Emotional Appeals. A second major class of diversions seeks to deflect attention from the merits of a claim by arousing strong feelings toward the person or subject the claim concerns. Prominent among diversions of this type are *appeals to pity and fear*.

1. *Appeal to Pity.* Appeals to pity are often found embedded in arguments offered in defense of an individual or group charged with some wrongdoing. By rehearsing the misfortunes that have befallen the accused or discussing the dire effects an unfavorable verdict would have on his wife and children, it is hoped that the sympathies of the reader or listener will be aroused and he will

act out of generosity or compassion, rather than being guided by an examination of the facts.

Besides being offered as excuses for wrongdoing, appeals to pity are also common when proposals designed to benefit an underprivileged segment of the population are considered. When introduced as part of the total complex of facts and reasons on which a wise decision depends, the condition of these individuals becomes a legitimate concern. When, however, this condition is made the sole criterion for decision, judgments tend to be impulsive rather than reflective. As a result, the action taken may lack those qualities of administrative convenience and economic feasibility an effective remedy must possess.

2. *Appeal to Fear.* Attempts to divert attention from the merits of a claim by arousing fear concerning the purposes or consequences of a proposed action are found in a wide range of subjects and situations. Arguments against rezoning a residential neighborhood to permit the construction of a corner filling station may carry the strong suggestion that such action would lead to a marked decline in property values, or arguments on behalf of increased appropriations for a state crime laboratory may be foregone entirely in favor of fear-arousing tales concerning the threat posed by the uncontrolled growth of organized crime.

Here again, the question is one of balance. Placed within the total context of the situation, the personal consequences stemming from such actions and policies are necessarily matters for concern. When made the sole basis for judgment, however, attention is diverted from other equally relevant factors.

Shifting Ground.   Instead of attacking the character or competence of a claim's author or clouding the issue by appeals to emotion, an arguer sometimes seeks to gain an unfair advantage by subtly shifting attention away from the claim he originally advanced and fastening it on one he is better able to defend.

Suppose, for instance, that during the course of a discussion concerning the merits of certain faculty members, Tom declares, "Professor Thomas of the economics department is the most effective lecturer in the college." Suppose further that, in response to this assertion, Paul offers by way of refutation the following facts: Professor Thomas's lectures often depart widely from the subject matter of the course, are frequently ill prepared, and more often than not contain data that clearly are out of date. Tom, seeing himself bested in the developing dispute, then declares, "Well, even you must admit that Thomas's lectures are always interesting."

In this example, Tom's action in shifting from his original claim to a narrower and presumably more defensible one is readily apparent. While shifts of this sort are often less pronounced or are made so gradually they are difficult to detect, they always have for their purpose diverting attention from the claim originally advanced and fixing it on a new claim that is easier to defend.

Silencers

A third group of stratagems in thought, instead of seeking to divert the attention of the reader or listener, have for their purpose silencing an opponent, thus assuring an easy victory for the claim presented. Among the silencers most commonly encountered in public and private discussions are *appeal to authority, appeal to tradition, use of technical language,* and *leveling a countercharge.*

Appeal to Authority.   Although under normal circumstances the judgments of authorities constitute a legitimate form of evidence, at times they may be introduced for the purpose of cowing an opponent and in this way leading him to concede the point at issue. An arguer, speaking in a confident or superior tone of voice, may declare, "What you say, my friend, is interesting, but clearly wrong. As the Governor himself pointed out to me privately only a few days ago, the state will finish the present fiscal year with a comfortable balance. Let us, therefore, go on to consider . . ." Sometimes the authority of the Constitution or Scriptures, or the pronouncement of an important figure of the past, is cited. Under such circumstances, the opponent is intimidated and further examination of the matter cut short.

Appeal to Custom or Tradition.   Closely related to appeal to authority is appeal to custom or tradition. Here, however, rather than citing the judgment of a prestigious person or document, the arguer recalls how the matter has always been dealt with in the past.

If, for instance, it is proposed that women be allowed to compete in the club's tennis tournament, a critic of the idea reminds the planning committee that, since its establishment more than half a century ago, the tournament has been limited to male players. Or if someone speaks approvingly of the shift from the draft to an all-volunteer army of professionals, the change is criticized on the grounds that the concept of the citizen soldier is one of our most cherished traditions.

There may, of course, be a number of perfectly valid reasons why the club's tennis tournament should be limited to men or why an all-volunteer army is not a good idea; and among these, perhaps, may be the fact that established customs and practices have survival value. To use an appeal to custom or tradition as the sole reason for opposing an idea, however, or to introduce it in such a way as to halt discussion, prevents the objective examination of those facts and reasons on which a sound judgment should be based.

Use of Technical Language.   A third sort of silencer consists of the use of technical language for the purpose of intimidating an opponent. Instead of presenting a legitimate argument against a claim with which he disagrees, someone may say, "I'm sure you realize that what you set forth is at best a *petitio principii* and may, in fact, be an out-and-out *non sequitur.*" Or he may turn aside an idea by declaring, "If you were familiar with Festinger's theory of cognitive dissonance or with Roger Brown's discussion of 'balance theories,' you would clearly not make that kind of statement." Thus confronted by language he does not understand or by theories he has never heard of, the author of the claim, reluctant to display his ignorance, may grant the point or fall silent.

In some circumstances the use of technical language may be essential to the full and fair discussion of a matter, and anyone who seriously advances a claim obviously ought to understand the terms and theories relevant to it. The use of such materials for the deliberate purpose of confusing or embarrassing an opponent is, however, patently unfair.

Leveling a Countercharge.   When a claim takes the form of an accusation or charge, the person who is accused, rather than advancing evidence and reasoning on behalf of his position or answering the charge in some other legitimate way, sometimes tries to defend himself by leveling a countercharge against his critics.

The politician charged with corruption may reply by alleging that his accuser is not above suspicion so far as the full and accurate reporting of campaign expenditures is concerned. Or the baseball fan confronted with the taunt "What happened to your Cubs this year?" may respond by asking his taunter, "Well, what happened to *your* Giants?"

If a countercharge strikes home, the individual advancing the original claim may, in order to avoid embarrassment, either drop his accusation or soften it considerably. Whatever victory may be gained by this method, is, however, more apparent than real, for it grows not out of an examination of the pertinent facts, but rather out of a device or stratagem deliberately designed to avoid such examination.

Deceivers

A final group of stratagems in thought may, for want of a better name, be known as deceivers. Although the stratagems in this group vary considerably, they share the common purpose of making an unwary reader or listener believe an illegitimate proof is sound or a faulty piece of reasoning valid. Under this heading fall *appeal to ignorance, begging the question, forcing a dichotomy, fastening on a trivial point, bandwagon,* and *persuasive definition.*

Appeal to Ignorance. The appeal to ignorance urges acceptance of a claim because evidence to the contrary is lacking. A representative of the television networks might assert, "Since there is no hard evidence that violence in television programs has an undesirable effect on children, we must conclude that this is not the case." Or a member of a committee to pick the outstanding senior on campus might declare, "Clearly Bill Adams is the most esteemed member of the senior class. During his four years here I have never heard a single person say a word against him."

Although the absence of evidence to the contrary may provide a certain degree of presumption in favor of a claim, it can never be accepted as solid proof that the claim is true. Hard evidence to refute the claim that violence on television does not have an undesirable effect on children may be lacking because appropriate investigations into the problem have not yet been undertaken. Bill Adams' apparent popularity among his fellows may stem from the fact that persons who dislike him have kept their thoughts to themselves or the individual advancing the claim may not have heard the criticisms pointed in his direction.

Only when direct proofs in support of a claim are set forth in numbers and strength sufficient to establish it beyond reasonable doubt can we regard acceptance as warranted.

Begging the Question. Begging the question consists of assuming the truth or desirability of a claim in the absence of argument. This stratagem commonly takes one of two forms. The first, sometimes referred to as the use of question-begging epithets, results from the use of evaluative or emotionally loaded terms in the statement of the issue under discussion. Thus, in a debate on the practicality of establishing a free campus bus system, one of the participants might declare, "My purpose today is to prove to you that this fanciful and utopian proposal for the establishment of a free campus bus system should be rejected as impractical." Since the aim of the debate is to determine if such a system is indeed practical, to employ the words "fanciful" and "utopian" in stating one's purpose is to judge the matter in advance.

A second and more devious form of begging the question is circular reasoning, or using the claim one is attempting to establish as a premise or necessary precondition for the argument advanced. Here are some examples:

Intramural sports are worthwhile because they provide large numbers of students with an inexpensive way to get healthful exercise and have fun. And anything that provides this much exercise and fun at so modest a cost, we all must agree, is worthwhile.

Depressions invariably follow wars. Why, with only one or two exceptions, every major depression in the history of the world has been preceded by a war of some sort.

In both of these instances, as a moment's reflection will show, the reason offered in support of the claim is, despite certain minor changes in wording, merely a restatement of the claim itself. Consequently the argument, instead of proceeding in the customary fashion from accepted data to contested claim, turns back on itself and proves nothing.

Forcing a Dichotomy. The stratagem of forcing a dichotomy seeks to win a reader's or listener's assent to a proposition by presenting him with only two choices and then suggesting that, unless he endorses the one favored by the author of the argument, he necessarily falls into the camp of the opposition. It says, in effect, "If you are not for me, you are against me. Now make your choice."

It is true, of course, that from time to time everyone faces a situation in which, as a practical matter, he must choose one of two alternative values or courses of action. Such situations, however, tend to be the exception rather than the rule. On most decision-demanding occasions a number of choices are available. We may favor Candidate A or Candidate B, or abstain from voting. We may see virtues and evils in each of two proposals, and therefore favor a compromise position. Where these and similar possibilities exist, an attempt to lock a reader's or listener's thinking into an either-or mold and force him to choose on this basis constitutes a clear case of eliciting an unfair or unwarranted judgment.

Fastening upon a Trivial Point. This stratagem, which is often employed by arguers defending a weak or untenable position, consists of finding in an opponent's case some minor omission or defect, and then magnifying this slip out of all proportion in an effort to discredit his case as a whole.

In a discussion concerning the evils of electronic surveillance, one of the participants may erroneously attribute to the Attorney General a statement that actually was made by one of his assistants. Seizing on this error, the arguer's opponent dwells on it until a naive reader or listener assumes it to be the pivotal point on which the issue turns.

Admittedly, accuracy of statement and precision of inference are requisites of all sound argument. At the same time, however, the relative importance of various sorts of facts must be kept in perspective, and minor slips, while they clearly deserve notice, must be given no more emphasis than they deserve. Since the purpose of an argument is not to embarrass an opponent, but to contribute to the wise solution of a problem, the focus should always be on those matters that make a genuine difference to the question at hand.

Bandwagon.   Among the most common types of stratagem is the appeal to prevailing opinion, known familiarly as the bandwagon technique. Here an arguer, instead of advancing evidence and reasoning that support the claim directly, calls for the claim's acceptance on the ground that it embodies what most persons believe or desire.

The study of a foreign language, it is asserted, is useless because this is the view expressed by a majority of the students interviewed in a recent nationwide survey on the question. Or we are told that, come election day, we should vote for Black rather than Green because Black is leading in the public opinion polls.

In cases of this sort, the line between sound and unsound argument is not always easy to determine. How most people feel about a man or an issue is necessarily a factor to be reckoned with whenever a proposal for practical action is advanced. Nor can the moral judgments of a large number of thoughtful individuals concerning an issue be lightly dismissed. On the other hand, to make such opinions the sole criterion of a claim's worth and to appeal to them in such a way as to discourage the consideration of other pertinent facts cannot help but result in choices that are less informed and critical than they should be.

Persuasive Definition.   A final stratagem designed to deceive or confuse the unwary is the use of a persuasive definition. This consists of redrawing the commonly accepted definition of a term in such a way as to lend unwarranted credence to one's cause.

By way of illustrating this stratagem, let us imagine a conversation between Jane and Helen. Jane declares, "I certainly am disappointed in Mary. I always thought she was my friend, but the other day she criticized me to my face for telling Bob I couldn't go to the dance and then accepting a date with Ted." To which Helen replies, "Oh, Jane, how can you be so mistaken? A *true* friend is not someone who condones your actions, right or wrong. It is someone who frankly points out your faults in order to make you a better person. And that is just what Mary did."

The nature of Helen's response is obvious. Instead of arguing the point directly by defending Mary's action as justified or undertaking to show Jane that her own action was wrong, Helen sidestepped the issue by redefining the word "friend." A "friend," she asserted, is not someone who never criticizes what we do or disagrees with what we think. On the contrary, a person who is "really" or "truly" our friend candidly points out our shortcomings because of a concern for our welfare.

If properly supported by evidence and reasoning designed to confirm it, a revised definition such as Helen advanced may constitute the claim of a legitimate argument. Simply to preface the revision by the word "true" or "real," however, thus only suggesting rather than actually proving its correctness, is an unwarranted evasion of responsibility.

Stratagems in Tone or Manner

A third group of commonly encountered stratagems lie in the tone or manner in which an argument is presented. Of these, the first three may occur in written as well as spoken appeals; the last two are found in oral arguments only.

Use of Humor

Instead of addressing himself to the subject seriously, an arguer sometimes attempts to gain an unfair advantage for himself or the position he supports by adopting a light or humorous manner. Although humor in itself is not necessarily incompatible with sound argument, when intended for entertainment rather than enlightenment or when employed as a substitute for the critical analysis of an issue, it results in judgments based on irrelevant grounds.

Use of Ridicule

Instead of examining a claim objectively, an arguer may seek to turn it aside by ridiculing the ideas it contains. In their more obvious forms, these ploys are easy enough to detect and are usually discounted by a reader or listener. When used subtly or scattered throughout an extended argument, however, their true nature may be overlooked, with the result that they play an unwarranted part in the decision arrived at.

Use of Irony

Irony, by definition, is the use of words to signify the opposite of what they normally mean. Suppose two persons are engaged in a dispute about a matter of common interest and one says to the other. "You are obviously a great expert on the subject." By the tone of his voice or the context in which the remark is embedded, however, it is apparent that what he really means is that the person is almost completely ignorant of the topic under consideration. As a result, the prestige and self-confidence of his opponent are impaired; and unless that party exercises great restraint, he may divert his next remarks from the subject at hand to a defense of his competence or expertise.

Assuming a Forceful or Belligerent Manner

If the judgments resulting from argument are to be wise and productive, the worth of each appeal must be measured solely by the strength of the evidence and the cogency of the reasoning on which it is based. When, therefore, an arguer attempts to add to the force of his cause by speaking in a loud voice, advancing unqualified assertions with a confident air, or assuming a belligerent manner, he oversteps the bounds of legitimate argument and seeks to establish his claim by unfair or unwarranted means.

Assuming an Excessively Conciliatory or Humble Manner

Just as the adoption of a forceful, belligerent, or overly confident manner trangresses the bounds of sound argument, so does the calculated assumption of a humble or excessively conciliatry pose constitute a stratagem in the manner of presentation. Because the only reliable way to judge the worth of an argument is to examine the facts and reasons on which it is based, these should always be made to stand forth fully and clearly in their own right, uncolored by a manner of presentation that unfairly adds to or subtracts from their worth.

Checklist

I. **Stratagems in Language**
   A. Equivocation
   B. Ambiguity
   C. Vagueness
   D. Emotionally loaded language

II. **Stratagems in Thought**
   A. Extensions
      1. Overstatement
      2. Transfers
         a. Simple transfer
         b. Transfer from the parts to the whole
         c. Transfer from the whole to the parts
         d. Transfer from a discredited proof to an undiscredited claim
      3. Reducing a claim to absurdity
   B. Diversions
      1. Diversions from claim to author
         a. Attack upon the character or competence of the person advancing the claim.
         b. The charge of inconsistency
      2. Emotional appeals
         a. Appeal to pity
         b. Appeal to fear
      3. Shifting ground
   C. Silencers
      1. Appeal to authority
      2. Appeal to custom or tradition
      3. Use of technical language
      4. Leveling a countercharge
   D. Deceivers
      1. Appeal to ignorance
      2. Begging the question
         a. Use of question-begging epithets
         b. Circular reasoning
      3. Forcing a dichotomy
      4. Fastening upon a trivial point
      5. Bandwagon
      6. Persuasive definition

III. **Stratagems in Tone or Manner**
   A. Use of humor
   B. Use of ridicule
   C. Use of irony
   D. Assuming a forceful or belligerent manner
   E. Assuming an excessively conciliatory or humble manner

Exercises

1. Select from the following list the terms you regard as loaded, and defend your selection by supplying in each case a neutral or unloaded synonym.

typewriter	realist	neurotic	patriot
pinko	murder	internationalist	financier
statesman	utopian	activist	athlete
newspaper	soldier	teacher	hippie

2. Select from the following list the terms you regard as vague, and defend your selection by supplying a synonym that is more precise.

economic depression	self-reliant
inch	broad-minded
liberal	atom
stallion	sibling
mental illness	pamphlet
emerging nation	fine arts
"good-time Charlie"	snowmobile
happiness	higher education

3. Select from the following list the sentences you regard as ambiguous, and defend your selection by pointing out the different meanings that they carry.

   Serious unemployment means political unrest.
   All men are equal.
   He went to Washington and then to London by air.
   Close the door behind you.
   John is five feet and seven inches tall.
   The elements of chemistry are difficult to master.
   Every man should pray daily or communicate with his God.
   Death alone comes to us all.
   If you study hard enough, you will pass.
   Love me, love my dog.
   I will wear no clothes to distinguish me from others.
   And he said to them: saddle me the ass; and they saddled him the ass.

4. Point out the fallacy or stratagem in each of these statements.

   a. Thousands of successful men and women read the *Wall Street Journal* every day. Therefore, if you want to be successful, read the *Wall Street Journal*.

   b. Professional football players exercise daily. Therefore, the way to become a professional football player is to exercise.

   c. I conclude from Jones' bohemian life-style that he is either a writer or an artist. As we all know, many writers and artists adopt a bohemian life-style.

   d. At a recent hearing, Anderson contended he should not be charged with stealing books from the library. "Any of my associates," he said, "can testify that I am a good Christian and read my Bible every morning."

e. Since each person in his own life seeks happiness, the aim of government should be the happiness of all.

f. Whiteside College has a long tradition of excellence. Therefore Professor Brown, who is a member of the Whiteside faculty, must be an excellent teacher.

g. They don't care anything about the customer at the China Shop. Last year while I was doing my Christmas shopping, a clerk in the gift department kept me waiting for five minutes.

h. Why are you always on my back for not studying? Last semester your GPA fell nearly two points.

i. Freedom of the press is essential to the well-being of any nation, for the free flow of ideas promotes the well-being of its citizens.

j. Since everyone ought to contribute to the Community Chest, there would be no harm in a city ordinance which required them to do so.

k. Oysters and caviar are rare and delicious. Therefore, oysters are rare and caviar is delicious.

l. Since any individual who serves on a jury is liable to be biased in his judgment, we cannot place confidence in the decisions arrived at in trials by jury.

m. Staying in bed promotes the health of the ill. Hence it is also good for those who are not ill.

n. There is no use inquiring into the matter further. In yesterday's *Tribune* the editor declared that the proposed throughway across town is impractical, and that is all there is to say about it.

o. We should not allow students to sit on policy-determining committees of the college. This college is nearly two hundred years old, and in all that time students have never participated in policy decisions.

p. During the course of his speech yesterday, Senator Walters said that at the depths of the Great Depression some 10 percent of the work force was unemployed. The truth is that the unemployment figure was nearer 9.5 percent. How can we trust a man who is so careless with facts?

q. Go ahead and smoke marijuana. More than a third of all college students today do.

r. Nothing is better than a long, happy life. Anything is better than nothing. Therefore, anything is better than a long, happy life.

s. All Indian youths had to learn to undergo great hardships and endure great pain. As a result of this training, small bands of Indians were often able to hold off cavalry forces four or five times their number.

t. She must be a good housekeeper, for only women are good housekeepers, and she is certainly a woman.

u. It is proved that things cannot be other than they are, for since everything was made for a purpose, it follows that everything is made for the best purpose. *Voltaire*, Candide.

v.   Mistresses are like books. If you pore upon them too much they doze you and make you unfit for company; but if used discreetly, you are the fitter for conversation by 'em. *Wycherley*, The Country Wife.

w.   It would not seem open to a man to disown his father (though a father may disown his son); being in debt, he should repay, but there is nothing by doing which a son will have done the equivalent of what he has received, so that he is always in debt. But creditors can remit a debt; and a father can therefore do so too. *Aristotle*, Nicomachean Ethics.

x.   A majority taken collectively is only an individual, whose opinions, and frequently whose interest, are opposed to those of another individual, who is styled a minority. If it be admitted that a man possessing absolute power may misuse that power by wrongdoing his adversaries, why should not a majority be liable to the same reproach? Men do not change their characters by uniting with each other; nor does their patience in the presence of obstacles increase with their strength. For my own part, I cannot believe it; the power to do everything, which I should refuse to one of my equals, I will never grant to any number of them. *De Tocqueville*, Democracy in America.

y.   No man with a genius for legislation has appeared in America. They are rare in the history of the world. There are orators, politicians, and eloquent men, by the thousand; but the speaker has not yet opened his mouth to speak who is capable of settling the much-vexed problems of the day. *Thoreau, "Civil Disobedience."*

z.   A man must conform himself to Nature's laws, *be* verily in communion with Nature and the truth of things, or Nature will answer him, No, not at all! . . . Nature bursts up in fireflames, French Revolutions and such like, proclaiming with terrible veracity that forged notes are forged. *Carlyle*, Heroes, Heroe-worship.

aa. . . . a true critic in the perusal of a book, is like a dog at a feast, whose thoughts and stomach are wholly set upon what the guests fling away, and consequently apt to snarl most when there are the fewest bones. *Swift*, A Tale of a Tub.

bb. The shopkeeper thrives only by the irregularities of youth; the farmer by the high prices of corn; the architect by the destruction of houses; the officers of justice by lawsuits and quarrels. Ministers of religion derive their distinction and employment from our vices and our death. No physician rejoices in the health of his friends, no soldiers in the peace of their country, and so of the rest. Therefore, carelessness, calamity, pestilence, disease, and even death are economic blessings. *Montaigne.*

cc. It is high time that professors who distort the perspective of young minds, who advocate the overthrow of our system of government, who corrupt and pervert the educational process, be purged from our educational institutions. . . .

The social studies in particular are dominated by the high priests of radicalism, and it is little wonder that many American young people get a badly distorted picture of their country, its present and its past. . . .

There is something dreadfully wrong with college governing boards and administrations which allow faculties . . . to become overloaded with fuzzy-minded, phony liberals whose heroes are Che Guevara, Fidel Castro, Ho Chi Minh, and Mao Tse-tung. *Senator Robert C. Byrd of West Virginia, in a statement to the President's Commission on Campus Unrest, September 9, 1970.*

dd. . . . each person's happiness is a good to that person, and the general happiness, therefore, a good to the aggregate of all persons. *John Stuart Mill*, Utilitarianism.

ee. But can you doubt that air has weight when you have the clear testimony of Aristotle affirming that all the elements have weight including air, and excepting only fire? *Galileo*, Dialogues Concerning Two New Sciences.

ff. Every additional dollar spent on education in America increases income inequality, because the median income of teachers is higher than the median income of the work force. In redistributing income in this way, more of it comes from the bottom. *Daniel P. Moynihan, "A Liberal's Critical Look at Liberalism,"* Des Moines Register, *Sunday, December 10, 1972, p. 9C.*

gg. Seeing that eye and hand and foot and every one of our members has some obvious function, must we not believe that in like manner a human being has a function over and above these particular functions? *Aristotle*, Nicomachean Ethics.

hh. Before I came down here, one [political analyst] told me that Southern voters wouldn't listen to Republicans, Southern voters won't support Republicans, and Southerners won't vote Republican. He told me he was *never* wrong. And then he drove off in his Edsel. *Vice President Spiro Agnew at a Mississippi Republican dinner, Jackson, Mississippi, October 20, 1969.*

ii. And first, where that I affirm the empire of a woman to be a thing repugnant to nature, I mean not only that God by the order of his creation hath spoiled woman of authority and dominion, but also that man hath seen, proved and pronounced just causes why that it should be. Man, I say, in many other cases blind, doth in this behalf see very clearly. For the causes be so manifest, that they cannot be hid. For who can deny but it repugneth of nature that the blind shall be appointed to lead and conduct such as do see? That the weak, the sick, and impotent persons shall nourish and keep the whole and strong, and finally, that the foolish, mad and phrenetic shall govern the discreet and give counsel to such as be sober of mind? And such be all women, compared unto man in bearing of authority. For their sight in civil regiment is but blindness, their strength weakness, their counsel foolishness, and judgment frenzy, if it be rightly considered. *John Knox*, Regiment of Women.

Writing or Speaking Assignment

Find in some likely source—newspapers, magazines, textbooks, advertisements, television commercials, conversations with your friends, etc.—one or more examples of what seem to you to be defective or crooked thinking. Expose these defects in a short speech or essay. If the defect you are working with comes from a printed source, reproduce it exactly or in reasonable detail before you begin your analysis; if it is drawn from a television commercial or a conversation, give as full and accurate a description as you can. In your analysis look for subtle or hidden appeals, as well as for the more obvious ones.

OR

Study carefully and then review, either orally or in writing, one of the books listed below for additional reading.

OR

After appropriate research into the matter in sources suggested by your instructor, prepare a short speech or essay on one of these topics or a similar one.

The Concept of Cause
Fallacies of the Syllogism
Is Language by Nature Ambiguous?
In Defense of Emotional Appeals
Hasty Generalizations and the Stereotypes That Result
Is Analogy Really the Weakest Form of Argument?
The Evils of Two-Valued Orientation: Why Forced
    Dichotomies Lead to Misunderstanding and Conflict
Formal vs. Material Validity: An Important Distinction
Aristotle's Treatment of Pseudoproofs
Suggestion and Its Influence on Belief and Behavior

For Additional Reading

Eisenberg, **Abne M.**, and **Joseph A. Ilardo.** *Argument: An Alternative to Violence.* Englewood Cliffs, N.J.: Prentice-Hall, Inc., 1972. Chapter 4, "Exposing a Fallacy."

Fearnside, W. Ward, and **William B. Holter.** *Fallacy.* Englewood Cliffs, N.J.: Prentice-Hall, Inc., 1959.

Kahane, Howard. *Logic and Contemporary Rhetoric.* Belmont, Calif.: Wadsworth Publishing Co., Inc., 1971.

St. Aubyn, Giles. *The Art of Argument.* New York: Emerson Books, Inc., 1957.

Thouless, Robert H. *How to Think Straight.* New York: Hart Publishing Co., Inc., n.d. (originally published by Simon and Schuster, 1932.)

Tibbetts, A. M. *The Strategies of Rhetoric.* Glenview, Ill.: Scott, Foresman and Co., 1969. Chapter 10, "Fallacies."

Appendix I
Specimen Arguments for Study and Analysis

Is boycotting lettuce such a good idea?

(Editor's Note: The following article is by Douglas L. Pinney. "Equal time" is an attempt by the viewpoint staff to see that all opinions are presented.)

The effort to boycott lettuce has brought before the public the tragic life style of the migratory worker. Figures cited in the **Daily Iowan** pointed to the disgrace of 800,000 children under 16 years old at work, a life expectancy of only 49 years, an average income for a family of four of $2,700, and an infant mortality rate 120 percent higher than the national average. Hardship is experienced here as few who will read this paper have known. Action is called for, but not the action of a boycott.

Few people stop to think of the way in which a boycott works. First a boycott assumes that the industry operates on and is most sensitive to economic considerations. The boycott then sets out to affect those economic considerations by refusing to purchase the industry's product.

Daily Iowan, Tuesday, September 19, 1972, p. 5. Reprinted with permission.

If the boycott is successful in persuading a large enough group to not purchase the product, then the unfavorable economic result on the industry will cause it to alter its practices in order to regain the boycotting segment of its market. Here the boycott would force the lettuce industry to allow the formation of unions for its workers.

So far the reasoning seems to hold up, but now consider what the industry will do. The boycott of its product, head lettuce, will appear to it as a reduction in demand for its product. This reduction is a dismal realization because profits will be greatly reduced and the industry hurt. But since the industry is an economic animal, it will seek to minimize its own loss. How—by a reduction in its costs, notably their labor costs or the present income of the farm workers. The longer and the more effective the boycott, the more it hurts the industry and the more the industry reduces its payments to farmworkers who with the reduced product demand are not needed. With an effective boycott we now have an industry which feels the effect of the boycott, but we have a segment of the migrant workers which feels the lack of income on a much more desperate level.

A corporation does not need clothes or food for its children—a worker does. You cannot reduce a $2,700 income by much. When we take away, by means of a boycott, the need to harvest lettuce, we take money out of the pocket of the worker as well as the industry. Big business in one sense is merely a big payroll.

Some would contend that I have missed the point since the workers' current income is so small and unionization would benefit the workers from the time it was installed. Unfortunately people must view things from their own perspective and experience. Try and put yourself in the place of the farm worker.

Unionization seems great, but with a boycott and the temporary reduction in the need of your labor, you are not sure you can survive—you have no savings account or emergency loan office to fall back on, your children hardly have enough to eat as it is, and above all you have no skills with which to find another job.

You can, when you lose your job, apply for unemployment funds provided you know they are available and know the procedure for getting them. The very hardships a boycott sets out to eliminate are heightened.

What can be done? We cannot leave the migrant worker to suffer his plight nor can we boycott with a clean conscience. We need to look to the causes of this plight. The industry low wage level is not the result of industry oppression but the result of the low value of the work of a migrant worker. These workers are working at the best job they can get! Tragic as that sounds to us with our many job options, it is fact.

We need to raise the value of the work done by a migrant worker by: (1) Making his current work worth more,

(2) Training him in work that is valued more by society and industry. The first way can be accomplished by consuming more lettuce. The more lettuce that needs to be harvested the more migrant workers are needed. Or we should train the migrant worker in a skill with which he would have more earning power.

To hope that eventual unionization will bring relief is wrong not only because the boycott would hurt the worker, but because unionization has several defects. Unionization under the current conditions of the industry would result in more cost to the lettuce industry (this is why it doesn't want unionization in the first place): wage levels would be set, firing procedures standardized, fringe benefits added.

These benefits are a tremendous improvement, but only for those who are in the union and who stay employed. What happens to the worker who is discriminated against and not let into the union, or the worker who loses his job because his company cannot afford to operate under the added costs of unionization, or the worker who at the new wage level is now more expensive than a machine which does his function? Unionization benefits those who get and keep jobs under the new situation.

The most unskilled, the most unattractive, the most feeble, the workers with the most need are not in that new, smaller group.

All these things need to be considered and given their due weight. I have seen no treatment of the problems of a lettuce boycott as presented here. I have only described what would take place in a general sense, but I would need to be convinced that the worker could survive the boycott while the industry could not and that unionization would benefit all and not some new smaller group of migrant workers. Only then would I boycott lettuce. Until then I will continue to eat my four salads a day.

In support of boycott; reply to rationalization

The following is a reply to a recent piece advocating no support for the lettuce boycott. It is offered by contributor Fred A. Wilcox, a UI grad student.

★ ★

I think Mr. Pinney's article is an excellent example of America's unique ability to rationalize cruelty. It is an argument, not without historical precedents for maintaining the status quo, the status quo in this particular instance being the poverty and nineteenth-century working conditions of lettuce pickers.

The argument goes, inversely, that if we all buy more lettuce there will be more work for lettuce pickers. More work for lettuce pickers obviously means more profits for growers. And lo, the argument untangles, more money for the owners means that people won't starve while trying to form a union. In other words, things are bad but they could get worse. Attempting to form a union or boycotting lettuce will make things worse; therefore, leave things alone. Keep on eatin' your four salads a day.

Such a tired, shopworn argument. It is the same argument used against civil rights demonstrations during the sixties. If black people are left alone, said the bigots and racists all over America, black people will be happy. In fact, said the folks who knew all about blacks, they were happy, before the agitators came along. The very intrusion of these communists was causing the good black citizens to become disenchanted with singing "Old Black Joe" while they worked fifteen hours a day on The Man's Plantation.

Civil rights agitation, said the liberal apologists for America's genocidal policy against twenty million blacks, will simply set the cause of black people back ten years. Civil rights, wrote and spoke reasonable men who declared their devotion to "minority" groups, would come in due time. But patience, not non-violent demonstrations, would bring about those rights.

Black people had been patient for three hundred years. But just a little more patience would win their rights, the rights guaranteed in the Constitution. Malcolm X said forget it, the white liberal is a snake. The white liberal said, "Malcolm, you don't understand history, baby."

According to the argument "if you don't boycott lettuce things will eventually improve, or at least they won't get any worse for migrant workers," had the American public bought more dresses during the early twentieth century, child labor laws would have been automatically passed by Congress. And if the American public would have purchased more cars from Ford, he would not have locked out his workers and hired Pinkerton men to stomp and kill labor organizers.

If the coal mining interests could sell more coal, America would enforce its mining safety standards, such as they be, and fewer men would die underground. If the steel workers would have just worked harder and given their children less to eat and forgotten all that union nonsense, then the big steel companies would not have hired goons to club and machine-gun workers when they marched for a shorter working day or higher wages.

And obviously Upton Sinclair didn't understand how things work when he wrote **The Jungle.** If the thousands of immigrants who were working in the packing industry for starvation wages just would have pushed a little harder, then surely the quality of meat would have improved for the general public and the workers' wages would have risen by a penny per hour. When I worked on highrise construction in our nation's capitol,

Daily Iowan, Tuesday, September 26, 1972, p. 4. Reprinted with permission.

we had deadlines to meet. If we ignored safety precautions and risked our lives we would certainly be rewarded: Our reward was the possibility of a job the next winter, if we were still alive and in one piece. A lot of carpenters were not after a summer of racing to meet the demands of big builder profiteers.

The argument that a union is a closed shop which discriminates against those willing to work for low wages is nothing less than an apology for the capitalist system which keeps seventeen million people working full time for less than four thousand dollars a year.

The same argument, the argument that by forming a union some workers might be unable to secure employment, is a justification for keeping one quarter of the American population in poverty. Mr. Nixon used this argument, that things could get worse, to justify his genocidal policy in Vietnam. If you keep on bombing Vietnam, peace will come for "a generation." **And the best way to get the prisoners back is to bomb Hanoi "back to the stone age."** I've heard this **same argument used by anyone who wants to maintain things,** no matter how **wretched and inhuman, the way they are.** Keep the blacks in their place and they will eventually be assimilated into middle class America. Keep on bombing for peace. Keep on working for low wages and under painful, dirty, humiliating conditions and at least you keep on working. A union might mean you don't work. Keep on eating lettuce in order to **improve conditions for the migrant** workers. At least by gobbling green stuff you don't make things worse.

I suggest that people who believe this argument go back and read American history. Nothing has been gained for the working people in this country except through boycott, strike, demonstration, violent confrontation. If the CIO had not organized workers, and if the workers had not gone into the streets or sat down in their factories, my daughter who is now eight would be out making buttons in some dingy factory from six to six, and I would be more likely shoveling sh-t in the stock yards. Or, don't bother reading

American history. Most of it is as foolish and full of distortions as the argument for eating lettuce. Read Jack London. Things would be the same today for most of us, had it not been for millions of workers who chose unionization over perpetual indentured servitude.

How to make the city safe again

Get the cops, courts and jails out of the public-morals business

By Robert Daley

Former Deputy Commissioner, Public Affairs, New York City Police.

How to reduce crime—
How to reduce police corruption—
How to make the city safe again—
Of course I can offer suggestions. But one's first reaction is a feeling of impotence. It all seems so hopeless. The answers have been there so long they will sound like platitudes, and no one has the will and guts to act on them anyway.

Last winter I helped force through a decision by Commissioner Murphy that New York cops would no longer enforce the street-gambling laws. For decades the primary purpose of the police had been to suppress gambling—or so it seemed to every cop, each one, all of them. Some cops arrested gamblers and some pocketed gambling graft. Some did both. But gambling was on every cop's mind twenty-four hours a day, like sex on the mind of an adolescent boy.

The citizens, especially in the black enclaves, did not want these laws enforced, and in a city rife with muggers it seemed immoral for the cops to waste manpower enforcing them, and I so convinced Commissioner Murphy and the police hierarchy over a period of days. Eventually, Chief of Patrol Donald Cawley was ordered to promulgate a decree, and he did so in a secret meeting with his borough commanders, and I leaked this secret on schedule to the press. Then we all waited for the storm, but it never came.

And so, at the cost of a few days' arguments by police brass, the single most important police-corruption hazard was eliminated, and a few million police hours and dollars per year were turned off gambling and onto street crime.

It seemed a small enough step then, but I get more impressed as I look back. Commissioner Murphy won that battle hands down, and also an earlier one in which he declined any longer, in the absence of a specific complain, to enforce the Sabbath laws. More recently, to cut down on corruption, he ordered the noninvolvement of certain antinuisance laws at construction sites. There was some criticism, not much.

The New York Times Magazine, September 24, 1972, pp. 14, 91- 98.
Copyright © 1972 by The New York Times Company.
Reprinted by Permission.

There are three parts of the criminal justice system—the cops, the courts, and correction. The implementation of a few dramatic ideas by the other two parties would be at least as effective as "selective" enforcement by police, and would reduce crime and corruption out of all proportion to their cost:

Enforce the gun laws. Everybody caught with an illegal gun goes to jail, instantly, instead of free, as now. Get those guns off the street and crime might drop. You'd be surprised.

I keep saying instantly. We live in a supercharged, high-velocity world. Everything takes place fast, except justice, which drags on for years. No wonder criminals laugh at it. It doesn't match the world. Trials should take place within a week. Before the witnesses have forgotten, or disappeared. Eliminate the delays which judges, prosecutors, defense attorneys (lawyers all) are so willing to accord each other. After conviction allow one appeal, also within a week, at which point the convicted criminal goes to jail for the duration of any other appeals.

I was personally involved in the arrests of two of New York's most successful professional car thieves. This was in October, 1971. It was the fifth arrest that year for one suspect, the third for the other. In May, 1972, I phoned the assistant district attorney who had the case. It was pending, he said; the two car thieves were out on bail and had another "operation" going in Queens: "We're trying to get another arrest on them."

Why do cases pend?

The jails must be changed. Also, felons must come out with a job waiting, and with some money. This isn't coddling criminals. The alternative is that each convict hits a fellow citizen on the head within an hour, in order to get money to eat, which is what is happening now.

Whole categories of crime must be eliminated. Get the cops, courts, and jails out of the public-morals business. Let the Public Health Department cope with the prostitutes. Try summary justice: an instant fine. In France if you're stopped for a traffic violation, you must pay the gendarme the fine on the spot. Give the health inspectors this power and you can clear any street of prostitutes in a few seconds. At the sight of a health inspector they will sprint for the doorways. We admit we can't obliterate prostitution, right? We just want to control it, right?

Make heroin legal. Qualified buyers could purchase it at cost at the corner drugstore, with minimum practicable controls. Black leaders would call this genocide. We can't afford to listen to them, for they may be wrong. Doubtless when Prohibition ended, certain men called this genocide too. How would the Irish race resist its fatal attraction for the bottle? Still, many of the Irish resist manfully, even today.

A victimless crime is not one where there is no victim, but one where there is no complaint. Laws cannot be enforced without complainants. The narcotic laws can't be enforced, for there are too many buyers and sellers. I have been out with police undercover teams that spent all day to find a certain dealer and buy $16 worth of heroin, seal it, trot it to the lab, await the result. Count one undercover buyer and two backup cops. All day for one buy. The D.As demand two buys before prosecution. The arrest took place on a third day. Nine man-days for one arrest, plus court time, and an estimated 300,000 addicts buying and selling junk every day. It can't be done.

Make heroin legal. Wipe out the profit and you wipe out the pushers who hook our youth, and the organized crime overlords. Wipe out the expense of illegal heroin and you eliminate most of the 300,000 burglars, muggers, and armed robbers. Burglars need to steal five times as much per day as their habits cost. Robbers may have to commit several crimes to get enough cash for one day's fix.

Change takes time. More than that, it takes will, and there is little of that around this year. In its absence, a few men can take a few giant steps on their own, at once, as Commissioner Murphy did with regard to gambling enforcement. The alternative is our current treadmill backward into the past.

Make sure every American is given the opportunities

By Jack Greenberg

Director-Counsel, N.A.A.C.P. Legal Defense and Educational Fund.

Count me with the "bleeding-heart" liberals who believe that "the most significant action that can be taken against crime is action designed to eliminate slums and ghettos, to improve education, to provide jobs, to make sure that every American is given the opportunities and the freedoms that will enable him to assume his responsibilities." In 1967 these were the words of the President's Commission on Law Enforcement and Administration of Justice, which included Lewis F. Powell, President Nixon's recent Supreme Court appointment, Leon Jaworski and Ross Malone, past presidents of the American Bar Association, William Rogers, Secretary of State, and others, none of whom are soft on crime.

Overwhelmingly, black and Puerto Rican New Yorkers are not only law-abiding but are the most frequent victims of violent crime. These crimes which they and whites suffer originate largely in such conditions as ghetto slum living, abject poverty and broken families. Socialization and character-building essential to law-abidingness have a hard time developing in the chaos of such communities. (Non-violent, non-fear-provoking white-collar crime is the domain of deviant, better-off whites). The July 19 Census Bureau report depicts one-third of the black families in the New York area with incomes below $5,000, half below $7,000 and 63 per cent of the Puerto Rican families below $7,000. The National Advisory Commission on Civil Disorders reported that in 1962 42.4 per cent of New York's nonwhite-occupied housing units were deteriorated, dilapidated or without full plumbing. Since then, the situation has worsened. With a minuscule vacancy rate and high rentals compounded by racial discrimination in housing, it is nearly impossible for the ghetto dweller to escape to a less damaging environment. Yet when the State Urban Development Corporation recently proposed building a mere 100 subsidized apartments in each of nine Westchester towns, political uproar caused the plan to be shelved in five of the towns. The school busing backlash also reflects the reluctance of many white Americans to allow even part-time escape from the ghetto into their own better-off enclaves.

Not all remedies involve political and social controversies as sharp as those touched on above, nor financial cost so great. But resistance is heavy even to reforms that would have a direct impact on crime, the most important of which are: (1) Prison reform. Prisons generally instruct in crime rather than rehabilitate. (2) Sweeping changes in treatment of juveniles. Juvenile detention not only predictably sets young people off on lives of crime, but costs as much as the best psychiatric institutions or university educations. (3) Decriminalization of much socially disfavored conduct, e.g., drunkenness, consensual sex offenses, gambling. (4) Gun control. The most modest proposals for control face enormous opposition. (5) Increasing the number of police on the streets. This costs money and dislocates established police work patterns.

The Crime Commission recommended many such changes, large and small, five years ago. But the recommendations have been so unheeded that Prof. James Vorenberg of Harvard, its executive director, recently wrote: "I find it hard to point to anything that is being done that is likely to reduce crime even to the level of five years ago."

Perhaps in the next few years, a growth in the political power of minority groups and idealistic young people, along with an end to the Vietnam war, releasing funds and, more important, moral energies, will lead to a consensus in favor of essential social changes, or at least experiments. Then, too, the median age of the population is getting somewhat older, a trend that should help lower the rate of crime, since the young commit a disproportionate number of violent crimes.

It is impossible to discuss crime in New York without dealing with heroin addiction. The experts disagree vigorously over the solution to this problem, and we cannot afford to wait years for answers. Yet, if we take the wrong approach without full information, we may make things worse.

There is a phenomenon known as the Hawthorne effect, perceived in early sociological research (at Hawthorne, N. Y.) in which it was found that subjects of social experiments often responded affirmatively merely *because* they were the subjects of the experiments. It may be that a massive group of experiments directed at drug addiction will produce a Hawthorne effect—at least a temporary defection from heroin in the addict population, sufficient to interfere with or break the cycle of addiction in which one addict recruits another.

Methadone maintenance and drug-free programs should be expanded to the limits of the numbers of addicts who will enroll. At the same time, despite the civil liberties problems, I would be willing to see a small experiment with involuntary civil commitment of addicts, necessarily coupled with treatment. While it has been said that treatment will not work when the addict is confined against his will, some who are knowledgeable about addiction argue to the contrary. And while I believe that heroin maintenance is an ultimately destructive program, I would be willing to see a small experiment with it on the slight chance that something beneficial for the addict and/or society may turn up. And with all this I would intensify police work against sellers.

Perhaps after a few years of such crash programs there will be a relapse to the old condition, but by then the cycle of addiction leading to more addiction may be broken and we may have learned more about how to deal with the problem. Maybe even now there is enough sentiment to undertake the effort and pay the cost of dealing with addiction on this intensive basis. ■

Thomas S. Szasz, M.D.

THE ETHICS OF ADDICTION

An argument in favor of letting
Americans take
any drug they want to take

*Dr. Thomas Szasz has
written many books on
psychiatry and psychol-
ogy, among them* The
Myth of Mental Illness,
Law, Liberty and Psy-
chiatry, *and, most re-
cently,* The Manufac-
ture of Madness. *He is
professor of psychiatry
at the State University
of New York Upstate
Medical Center.*

To avoid clichés about "drug abuse," let us analyze its official definition. According to the World Health Organization, "Drug addiction is a state of periodic or chronic intoxication detrimental to the individual and to society, produced by the repeated consumption of a drug (natural or synthetic). Its characteristics include: 1) an overpowering desire or need (compulsion) to continue taking the drug and to obtain it by any means, 2) a tendency to increase the dosage, and 3) a psychic (psychological) and sometimes physical dependence on the effects of the drug."

Since this definition hinges on the harm done to both the individual and society, it is clearly an ethical one. Moreover, by not specifying what is "detrimental," it consigns the problem of addiction to psychiatrists who define the patient's "dangerousness to himself and others."

Next, we come to the effort to obtain the addictive substance "by any means." This suggests that the substance must be prohibited, or is very expensive, and is hence difficult for the ordinary person to obtain (rather than that the person who wants it has an inordinate craving for it). If there were an abundant and inexpensive supply of what the "addict" wants, there would be no reason for him to go to "any means" to obtain it. Thus by the WHO's definition, one can be addicted only to a substance that is illegal or otherwise difficult to obtain. This surely removes the problem of addiction from the realm of medicine and psychiatry, and puts it squarely into that of morals and law.

Harper's Magazine, April 1972, pp. 74-79. Copyright ©
1972 by Minneapolis Star and Tribune Co., Inc. Reprinted
from the April 1972 issue of *Harper's Magazine* by
permission of the author.

In short, drug addiction or drug abuse cannot be defined without specifying the proper and improper uses of certain pharmacologically active agents. The regular administration of morphine by a physician to a patient dying of cancer is the paradigm of the proper use of a narcotic; whereas even its occasional self-administration by a physically healthy person for the purpose of "pharmacological pleasure" is the paradigm of drug abuse.

I submit that these judgments have nothing whatever to do with medicine, pharmacology, or psychiatry. They are moral judgments. Indeed, our present views on addiction are astonishingly similar to some of our former views on sex. Until recently, masturbation—or self-abuse, as it was called—was professionally declared, and popularly accepted, as both the cause and the symptom of a variety of illnesses. Even today, homosexuality—called a "sexual perversion"—is regarded as a disease by medical and psychiatric experts as well as by "well-informed" laymen.

To be sure, it is now virtually impossible to cite a contemporary medical authority to support the concept of self-abuse. Medical opinion holds that whether a person masturbates or not is medically irrelevant; and that engaging in the practice or refraining from it is a matter of personal morals or life-style. On the other hand, it is virtually impossible to cite a contemporary medical authority to oppose the concept of drug abuse. Medical opinion holds that drug abuse is a major medical, psychiatric, and public health problem; that drug addiction is a disease similar to diabetes, requiring prolonged (or lifelong) and careful, medically supervised treatment; and that taking or not taking drugs is primarily, if not solely, a matter of medical responsibility.

Thus the man on the street can only believe what he hears from all sides—that drug addiction is a disease, "like any other," which has now reached "epidemic proportions," and whose "medical" containment justifies the limitless expenditure of tax monies and the corresponding aggrandizement and enrichment of noble medical warriors against this "plague."

L IKE ANY SOCIAL POLICY, our drug laws may be examined from two entirely different points of view: technical and moral. Our present inclination is either to ignore the moral perspective or to mistake the technical for the moral.

Since most of the propagandists against drug abuse seek to justify certain repressive policies because of the alleged dangerousness of various drugs, they often falsify the facts about the true pharmacological properties of the drugs they seek to prohibit. They do so for two reasons: first, because many substances in daily use are just as harmful as the substances they want to prohibit; second, because they realize that dangerousness alone is never a sufficiently persuasive argument to justify the prohibition of any drug, substance, or artifact. Accordingly, the more they ignore the moral dimensions of the problem, the more they must escalate their fraudulent claims about the dangers of drugs.

To be sure, some drugs are more dangerous than others. It is easier to kill oneself with heroin than with aspirin. But it is also easier to kill oneself by jumping off a high building than a low one. In the case of drugs, we regard their potentiality for self-injury as justification for their prohibition; in the case of buildings, we do not.

Furthermore, we systematically blur and confuse the two quite different ways in which narcotics may cause death: by a deliberate act of suicide or by accidental overdosage.

Every individual is capable of injuring or killing himself. This potentiality is a fundamental expression of human freedom. Self-destructive behavior may be regarded as sinful and penalized by means of informal sanctions. But it should not be regarded as a crime or (mental) disease, justifying or warranting the use of the police powers of the state for its control.

Therefore, it is absurd to deprive an adult of a drug (or of anything else) because he might use it to kill himself. To do so is to treat everyone the way institutional psychiatrists treat the so-called suicidal mental patient: they not only imprison such a person but take everything away from him—shoelaces, belts, razor blades, eating utensils, and so forth—until the "patient" lies naked on a mattress in a padded cell—lest he kill himself. The result is degrading tyrannization.

Death by accidental overdose is an altogether different matter. But can anyone doubt that this danger now looms so large precisely because the sale of narcotics and many other drugs is illegal? Those who buy illicit drugs cannot be sure what drug they are getting or how much of it. Free trade in drugs, with governmental action limited to safeguarding the purity of the product and the veracity of the labeling, would reduce the risk of accidental overdose with "dangerous drugs" to the same levels that prevail, and that we find acceptable, with respect to other chemical agents and physical artifacts that abound in our complex technological society.

This essay is not intended as an exposition on the pharmacological properties of narcotics and other mind-affecting drugs. However, I want to make it clear that in my view, *regardless* of their danger, all drugs should be "legalized" (a misleading term I employ reluctantly as a concession to common usage). Although I recognize that some drugs—notably heroin, the amphetamines, and LSD, among those now in vogue—may have undesirable or dangerous consequences, I favor free trade in drugs for the same reason the Founding Fathers favored free trade in ideas. In an open society, it is none of the government's business what idea a man puts into his mind; likewise, it should be none of the government's business what drug he puts into his body.

"If ingesting alcohol is a Constitutional right, is ingesting opium, or heroin, or barbiturates, or anything else, not such a right?"

Withdrawal pains from tradition

IT IS A FUNDAMENTAL characteristic of human beings that they get used to things: one becomes habituated, or "addicted," not only to narcotics, but to cigarettes, cocktails before dinner, orange juice for breakfast, comic strips, and so forth. It is similarly a fundamental characteristic of living organisms that they acquire increasing tolerance to various chemical agents and physical stimuli: the first cigarette may cause nothing but nausea and headache; a year later, smoking three packs a day may be pure joy. Both alcohol and opiates are "addictive" in the sense that the more regularly they are used, the more the user craves them and the greater his tolerance for them becomes. Yet none of this involves any mysterious process of "getting hooked." It is simply an aspect of the universal biological propensity for *learning*, which is especially well developed in man. The opiate habit, like the cigarette habit or food habit, can be broken—and without any medical assistance— provided the person wants to break it. Often he doesn't. And why, indeed, should he, if he has nothing better to do with his life? Or, as happens to be the case with morphine, if he can live an essentially normal life while under its influence?

Actually, opium is much less toxic than alcohol. Just as it is possible to be an "alcoholic" and work and be productive, so it is (or, rather, it used to be) possible to be an opium addict and work and be productive. According to a definitive study published by the American Medical Association in 1929, ". . . morphine addiction is not characterized by physical deterioration or impairment of physical fitness . . . There is no evidence of change in the circulatory, hepatic, renal, or endocrine functions. When it is considered that these subjects had been addicted for at least five years, some of them for as long as twenty years, these negative observations are highly significant." In a 1928 study, Lawrence Kolb, an Assistant Surgeon General of the United States Public Health Service, found that of 119 persons addicted to opiates through medical practice, "90 had good industrial records and only 29 had poor ones . . . Judged by the output of labor and their own statements, none of the normal persons had [his] efficiency reduced by opium. Twenty-two of them worked regularly while taking opium for twenty-five years or more; one of them, a woman aged 81 and still alert mentally, had taken 3 grains of morphine daily for 65 years. [The usual therapeutic dose is one-quarter grain, three to four grains being fatal for the nonaddict.] She gave birth to and raised six children, and managed her household affairs with more than average efficiency. A widow, aged 66, had taken 17 grains of morphine

daily for most of 37 years. She is alert mentally
... does physical labor every day, and makes
her own living."

I am not citing this evidence to recommend
the opium habit. The point is that we must, in
plain honesty, distinguish between pharmacological effects and personal inclinations. Some
people take drugs to help them function and conform to social expectations; others take them for
the very opposite reason, to ritualize their refusal to function and conform to social expectations. Much of the "drug abuse" we now witness
—perhaps nearly all of it—is of the second type.
But instead of acknowledging that "addicts" are
unfit or unwilling to work and be "normal," we
prefer to believe that they act as they do because
certain drugs—especially heroin, LSD, and the
amphetamines—make them "sick." If only we
could get them "well," so runs this comforting
view, they would become "productive" and "useful" citizens. To believe this is like believing that
if an illiterate cigarette smoker would only stop
smoking, he would become an Einstein. With a
falsehood like this, one can go far. No wonder
that politicians and psychiatrists love it.

The concept of free trade in drugs runs counter
to our cherished notion that everyone must work
and idleness is acceptable only under special
conditions. In general, the obligation to work is
greatest for healthy, adult, white men. We tolerate idleness on the part of children, women,
Negroes, the aged, and the sick, and even accept
the responsibility to support them. But the new
wave of drug abuse affects mainly young adults,
often white males, who are, in principle at least,
capable of working and supporting themselves.
But they refuse: they "drop out"; and in doing
so, they challenge the most basic values of our
society.

The fear that free trade in narcotics would result in vast masses of our population spending
their days and nights smoking opium or mainlin-
ing heroin, rather than working and taking care
of their responsibilities, is a bugaboo that does
not deserve to be taken seriously. Habits of work
and idleness are deep-seated cultural patterns.
Free trade in abortions has not made an indus-
trious people like the Japanese give up work for

fornication. Nor would free trade in drugs convert such a people from hustlers to hippies. Indeed, I think the opposite might be the case: it is questionable whether, or for how long, a responsible people can tolerate being treated as totally irresponsible with respect to drugs and drug-taking. In other words, how long can we live with the inconsistency of being expected to be responsible for operating cars and computers, but not for operating our own bodies?

ALTHOUGH MY ARGUMENT about drug-taking is moral and political, and does not depend upon showing that free trade in drugs would also have fiscal advantages over our present policies, let me indicate briefly some of its economic implications.

The war on addiction is not only astronomically expensive; it is also counterproductive. On April 1, 1967, New York State's narcotics addiction control program, hailed as "the most massive ever tried in the nation," went into effect. "The program, which may cost up to $400 million in three years," reported the *New York Times*, "was hailed by Governor Rockefeller as 'the start of an unending war.'" Three years later, it was conservatively estimated that the number of addicts in the state had tripled or quadrupled. New York State Senator John Hughes reports that the cost of caring for each addict during this time was $12,000 per year (as against $4,000 per year for patients in state mental hospitals). It's been a great time, though, for some of the ex-addicts. In New York City's Addiction Services Agency, one ex-addict started at $6,500 a year in 1967, and was making $16,000 seven months later. Another started at $6,500 and soon rose to $18,100. The salaries of the medical bureaucrats in charge of these programs are similarly attractive. In short, the detection and rehabilitation of addicts is good business. We now know that the spread of witchcraft in the late Middle Ages was due more to the work of witchmongers than to the lure of witchcraft. Is it not possible that the spread of addiction in our day is due more to the work of addictmongers than to the lure of narcotics?

Let us see how far some of the monies spent

on the war on addiction could go in supporting people who prefer to drop out of society and drug themselves. Their "habit" itself would cost next to nothing; free trade would bring the price of narcotics down to a negligible amount. During the 1969-70 fiscal year, the New York State Narcotics Addiction Control Commission had a budget of nearly $50 million, excluding capital construction. Using these figures as a tentative base for calculation, here is what we come to: $100 million will support 30,000 drug addicts at $3,300 per year. Since the population of New York State is roughly one-tenth that of the nation, if we multiply its operating budget for addiction control by ten, we arrive at a figure of $500 million, enough to support 150,000 addicts.

I am not advocating that we spend our hard-earned money in this way. I am only trying to show that free trade in narcotics would be more economical for those of us who work, even if we had to support legions of addicts, than is our present program of trying to "cure" them. Moreover, I have not even made use, in my economic estimates, of the incalculable sums we would save by reducing crimes now engendered by the illegal traffic in drugs.

The right of self-medication

CLEARLY, the argument that marijuana—or heroin, methadone, or morphine—is prohibited because it is addictive or dangerous cannot be supported by facts. For one thing, there are many drugs, from insulin to penicillin, that are neither addictive nor dangerous but are nevertheless also prohibited; they can be obtained only through a physician's prescription. For another, there are many things, from dynamite to guns, that are much more dangerous than narcotics (especially to others) but are not prohibited. As everyone knows, it is still possible in the United States to walk into a store and walk out with a shotgun. We enjoy this right not because we believe that guns are safe but because we believe even more strongly that civil liberties are precious. At the same time, it is not possible in the United States to walk into a store and walk out with a bottle of barbiturates, codeine, or other drugs.

I believe that just as we regard freedom of speech and religion as fundamental rights, so we should also regard freedom of self-medication as a fundamental right. Like most rights, the right of self-medication should apply only to adults; and it should not be an unqualified right. Since these are important qualifications, it is necessary to specify their precise range.

John Stuart Mill said (approximately) that a person's right to swing his arm ends where his neighbor's nose begins. And Oliver Wendell Holmes said that no one has a right to shout "Fire!" in a crowded theater. Similarly, the limiting condition with respect to self-medication should be the inflicting of actual (as against symbolic) harm on others.

Our present practices with respect to alcohol embody and reflect this individualistic ethic. We have the right to buy, possess, and consume alcoholic beverages. Regardless of how offensive drunkenness might be to a person, he cannot interfere with another person's "right" to become inebriated so long as that person drinks in the privacy of his own home or at some other appropriate location, and so long as he conducts himself in an otherwise law-abiding manner. In short, we have a right to be intoxicated—in private. Public intoxication is considered an offense to others and is therefore a violation of the criminal law. It makes sense that what is a "right" in one place may become, by virtue of its disruptive or disturbing effect on others, an offense somewhere else.

The right to self-medication should be hedged in by similar limits. Public intoxication, not only with alcohol but with any drug, should be an offense punishable by the criminal law. Furthermore, acts that may injure others—such as driving a car—should, when carried out in a drug-intoxicated state, be punished especially strictly and severely. The right to self-medication must thus entail unqualified responsibility for the effects of one's drug-intoxicated behavior on others. For unless we are willing to hold ourselves responsible for our own behavior, and hold others responsible for theirs, the liberty to use drugs (or to engage in other acts) degenerates into a license to hurt others.

"It is absurd to deprive an adult of a drug (or anything else) because he might use it to kill himself."

S UCH, THEN, WOULD BE the situation of adults, if we regarded the freedom to take drugs as a fundamental right similar to the freedom to read and worship. What would be the situation of children? Since many people who are now said to be drug addicts or drug abusers are minors, it is especially important that we think clearly about this aspect of the problem.

I do not believe, and I do not advocate, that children should have a right to ingest, inject, or otherwise use any drug or substance they want. Children do not have the right to drive, drink, vote, marry, or make binding contracts. They acquire these rights at various ages, coming into their full possession at maturity, usually between the ages of eighteen and twenty-one. The right to self-medication should similarly be withheld until maturity.

In short, I suggest that "dangerous" drugs be treated, more or less, as alcohol is treated now. Neither the use of narcotics, nor their possession, should be prohibited, but only their sale to minors. Of course, this would result in the ready availability of all kinds of drugs among minors —though perhaps their availability would be no greater than it is now, but would only be more visible and hence more easily subject to proper controls. This arrangement would place responsibility for the use of all drugs by children where it belongs: on parents and their children. This is where the major responsibility rests for the use of alcohol. It is a tragic symptom of our refusal to take personal liberty and responsibility seriously that there appears to be no public desire to assume a similar stance toward other "dangerous" drugs.

Consider what would happen should a child bring a bottle of gin to school and get drunk there. Would the school authorities blame the local liquor stores as pushers? Or would they blame the parents and the child himself? There is liquor in practically every home in America and yet children rarely bring liquor to school. Whereas marijuana, Dexedrine, and heroin— substances children usually do not find at home and whose very possession is a criminal offense— frequently find their way into the school.

Our attitude toward sexual activity provides

another model for our attitude toward drugs. Although we generally discourage children below a certain age from engaging in sexual activities with others, we do not prohibit such activities by law. What we do prohibit by law is the sexual seduction of children by adults. The "pharmacological seduction" of children by adults should be similarly punishable. In other words, adults who give or sell drugs to children should be regarded as offenders. Such a specific and limited prohibition—as against the kinds of generalized prohibitions that we had under the Volstead Act or have now with respect to countless drugs—would be relatively easy to enforce. Moreover, it would probably be rarely violated, for there would be little psychological interest and no economic profit in doing so.

The True Faith: scientific medicine

WHAT I AM SUGGESTING is that while addiction is ostensibly a medical and pharmacological problem, actually it is a moral and political problem. We ought to know that there is no necessary connection between facts and values, between what is and what ought to be. Thus, objectively quite harmful acts, objects, or persons may be accepted and tolerated—by minimizing their dangerousness. Conversely, objectively quite harmless acts, objects, or persons may be prohibited and persecuted—by exaggerating their dangerousness. It is always necessary to distinguish—and especially so when dealing with social policy—between description and prescription, fact and rhetoric, truth and falsehood.

In our society, there are two principal methods of legitimizing policy: social tradition and scientific judgment. More than anything else, time is the supreme ethical arbiter. Whatever a social practice might be, if people engage in it, generation after generation, that practice becomes acceptable.

Many opponents of illegal drugs admit that nicotine may be more harmful to health than marijuana; nevertheless, they urge that smoking cigarettes should be legal but smoking marijuana should not be, because the former habit is socially accepted while the latter is not. This is a perfectly reasonable argument. But let us understand it for what it is—a plea for legitimizing old and accepted practices, and for illegitimizing novel and unaccepted ones. It is a justification that rests on precedent, not evidence.

The other method of legitimizing policy, ever more important in the modern world, is through the authority of science. In matters of health, a vast and increasingly elastic category, physicians play important roles as legitimizers and illegitimizers. This, in short, is why we regard being medicated by a doctor as drug use, and self-medication (especially with certain classes of drugs) as drug abuse.

This, too, is a perfectly reasonable arrangement. But we must understand that it is a plea for legitimizing what doctors do, because they do it with "good therapeutic" intent; and for illegitimizing what laymen do, because they do it with bad self-abusive ("masturbatory" or mind-altering) intent. This justification rests on the principles of professionalism, not of pharmacology. Hence we applaud the systematic medical use of methadone and call it "treatment for heroin addiction," but decry the occasional non-medical use of marijuana and call it "dangerous drug abuse."

Our present concept of drug abuse articulates and symbolizes a fundamental policy of scientific medicine—namely, that a layman should not medicate his own body but should place its medical care under the supervision of a duly accredited physician. Before the Reformation, the practice of True Christianity rested on a similar policy—namely, that a layman should not himself commune with God but should place his spiritual care under the supervision of a duly accredited priest. The self-interests of the church and of medicine in such policies are obvious enough. What might be less obvious is the interest of the laity: by delegating responsibility for the spiritual and medical welfare of the people to a class of authoritatively accredited specialists, these policies—and the practices they ensure— relieve individuals from assuming the burdens of responsibility for themselves. As I see it, our present problems with drug use and drug abuse are just one of the consequences of our pervasive ambivalence about personal autonomy and responsibility.

I propose a medical reformation analogous to the Protestant Reformation: specifically, a "protest" against the systematic mystification of man's relationship to his body and his professionalized separation from it. The immediate aim of this reform would be to remove the physician as intermediary between man and his body and to give the layman direct access to the language and contents of the pharmacopoeia. If man had unencumbered access to his own body and the means of chemically altering it, it would spell the end of medicine, at least as we now know it. This is why, with faith in scientific medicine so strong, there is little interest in this kind of medical reform. Physicians fear the loss of their privileges; laymen, the loss of their protections.

Finally, since luckily we still do not live in the utopian perfection of "one world," our technical approach to the "drug problem" has led, and will undoubtedly continue to lead, to some curious attempts to combat it.

Here is one such attempt: the American government is now pressuring Turkey to restrict its farmers from growing poppies (the source of morphine and heroin). If turnabout is fair play, perhaps we should expect the Turkish government to pressure the United States to restrict its farmers from growing corn and wheat. Or should we assume that Muslims have enough self-control to leave alcohol alone, but Christians need all the controls that politicians, policemen, and physicians can bring to bear on them to enable them to leave opiates alone?

Life, liberty, and the pursuit of highs

SOONER OR LATER we shall have to confront the basic moral dilemma underlying this problem: does a person have the right to take a drug, any drug—not because he needs it to cure an illness, but because he wants to take it?

The Declaration of Independence speaks of our inalienable right to "life, liberty, and the pursuit of happiness." How are we to interpret this? By asserting that we ought to be free to pursue happiness by playing golf or watching television, but not by drinking alcohol, or smoking marijuana, or ingesting pep pills?

The Constitution and the Bill of Rights are silent on the subject of drugs. This would seem to imply that the adult citizen has, or ought to have, the right to medicate his own body as he sees fit. Were this not the case, why should there have been a need for a Constitutional Amendment to outlaw drinking? But if ingesting alcohol was, and is now again, a Constitutional right, is ingesting opium, or heroin, or barbiturates, or anything else, not also such a right? If it is, then the Harrison Narcotic Act is not only a bad law but is unconstitutional as well, because it prescribes in a legislative act what ought to be promulgated in a Constitutional Amendment.

The questions remain: as American citizens, should we have the right to take narcotics or other drugs? If we take drugs and conduct ourselves as responsible and law-abiding citizens, should we have a right to remain unmolested by the government? Lastly, if we take drugs and break the law, should we have a right to be treated as persons accused of crime, rather than as patients accused of mental illness?

These are fundamental questions that are conspicuous by their absence from all contemporary discussions of problems of drug addiction and drug abuse. The result is that instead of debating the use of drugs in moral and political terms, we define our task as the ostensibly narrow technical problem of protecting people from poisoning themselves with substances for whose use they cannot possibly assume responsibility. This, I think, best explains the frightening national consensus against personal responsibility for taking drugs and for one's conduct while under their influence. In 1965, for example, when President Johnson sought a bill imposing tight federal controls over pep pills and goof balls, the bill cleared the House by a unanimous vote, 402 to 0.

The failure of such measures to curb the "drug menace" has only served to inflame our legislators' enthusiasm for them. In October 1970 the Senate passed, again by a unanimous vote (54 to 0) "a major narcotics crackdown bill."

To me, unanimity on an issue as basic and

"The concept of free trade in drugs runs counter to our cherished notion that everyone must work and idleness is acceptable only under special conditions."

complex as this means a complete evasion of the actual problem and an attempt to master it by attacking and overpowering a scapegoat—"dangerous drugs" and "drug abusers." There is an ominous resemblance between the unanimity with which all "reasonable" men—and especially politicians, physicians, and priests—formerly supported the protective measures of society against witches and Jews, and that with which they now support them against drug addicts and drug abusers.

AFTER ALL IS SAID AND DONE, the issue comes down to whether we accept or reject the ethical principle John Stuart Mill so clearly enunciated: "The only purpose [he wrote in *On Liberty*] for which power can be rightfully exercised over any member of a civilized community, against his will, is to prevent harm to others. His own good, either physical or moral, is not a sufficient warrant. He cannot rightfully be compelled to do or forbear because it will make him happier, because in the opinions of others, to do so would be wise, or even right . . . In the part [of his conduct] which merely concerns himself, his independence is, of right, absolute. Over himself, over his own body and mind, the individual is sovereign."

By recognizing the problem of drug abuse for what it is—a moral and political question rather than a medical or therapeutic one—we can choose to maximize the sphere of action of the state at the expense of the individual, or of the individual at the expense of the state. In other words, we could commit ourselves to the view that the state, the representative of many, is more important than the individual; that it therefore has the right, indeed the duty, to regulate the life of the individual in the best interests of the group. Or we could commit ourselves to the view that individual dignity and liberty are the supreme values of life, and that the foremost duty of the state is to protect and promote these values.

In short, we must choose between the ethic of collectivism and individualism, and pay the price of either—or of both. ☐

The Building
of the Gilded Cage

Jo Freeman

Hidden somewhere in the byways of social science is an occasionally discussed, seldom studied, frequently employed, and rarely questioned field generally referred to as social control. We have so thoroughly absorbed our national ideology about living in a "free society" that whatever else we may question, as radicals or academics, we are reluctant to admit that all societies, ours included, do an awful lot of controlling of *everyone's* lives. We are even more reluctant to face the often subtle ways that our own attitudes and our own lives are being controlled by that same society.

This is why it has been so difficult for materially well-off, educated whites—women as well as men—to accept the idea that women are oppressed. "Women can have a career (or do something else) if they really want to" is the oft-heard refrain. "Women are where they are because they like it" is another. There are many more. "Women are their own worst enemies." "Women prefer to be wives and mothers rather than compete in the hard, aggressive male world." "Women enjoy being feminine. They like to be treated like ladies." These are just variations on the same "freedom of choice" argument which maintains that women are free (don't forget, we are living in a *free* society) to do what they want and never question why they think they want what they say they want.

But what people think they want is precisely what society must control if it is to maintain the *status quo*. As the Bems put it, "We overlook the fact that the society that has spent twenty years carefully marking the woman's ballot for her has nothing to lose in that twenty-first year by pretending to let her cast it for the alternative of her choice. Society has controlled not her alternatives but her motivation to choose any but one of those alternatives."[1]

There are many mechanisms of social control and some are more subtle than others. The socialization process, the climate of opinion in which people live, the group ideology (political or religious), the kind of social structures available, the legal system, and the police are just some of the means society has at its disposal to channel people into the roles it finds necessary for its maintenance. They are all worthy of study, but here

[1] Sandra Bem and Daryl Bem, "We're All Non-Conscious Sexists," *Psychology Today*, Vol. 4 (November 1970), p. 26.

From *The Second Wave: A Magazine of the New Feminism,* I (Spring 1971), pp. 7-9, 33-39. Copyright © 1970, 1973 by Jo Freeman. All rights reserved. Reprinted by permission.

we are only going to look at two of them—one overt and one covert—to see what they can tell us about women.

The easiest place to start when trying to determine the position of any group of people is with the legal system. This may strike us as a little strange since our national ideology also says that "all men are equal under the law" until we remember that the ideology is absolutely correct in its restriction of this promise to "men." Now there are three groups who have never been accorded the status and the rights of manhood—blacks, children (minors), and women. Children at least are considered to be in their inferior, dependent status only temporarily because some of them (white males) eventually graduate to become men. Blacks (the 47% who are male) have "been denied their manhood" since they were kidnapped from Africa and are currently demanding it back. But women (51% of the population, black and white)—how can a woman have manhood?

This paradox illustrates the problem very well; because there is a long-standing legal tradition, reaching back to early Roman law, which says that women are perpetual children and the only adults are men. This tradition, known as the "Perpetual Tutelage of Women,"[2] has had its ups and downs, been more or less enforced, but the definition of women as minors who never grow up, who therefore must always be under the guidance of a male (father, brother, husband, or son), has been carried down in modified form to the present day and vestiges of it can still be seen in our legal system.

Even Roman law was an improvement over Greek society. In that cradle of democracy only men could be citizens in the polis. In fact most women were slaves, and most slaves were women.[3] In ancient Rome the status of both women and slaves improved slightly as they were incorporated into the family under the rule of *Patria potestas*, or Power of the Father. This term designated not so much a familial relationship as a property relationship. All land was owned by families, not individuals, and was under the control of the oldest male. Women and slaves could not assume proprietorship and in fact frequently were considered to be forms of property. A woman in particular had to turn any income she might receive over to the head of the household and had no rights to her own children, to divorce, or to any life outside the family. The relationship of woman to man was designated by the concept of *manus* (hand), under which the woman stood. Woman had no rights under law—not even legal recognition. In any civil or criminal case she had to be represented by the *Pater* who accepted legal judgment on himself and in turn judged her according to his whims. Unlike slaves, women could not be *emancipated* (removed from under the hand). They could only go from under one hand to another. This was the nature of the marital relationship (from which comes our modern practice "to ask a woman's father for her *hand* in marriage"). At marriage women were "born again" into the household of

---

[2] Sir Henry Sumner Maine, *Ancient Law* (London: John Murray, 1905), p. 135.
[3] Alvin W. Gouldner, *Enter Plato* (New York: Basic Books, 1965), p. 10.

the bridegroom's family and became the "daughter of her husband." [4]

Although later practice of Roman law was much less severe than the ancient rules, some of the most stringent aspects were incorporated into canon law and from there passed to the English common law. Interpretation and spread of the Roman law varied throughout Europe, but it was through the English common law that it was brought to this country and made part of our own legal tradition.

9 Even here history played tricks on women. Throughout the sixteenth and seventeenth centuries tremendous liberalizations were taking place in the common law attitude toward women. This was particularly true in the American colonies where rapidly accelerating commercial expansion often made it profitable to ignore the old social rules. In particular, the development of property other than land facilitated this process as women had always been held to have some right in *movable* property while only male heirs could inherit the family lands. [5]

10 But when Blackstone wrote his soon-to-be-famous *Commentaries on the Laws of England*, he chose to ignore these new trends in favor of codifying the old common law rules. Published in 1765, his work was used in Britain as a textbook. But in the Colonies and new Republic it became a legal bible. Concise and readable, it was frequently the only book to be found in most law libraries in the United States up until the middle of the nineteenth century, and incipient lawyers rarely delved past its pages when seeking the roots of legal tradition. [6] Thus when Edward Mansfield wrote the first major analysis of *The Legal Rights, Liabilities and Duties of Women* in 1845, he still found it necessary to pay homage to the Blackstone doctrine that "the husband and wife are as one and that one is the husband." As he saw it three years before the Seneca Falls Convention would write the *Woman's Declaration of Independence*, "It appears that the husband's control over the person of his wife is so complete that he may claim her society altogether; that he may reclaim her if she goes away or is detained by others; that he may use constraint upon her liberty to prevent her going away, or to prevent improper conduct; that he may maintain suits for injuries to her person; that she cannot sue alone; and that she cannot execute a deed or valid conveyance without the concurrence of her husband. In most respects she loses the power of personal independence, and altogether that of separate action in legal matters." [7] The husband also had almost total control over all the wife's real and personal property or income.

11 Legal traditions die hard even when they are mythical ones. So the

---

[4] Numa Denis Fustel de Coulanges, *The Ancient City* (Garden City, N. Y.: Doubleay & Company, 1873), pp. 42–94.

[5] Richard B. Morris, *Studies in the History of American Law* (Philadelphia: Mitchell & Co., 1959), pp. 126–128.

[6] Mary Beard, *Woman as Force in History* (New York: The Macmillan Company, 1946), pp. 108–109.

[7] Edward Mansfield, *The Legal Rights, Liabilities and Duties of Women* (Salem, Mass.: Jewett & Co., 1845), p. 273.

bulk of the activities of feminists in the nineteenth century were spent chipping away at the legal nonexistence that Blackstone had defined for married women. Despite the passage of Married Women's Property Acts and much other legislative relief during the nineteenth century, the core idea of the common law that husbands and wives have reciprocal—not equal—rights and duties remains. The husband must support the wife and children, and she in return must render services to the husband. Thus the woman is legally required to do the domestic chores, to provide marital companionship and sexual consortium. Her first obligation is to him. If he moves out of town, she cannot get unemployment compensation if she quits her job to follow him, but he can divorce her on grounds of desertion if she doesn't. Likewise, unless there has been a legal separation, she cannot deny him access to their house even if she has good reason to believe that his entry on a particular occasion would result in physical abuse to her and her children. He must maintain her, but the amount of support beyond subsistence is at his discretion. She has no claim for direct compensation for any of the services rendered.[8]

Crozier commented on this distribution of obligations: "Clearly, that economic relationship between A and B whereby A has an original ownership of B's labor, with the consequent necessity of providing B's maintenance, is the economic relationship between an owner and his property rather than that between two free persons. It was the economic relationship between a person and his domesticated animal. In the English common law the wife was, in economic relationship to the husband, his property. The financial plan of marriage law was founded upon the economic relationship of owner and property."[9]

This basic relationship still remains in force today. The "domesticated animal" has acquired a longer leash, but the legal chains have yet to be broken. Common law practices, assumptions, and attitudes still dominate the law. The property, real and personal, brought by the woman to the marriage now remains her separate estate, but such is not always the case for that acquired during the marriage.

There are two types of property systems in the United States—common law and community. In the nine community property states (Arizona, California, Hawaii, Idaho, Louisiana, Nevada, New Mexico, Texas, and Washington) all property or income acquired by either husband or wife is community property and is equally divided upon divorce. However, "the general rule is that the husband is the head of the 'community' and the duty is his to manage the property for the benefit of his wife and family. Usually, as long as the husband is capable of managing the community, the wife has no power of control over it and, acting alone, cannot contract debts chargeable against it."[10] Included in the property is

[8] Sophonisba Breckinridge, *The Family and the State* (Chicago: University of Chicago Press, 1934), pp. 109–110.
[9] Blanche Crozier, "Marital Support," *Boston University Law Review*, Vol. 15, (1935).
[10] Philip Francis, *The Legal Status of Women* (New York: Oceana Publications, 1963), p. 23.

the income of a working wife which, under the law, is managed by the husband with the wife having no legal right to a say in how it shall be spent.

In common law states each spouse has a right to manage his own income and property. However, unlike community property states, this principle does not recognize the contribution made by a wife who works only in the home. Although the wife generally contributes domestic labor to the maintenance of the home far in excess of that of her husband she has no right to an allowance, wages or an income of any sort. Nor can she claim joint ownership upon divorce.[11]

Marriage incurs a few other disabilities as well. A married woman cannot contract on the same basis as her husband or a single woman in most states. In only five states does she have the same right to her own domicile. In many states a married woman can now live separately from her husband, but his domicile is still her address for purposes of taxation, voting, jury service, etc.[12]

Along with the domicile regulations, those concerning names are most symbolic of the theory of the husband's and wife's legal unity. Legally, every married woman's surname is that of her husband and no court will uphold her right to go by a different name. Pragmatically, she can use another name only so long as her husband does not object. If he were legally to change his name, hers would automatically change too, though such would not necessarily be the case for the children. "In a very real sense, the loss of a woman's surname represents the destruction of an important part of her personality and its submersion in that of her husband."[13]

When we move out of the common law and into the statutory law, we find an area in which, until recently, the dual legal status of women has increased in the last seventy years. This assault was particularly intense around the turn of the century, but has solidified considerably since then. Some of the earliest sex discriminatory legislation was against prostitutes; but this didn't so much prohibit the practice of their profession as regulate their hours and place of work. The big crackdown against prostitutes didn't come until World War I when there was fear that the soldiers would contact venereal disease.[14]

There was also a rise in the abortion laws. Originally abortion was illegal only when performed without the husband's consent and the only

[11] Citizens Advisory Council on the Status of Women, *Report of the Task Force on Family Law and Policy*, 1968, p. 2.
[12] *Ibid.*, p. 39.
[13] Leo Kanowitz, *Women and the Law: The Unfinished Revolution* (Albuquerque: University of New Mexico Press, 1969), p. 41.

[14] George Gould and Ray F. Dickenson, The American Social Hygiene Association, *Digest of State and Federal Laws Dealing with Prostitution and Other Sex Offenses*, 1942.

crime was a "wrong to the husband in depriving him of children."[15] Prior to passage of the nineteenth-century laws which made it a criminal offense it was largely regarded as a Church offense punishable by religious penalties.[16]

The most frequent new laws were sex-specific labor legislation. Under common law and in the early years of this country there was very little restrictive legislation on the employment of women. It was not needed. Custom and prejudice alone sufficed to keep the occupations in which women might be gainfully employed limited to domestic servant, factory worker, governess, and prostitute. As women acquired education and professional skills in the wake of the Industrial Revolution, they increasingly sought employment in fields which put them in competition with men. In some instances men gave way totally, and the field became dominated by women, losing prestige, opportunities for advancement and pay in the process. The occupation of secretary is the most notable. In most cases men fought back and were quick to make use of economic, ideological, and legal weapons to reduce or eliminate their competition. "They excluded women from trade unions, made contracts with employers to prevent their hiring women, passed laws restricting the employment of married women, caricatured working women, and carried on ceaseless propaganda to return women to the home or to keep them there."[17]

The restrictive labor laws were the main weapon. Among the earliest were those prohibiting women from practicing certain professions, such as law and medicine. But most were directed toward regulating work conditions in factories. Initially such laws were aimed at protecting both men and women workers from the sweatshop conditions that prevailed during the nineteenth century. The extent to which women, and children, were protected more than men varied from state to state, but in 1905 the heated struggle to get the state to assume responsibility for the welfare of workers received a major setback. The Supreme Court invalidated a New York law that no male or female worker could be required or permitted to work in bakeries more than sixty hours a week and in so doing made all such protective laws unconstitutional.[18]

Three years later the Court upheld an almost identical Oregon statute that applied to females only, on the grounds that their physical inferiority and their function as "mothers to the race" justified special class legislation.[19] With this decision as a precedent, the drive for protective legislation became distorted into a push for laws that applied to women only. It made some strange allies, who had totally opposing

[15] Bernard M. Dickens, *Abortion and the Law* (Bristol: MacGibbon & Kee, Ltd., 1966), p. 15.

[16] Alan F. Guttmacher, "Abortion—Yesterday, Today and Tomorrow," in Alan F. Guttmacher, ed., *The Case for Legalized Abortion Now* (Berkeley: Diablo Press, 1967), p. 4.

[17] Helen Mayer Hacker, "Women as a Minority Group," *Social Forces*, Vol. 31 (October 1951), p. 67.

[18] *Lockner* v. *New York*, 198 U. S. 45 (1905).

[19] *Mueller* v. *Oregon*, 208 U. C. 412 (1908).

reasons for supporting such laws. On the one hand social reformers and many feminists were in favor of them on the principle that half a loaf was better than none and the hope that at some time in the future the laws would apply to men as well.[20] Many male union leaders were also in favor of them, but not because they would protect women. As President Strasser of the International Cigarmakers Union expressed it, "We cannot drive the females out of the trade but we can restrict this daily quota of labor through factory laws." [21]

Strasser soon proved to be right, as the primary use of "protective" laws has been to protect the jobs of men by denying overtime pay, promotions, and employment opportunities to women. The Supreme Court has long since rejected its ruling that prevented protective legislation from applying to men yet there has been no move by male workers to have the laws extended to them. Most of the real benefits made available by such laws have been obtained through federal law or collective bargaining, while the state restrictive laws have been quoted by unions and employers alike to keep women in an inferior competitive position. The dislike of these laws felt by the women they affect can be seen in the numerous cases challenging their legitimacy that have been filed since Title VII of the Civil Rights Act was passed (prohibiting sex discrimination in employment).

These laws do more than restrict the hours which women may work. An examination of the state labor laws reveals a complex, confusing, inconsistent chaos. As of 1970, before the courts began voiding many sex-specific labor laws on the grounds they were in conflict with Title VII, thirteen states had minimum wage laws which applied only to women and minors, and two which applied only to women. Adult women were prohibited from working in specified occupations or under certain working conditions considered hazardous in twenty-six states; in ten of these women could not work in bars.

Laws restricting the number of hours a woman might work—generally to eight per day and forty-eight per week-were found in forty-one states and the District of Columbia. Twenty states prohibited night work and limitations were made in twelve on the amount of weight that could be lifted by a woman. These maximums ranged from fifteen to thirty-five pounds (the weight of a small child).[23]

The "weight and hours" laws have proved to be the most onerous and are the ones usually challenged in the courts. In *Mengelkoch et al. v. the Industrial Welfare Commission of California and North American Aviation, Inc.*, the defending corporation has admitted that the women

---

[20] British feminists always opposed such laws for their country on the grounds that any sex specific laws were fraught with more evil than good.

[21] Alice Henry, *The Trade Union Woman* (New York: Appleton and Co., 1915), p. 24.

[22] U. S. Department of Labor, *Summary of State Labor Laws for Women*, February 1967, passim.

[23] *Ibid.*

were denied overtime and promotions to positions requiring overtime, justifying their actions by the California maximum hours law. In *Roig* v. *Southern Bell Telephone and Telegraph Co.*, the plaintiffs are protesting that their current job is exempt from the Louisiana maximum hours but that the higher paying job to which they were denied promotion is not. One major case which challenged the Georgia weight-lifting law is *Weeks* v. *Southern Bell Telephone and Telegraph*. It received a favorable ruling from the Fifth Circuit Court, but the plaintiff has yet to be given the promotion for which she sued.

But perhaps most illustrative of all is an Indiana case,[24] in which the company tried to establish maximum weight-lifting restrictions even though its plant and the plaintiffs were located in a state which did not have such laws. By company policy, women were restricted to jobs whose highest pay rate was identical with the lowest pay rate for men. Many of the women, including the defendants, were laid off, while men with less seniority were kept on, on the grounds that the women could not lift over 35 pounds. This policy resulted in such anomalies as women having to lift seventeen and one-half tons of products a day in separate ten-pound loads, while the male supervisors sat at the head of the assembly line handling the controls and lifting one forty-pound box of caps each hour. "In a number of other instances, women were doing hard manual labor until the operations were automated; then they were relieved of their duties, and men were employed to perform the easier and more pleasant jobs."[25] In its defense, the company claimed it reached this policy in accordance with the union's wishes, but the Seventh Circuit Court unanimously ruled against it anyway. This is only one of many instances in which corporations and male-run unions have taken advantage of "protective" legislation in order to protect themselves from giving women equal job opportunities and equal pay.

With the passage of Title VII the restrictive labor legislation is slowly being dissolved by the courts. But these laws are just vestiges of what has been an entirely separate legal system applicable particularly to women. At their base lies the fact that the position of women under the Constitution is not the same as that of men. The Supreme Court has ruled several times that the Fourteenth Amendment prohibits any arbitrary class legislation, except that based on sex. The last case was decided in 1961, but the most important was in 1874. In *Minor* v. *Happerset* (88 U. S. 21 Wall. 162 1873), the Court first defined the concept of "second-class citizenship" by saying that some citizens could be denied rights which others had. The "equal protection" clause of the Fourteenth Amendment did not give women equal rights with men.

Other groups in society have also had special bodies of law created for them as a means of social control. Thus an examination of the statutes

---

[24] *Sellers, Moore and Case* v. *Colgate Palmolive Co. and the International Chemical Workers Union, Local No. 15*, 272 Supp. 332; *Minn. L. Rev.* Vol. 52, p. 1091.

[25] *Brief for the Plaintiffs/ Appellants in the Seventh Circuit Court of Appeals*, No. 16, 632, p. 5.

can clearly delineate those groups which society feels it necessary to control.

The statutes do not necessarily indicate *all* of the groups which a particular society excludes from full participation, but they do show those which it most adamantly excludes. In virtually every society that has existed, the caste cleavages, as distinct from the class lines, have been imbedded in the law. Differentiating between class and caste is often difficult as the two differ in degree that only at the extremes is seen as a difference in kind. It is made more difficult by our refusal to acknowledge that castes exist in our society. Here too we have allowed our thinking to be subverted by our national ideology. Our belief in the potentiality, if not the current existence, of high social mobility determined only by the individual's talents leads us to believe that mobility is hampered by one's socio-economic origins but not that it is made impossible if one comes from the wrong caste. Only recently have we reluctantly begun to face the reality of the "color-line" as a caste boundary. Our consciousness of the caste nature of the other boundaries, particularly that of sex, is not yet this high.

The law not only shows the caste boundaries, it also gives a fairly good history of the changes in boundaries. If the rigidity of caste lines fades into more permeable class lines, the legislation usually changes with it. The Middle Ages saw separate application of the law to the separate estates. In the early years of this country certain rights were reserved to those possessing a minimum amount of property. Today, nobility of birth or amount of income may affect the treatment one receives from the courts, but it is not expressed in the law itself. For the past 150 years, the major caste divisions have been along the lines of age, sex, and ethnic origin; these have been the categories for which special legislation has existed.

The law further indicates when restricted castes are seen to be most threatening and the ways in which they are felt to be threatening. If members of a group will restrict their own activities, or these activities are inconsequential, law is unnecessary. No law need be made to keep people out of places they never considered going. It is when certain prerogatives are threatened by an outgroup that it must be made illegal to violate them. Thus Jim Crow laws were not necessary during slavery and restrictive labor legislation was not extensively sought for until women entered the job market in rapidly accelerating numbers at the end of the nineteenth century.

Frequently, members of the lower castes are lumped together and the same body of special law applied to all. Most of the labor legislation discussed earlier applies to "women and minors." The state of New York once worded its franchise law to include everyone but "women, minors, convicts and idiots." When a legal status had to be found for Negro slaves in the seventeenth century, the "nearest and most natural analogy was the status of women." [26] But the clearest analogy of all was stated by the Southern slave-owning class when trying to defend the system prior to the Civil War. One of the most widely read rationalizations was that of George Fitzhugh who wrote in his 1854 *Sociology for the South* that " the kind of slavery is adapted to the men enslaved. Wives and apprentices are slaves, not in theory only, but often in fact. Children are slaves to their parents, guardians, and teachers. Imprisoned culprits are slaves. Lunatics and idiots are slaves also." [27]

The progress of "out castes," particularly those of the wrong race and sex, also has been parallel. The language of the Nineteenth Amendment was borrowed directly from that of the Fifteenth. The "sex" provision of Title VII (only the second piece of corrective legislation pertaining to women that has been passed) [28] was stuck into the Civil Rights Act of 1964 as a joke by octogenarian representative Howard W. Smith of Virginia.[29]

Many of the same people were involved in both movements as well. Sojourner Truth and Douglass were staunch feminists. Douglass urged the first Convention at Seneca Falls in 1848 to demand the franchise when many of the women were reluctant to do so. Similarly, the early feminists were ardent abolitionists. The consciousness of two of the most active is dated from the World Anti-Slavery Convention in London in 1840 when Lucretia Mott and Elizabeth Cady Stanton were compelled to sit in the galleries rather than participate in the convention.[30] Many of today's new feminists also come out of an active background in the civil rights and other social movements.[31] Almost without exception, when one of the lower castes in our society begins to revolt, the others quickly perceive the similarities to their own condition and start the battle on their own grounds.

Thus it is not surprising that these groups quickly find that they have more in common than having a similar legal situation. All of them, when comparing themselves to the culture of the middle-aged white male,[32] find that they are distinctly in the minority position. This minority position involves a good deal more than laws and a good deal more than economic and social discrimination. Discrimination *per se* is only one aspect of oppression and not always the most significant one. There are many other social and psychological aspects. Likewise, being subject to separate laws and poorer access to the socio-economic system are only

---

[26] Gunnar Myrdal, *An American Dilemma* (New York: Harper & Row, Publishers, 1944), p. 1073.

[27] George Fitzhugh, *Sociology for the South* (Richmond, Va.: A. Morris, 1854), p. 86.

[28] The first was the Equal Pay Act of 1963 which took 94 years to get through Congress.

[29] Caroline Bird, *Born Female: The High Cost of Keeping Women Down* (New York: David McKay Co., 1968), chapter I.

[30] Eleanor Flexner, *Century of Struggle* (New York: Atheneum, 1959), p. 71. They were joined by one white and one black man, William Lloyd Garrison and John Cronan.

[31] Jo Freeman, "The New Feminists," *Nation*, Vol. 208 (February 24, 1969), p. 242.

[32] Myrdal, p. 1073.

some of the characteristics of being in a minority group. This point has been well explored by Hacker.[33]

The Negro analogy has been challenged many times on the grounds that women do not suffer from the same overt segregation as blacks. This point is well noted. But it is important to realize that blatant discrimination is just one mechanism of social control. There are many more subtle ones employed long before such coercion becomes necessary. It is only when these other methods fail to keep a minority group in its place that harsher means must be found. Given that a particular society needs the subservience of several different groups of people, it will use its techniques to a different degree with each of them, depending on what is available and what they are most susceptible to. It is a measure of the blacks' resistance to the definition which white society has tried to impose on them that such violent extremes have had to be used to keep the caste lines intact.

Women, however, have not needed such stringent social chains. Their bodies can be left free because their minds are chained long before they became functioning adults. Most women have so thoroughly internalized the social definitions that their only significant role is to serve men as wives and raise the next generation of men and their servants that no laws are necessary to enforce this.

The result is that women, even more than other minority groups, have their identities derived first as members of a group and only second, if at all, as unique persons. "Consider the following—When a boy is born, it is difficult to predict what he will be doing twenty-five years later. We cannot say whether he will be an artist or a doctor or a college professor because he will be permitted to develop and fulfill his own identity. But if the newborn child is a girl, we can predict with almost complete certainty how she will be spending her time twenty-five years later. Her individuality does not have to be considered; it is irrelevant."[34]

Yet until very recently, most women have refused to recognize their own oppression. They have openly accepted the social definition of who and what they are. They have refused to be conscious of the fact that they are seen and treated, before anything else, as women. Many still do. This very refusal is significant because no group is so oppressed as one which will not recognize its own oppression. Women's denial that they must deal with their oppression is a reflection of just how far they still have to go.

There are many reasons why covert mechanisms of social control have been so much more successful with women than with most other minority groups. More than most they have been denied any history. Their tradition of subjection is long, and even this history is purged from the books so women cannot compare the similarities of their current condition with that of the past. In a not-so-subtle way both men and women

---

[33] Hacker, pp. 10–19.

[34] Bem and Bem, p. 7.

are told that only men make history and women are not important enough to study.

Further, the agents of social control are much nearer to hand than those of any other group. No other minority lives in the same household with its master, separated totally from its peers and urged to compete with them for the privilege of serving the majority group. No other minority so thoroughly accepts the standards of the dominant group as its own and interprets any deviance from those values as a sign of degeneracy. No other minority so readily argues for the maintenance of its own position as one that is merely "different" without questioning whether one must be the "same" to be equal.

Women reach this condition, this acceptance of their secondary role as right and just, through the most insidious mechanism of social control yet devised—the socialization process. That is the mechanism that we want to analyze now.

To understand how most women are socialized we must first understand how they see themselves and are seen by others. Several studies have been done on this. Quoting one of them, McClelland stated that "the female image is characterized as small, weak, soft and light. In the United States it is also dull, peaceful, relaxed, cold, rounded, passive and slow." [35] A more thorough study which asked men and women to choose out of a long list of adjectives those which most clearly applied to themselves showed that women strongly felt themselves to be such things as uncertain, anxious, nervous, hasty, careless, fearful, full, childish, helpless, sorry, timid, clumsy, stupid, silly, and domestic. On a more positive side women felt they were understanding, tender, sympathetic, pure, generous, affectionate, loving, moral, kind, grateful, and patient. [36]

This is not a very favorable self-image, but it does correspond fairly well with the social myths about what women are like. The image has some nice qualities, but they are not the ones normally required for that kind of achievement to which society gives its highest social rewards. Now one can justifiably question both the idea of achievement and the qualities necessary for it, but this is not the place to do so. Rather, because the current standards are the ones which women have been told they do not meet, the purpose here will be to look at the socialization process as a mechanism to keep them from doing so. We will also need to analyze some of the social expectations about women and about what they define as a successful *woman* (not a successful person) because they are inextricably bound up with the socialization process. All people are socialized to meet the social expectations held for them, and it is only when this process fails to do so (as is currently happening on several fronts) that it is at all questioned.

---

[35] David McClelland, "Wanted: A New Self-Image for Women," in Robert J. Lifton, ed., *The Woman in America* (Boston: Beacon Press, 1965), p. 173.
[36] Edward M. Bennett and Larry R. Cohen, "Men and Women: Personality Patterns and Contrasts," *Genetic Psychology Monographs*, Vol. 59 (1959), pp. 101–155.

First, let us further examine the effects on women of minority group status. Here another interesting parallel emerges, but it is one fraught with more heresy than any previously observed. When we look at the *results* of female socialization we find a strong similarity between what our society labels, even extols, as the typical "feminine" character structure and that of oppressed peoples in this country and elsewhere.

In his classic study, *The Nature of Prejudice*, Allport devotes a chapter to "Traits Due to Victimization." Included are such personality characteristics as sensitivity, submission, fantasies of power, desire for protection, indirectness, ingratiation, petty revenge and sabotage, sympathy, extremes of both self and group hatred and self and group glorification, display of flashy status symbols, compassion for the underprivileged, identification with the dominant group's norms, and passivity.[37] Allport was primarily concerned with Jews and Negroes, but compare his characterization with the very thorough review of the literature on sex differences among young children made by Terman and Tyler. For girls, they listed such traits as sensitivity, conformity to social pressures, response to environment, ease of social control, ingratiation, sympathy, low levels of aspiration, compassion for the underprivileged, and anxiety. They found that girls compared to boys were more nervous, unstable, neurotic, socially dependent, submissive, had less self-confidence, lower opinions of themselves and of girls in general, and were more timid, emotional, ministrative, fearful, and passive.[38] These are also the kinds of traits found in the Indians when under British rule,[39] in the Algerians under the French,[40] and elsewhere.

Two of the most essential aspects of this "minority group character structure" are the extent to which one's perceptions are distorted and one's group is denigrated. These two things in and of themselves are very effective means of social control. If one can be led to believe in one's own inferiority, then one is much less likely to resist the status that goes with that inferiority.

When we look at women's opinion of women, we find the notion that they are inferior prevalent just about everywhere. Young girls get off to a very good start. They begin speaking, reading, and counting sooner. They articulate more clearly and put words into sentences earlier. They have fewer reading and stuttering problems. Girls are even better in math in the early school years. They also make a lot better grades than boys do until late high school. But when they are asked to compare their achievements with those of boys, they rate boys higher in virtually every respect. Despite factual evidence to the contrary, girls' opinion of girls grows

---

[37] Gordon W. Allport, *The Nature of Prejudice* (Reading, Mass.: Addison-Wesley Publishing Co., 1954), pp. 142-161.

[38] Lewis M. Terman and Leona E. Tyler, "Psychological Sex Differences," in Leonard Carmichael, ed., *Manual of Child Psychology* (New York: John Wiley & Sons, 1954), pp. 1080–1100.

[39] Lewis Fisher, *Gandhi* (New York: New American Library, 1954).

[40] Franz Fanon, *The Wretched of the Earth* (New York: Grove Press, 1963).

progressively worse with age, while their opinion of boys and boys' abilities grows better. Boys, likewise, have an increasingly better opinion of themselves and worse opinion of girls as they grow older.[41]

These distortions become so gross that, according to Goldberg, by the time girls reach college they have become prejudiced against women. He gave college girls sets of booklets containing six identical professional articles in traditional male, female, and neutral fields. The articles were identical, but the names of the authors were not. For example, an article in one set would bear the name "John T. McKay" and in another set the same article would be authored by "Joan T. McKay." Questions at the end of each article asked the students to rate the articles on value, persuasiveness, and profundity, and the authors for writing style and competence. The male authors fared better in every field, even in such "feminine" areas as Art History and Dietetics. Goldberg concluded that "women are prejudiced against female professionals and, regardless of the actual accomplishments of these professionals, will firmly refuse to recognize them as the equals of their male colleagues."[42]

But these unconscious assumptions about women can be very subtle and cannot help but to support the myth that women do not produce high-quality professional work. If the Goldberg findings hold in other situations, and the likelihood is great that they do, it explains why women's work must be of a much higher quality than that of men to be acknowledged as merely equal. People in our society simply refuse to believe that a woman can cross the caste lines and be competent in a "man's world."

However, most women rarely get to the point of writing professional articles or doing other things which put them in competition with men. They seem to lack what psychologists call the "Achievement Motive."[43] When we look at the little research that has been done, we can see why this is the case. Horner's recent study of undergraduates at the University of Michigan showed that 65 percent of the women but only 10 percent of the men associated academic success with having negative consequences. Further research showed that these college women had what Horner termed a "motive to avoid success" because they perceived it as leading to social rejection and role conflict with their concept of "feminity."[44] Lipinski has also shown that women students associate success in the usual sense as something which is achieved by men but not by women.[45] Pierce suggested that girls did in fact have achievement motiva-

[41] S. Smith, "Age and Sex Differences in Children's Opinion Concerning Sex Differences," *Journal of Genetic Psychology*, Vol. 54 (1939), pp. 17–25.

[42] Philip Goldberg, "Are Women Prejudiced Against Women?" *Transaction*, Vol. 5 (April 1968), pp. 28 ff.

[43] McClelland, passim.

[44] Matina S. Horner, "Woman's Will to Fail," *Psychology Today*, Vol. 3 (November 1969), p. 36. See also, Matina S. Horner, *Sex Differences in Achievement Motivation and Performance in Competitive and Non-Competitive Situations.* Unpublished doctoral dissertation, University of Michigan, 1968.

[45] Beatrice Lipinski, *Sex-Role Conflict and Achievement Motivation in College Women.* Unpublished doctoral dissertation, University of Cincinnati, 1965.

tion but that they had different criteria for achievement than did boys. He went on to show that high achievement motivation in high school women correlates much more strongly with early marriage than it does with success in school.[46]

Some immediate precedents for the idea that women should not achieve too much academically can be seen in high school, for it is here that the performance of girls begins to drop drastically. It is also at this time that peer-group pressures on sex-role behavior increase and conceptions of what is "properly feminine" or "masculine" become more narrow.[47] One need only recall Asch's experiments to see how peer-group pressures, coupled with our rigid ideas about "femininity" and "masculinity," could lead to the results found by Horner, Lipinski, and Pierce. Asch found that some 33 percent of his subjects would go contrary to the evidence of their own senses about something as tangible as the comparative length of two lines when their judgments were at variance with those made by the other group members.[48] All but a handful of the other 67 percent experienced tremendous trauma in trying to stick to their correct perceptions.

These experiments are suggestive of how powerful a group can be in imposing its own definition of a situation and suppressing the resistance of individual deviants. When we move to something as intangible as sex-role behavior and to social sanctions far greater than simply the displeasure of a group of unknown experimental stooges, we can get an idea of how stifling social expectations can be. It is not surprising, in light of our cultural norm that a girl should not appear too smart or surpass boys in anything, that those pressures to conform, so prevalent in adolescence, prompt girls to believe that the development of their minds will have only negative results.

But this process begins long before puberty. It begins with the kind of toys young children are given to play with, with the roles they see their parents in, with the stories in their early reading books, and the kind of ambitions they express or actions they engage in that receive rewards from their parents and other adults. Some of the early differentiation along these lines is obvious to us from looking at young children and reminiscing about our own lives. But some of it is not so obvious, even when we engage in it ourselves. It consists of little actions which parents and teachers do every day that are not even noticed but can profoundly affect the style and quality of a child's developing mind.

Adequate research has not yet been done which irrefutably links up child-rearing practices with the eventual adult mind, but there is evidence

[46] James V. Pierce, "Sex Differences in Achievement Motivation of Able High School Students," Co-operative Research Project No. 1097, University of Chicago, December 1961.

[47] Lionel J. Neiman, "The Influence of Peer Groups Upon Attitudes Toward the Feminine Role," *Social Problems*, Vol. 2 (1954), pp. 104–111.

[48] S. E. Asch, "Studies of Independence and Conformity. A Minority of One Against a Unanimous Majority," *Psychological Monographs*, Vol. 70, No. 9 (1956).

to support some hypotheses. Let us take a look at one area where strong sex differences show up relatively early—mathematical reasoning ability. No one has been able to define exactly what this ability is, but it has been linked up with number ability and spatial perception, or the ability to visualize objects out of their context. As on other tests, girls score higher on number ability until late high school, but such is not the case with analytic and spatial perception tests. These tests indicate that boys perceive more analytically, while girls are more contextual—although the ability to "break set" or be "field independent" also does not seem to appear until after the fourth or fifth year.[19]

According to Maccoby, this contextual mode of perception common to women is a distinct disadvantage for scientific production. "Girls on the average develop a somewhat different way of handling incoming information—their thinking is less analytic, more global, and more perseverative—and this kind of thinking may serve very well for many kinds of functioning, but it is not the kind of thinking most conducive to high-level intellectual productivity, especially in science."[50]

Several social psychologists have postulated that the key developmental characteristic of analytic thinking is what is called early "independence and mastery training," or "whether and how soon a child is encouraged to assume initiative, to take responsibility for himself, and to solve problems by himself, rather than rely on others for the direction of his activities."[51] In other words, analytically inclined children are those who have not been subject to what Bronfenbrenner calls "over-socialization,"[52] and there is a good deal of indirect evidence that such is the case. Levy has observed that "overprotected" boys tend to develop intellectually like girls.[53] Bing found that those girls who were good at spatial tasks were those whose mothers left them alone to solve the problems by themselves, while the mothers of verbally inclined daughters insisted on helping them.[54] Witkin similarly found that mothers of analytic children had encouraged their initiative, while mothers of non-analytic children had encouraged dependence and discouraged self-assertion.[55] One writer com-

[49] Eleanor E. Maccoby, "Sex Differences in Intellectual Functioning," in Eleanor Maccoby, ed., *The Development of Sex Differences* (Stanford University Press, 1966), p. 26 ff. The three most common tests are the Rod and Frame test. which requires the adjustment of a rod to a vertical position regardless of the tilt of a frame around it; the Embedded Figures Test, which determines the ability to perceive a figure embedded in a more complex field; and an analytic test in which one groups a set of objects according to a common element.
[50] Eleanor E. Maccoby, "Woman's Intellect" in Seymour M. Farber and Roger H. L. Wilson, eds., *Man and Civilization: The Potential of Women, A Symposium,* (New York: McGraw-Hill, 1963), p. 30.
[51] Maccoby, *Ibid.,* p. 31. See also Julia A. Sherman, "Problems of Sex Differences in Space Perception and Aspects of Intellectual Functioning," *Psychological Review,* Vol. 74 (July 1967), pp. 290–299; and Philip E. Vernon, "Ability Factors and Environmental Influences," *American Psychologist,* Vol. 20 (September 1965), pp. 723–733.
[52] Urie Bronfenbrenner, "Some Familial Antecedents of Responsibility and Leadership in Adolescents," in Luigi Petrullo and Bernard M. Bass, eds., *Leadership and Interpersonal Behavior* (New York: Holt, Rinehart and Winston, 1961), p. 260.
[53] D. M. Levy, *Maternal Overprotection* (New York: Columbia University Press, 1943).
[54] Maccoby, *Ibid.,* p. 31.
[55] Herman A. Witkin *et al., Psychological Differentiation* (New York: John Wiley & Sons, 1962).

mented on these studies that "this is to be expected, for the independent child is less likely to accept superficial appearances of objects without exploring them for himself, while the dependent child will be afraid to reach out on his own and will accept appearances without question. In other words, the independent child is likely to be more *active*, not only psychologically but physically, and the physically active child will naturally have more kinesthetic experience with spatial relationships in his environment." [56]

When we turn to specific child-rearing practices, we find that the pattern repeats itself according to the sex of the child. Although comparative studies of parental treatment of boys and girls are not extensive, those that have been made indicate that the traditional practices applied to girls are very different from those applied to boys. Girls receive more affection, more protectiveness, more control, and more restrictions. Boys are subjected to more achievement demands and higher expectations.[57] In short, while girls are not always encouraged to be dependent *per se*, they are usually not encouraged to be *independent* and physically active. "Such findings indicate that the differential treatment of the two sexes reflects in part a difference in goals. With sons, socialization seems to focus primarily on directing and constraining the boys' impact on the environment. With daughters, the aim is rather to protect the girl from the impact of environment. The boy is being prepared to mold his world, the girl to be molded by it." [58]

This relationship holds true cross-culturally even more than it does in our own society. In studying child socialization in 110 non-literate cultures, Barry, Bacon, and Child found that "pressure toward nurturance, obedience, and responsibility is most often stronger for girls, whereas pressure toward achievement and self-reliance is most often stronger for boys." [59] They also found that strong differences in socialization practices were consistent with highly differentiated adult sex roles.

These cross-cultural studies show that dependency training for women is widespread and has results beyond simply curtailing analytic ability. In all these cultures women were in a relatively inferior status position compared to males. In fact, there was a correlation with the degree of rigidity of sex-role socialization and the subservice of women to men.

In our society also, analytic abilities are not the only ones valued. Being person-oriented and contextual in perception are very valuable attributes for many fields where, nevertheless, very few women are found. Such characteristics are valuable in the arts and the social sciences

[56] James Clapp, "Sex Differences in Mathematical Reasoning Ability," unpublished paper, 1968.
[57] Robert R. Sears *et al.*, *Patterns of Child Rearing* (Evanston, Ill.: Row and Peterson, 1957).
[58] Bronfenbrenner, *Ibid.*, p. 260.
[59] Herbert Barry, M. K. Bacon, and Irving L. Child, "A Cross-Cultural Survey of Some Sex Differences in Socialization," *Journal of Abnormal and Social Psychology*, Vol. 55 (November 1957), p. 328.

where women are found more than in the natural sciences—yet even here their achievement is still not deemed equivalent to that of men. One explanation of this, of course, is the repressive effect of role conflict and peer-group pressures discussed earlier. But when one looks further it appears that there is an earlier cause here as well.

As several studies have shown, the very same early independence and mastery training which has such a beneficial effect on analytic thinking also determines the extent of one's achievement orientation [60]—that drive which pushes one to excel beyond the need of survival. And it is precisely this kind of training that women fail to receive. They are encouraged to be dependent and passive—to be "feminine." In that process the shape of their mind is altered and their ambitions are dulled or channeled into the only socially rewarded achievement for a woman—marriage.

Now we have come almost full circle and can begin to see the vicious nature of the trap in which our society places women. When we become conscious of the many subtle mechanisms of social control—peer-group pressures, cultural norms, parental training, teachers, role expectations, and negative self-concept—it is not hard to see why girls who are better at most everything in childhood do not excel at much of anything as adults.

Only one link remains and that requires taking a brief look at those few women who do manage to slip through a chance loophole. Maccoby provided the best commentary on this when she noted that the girl who does not succumb to overprotection and develop the appropriate personality and behavior for her sex has a major price to pay: the anxiety that comes from crossing the caste lines. She feels that "it is this anxiety which helps to account for the lack of productivity among those women who do make intellectual careers—because [anxiety] is especially damaging to creative thinking." The combination of all these factors together tell "something of a horror story. It would appear that even when a woman is suitably endowed intellectually and develops the right temperament and habits of thought to make use of her endowment, she must be fleet of foot indeed to scale the hurdles society has erected for her and to remain a whole and happy person while continuing to follow her intellectual bent."[61]

The plot behind this horror story should by now be clearly evident. There is more to oppression than discrimination and more to the condition of women than whether or not they want to be free of the home. All societies have many ways to keep people in their places, and we have only discussed a few of the ones used to keep women in theirs. Women have been striving to break free of these bonds for many hundreds of years and

[60] Marian R. Winterbottom, "The Relation of Need for Achievement to Learning Experiences in Independence and Mastery," in Harold Proshansky and Bernard Seidenberg, eds., *Basic Studies in Social Psychology* (New York: Holt, Rinehart and Winston, 1965), pp. 294–307.
[61] Maccoby, *Ibid.*, p. 37.

once again are gathering their strength for another try. It will take more than a few changes in the legal system to significantly change the condition of women, although those changes will be reflective of more profound changes taking place in society. Unlike blacks, the women's liberation movement does not have the thicket of Jim Crow laws to cut through. This is a mixed blessing. On the one hand, the women's liberation movement lacks the simple handholds of oppression which the early civil rights movement had; but at the same time it does not have to waste time wading through legal segregation before realizing that the real nature of oppression lies much deeper. It is the more basic means of social control that will have to be attacked as women and men look into their lives and dissect the many factors that made them what they are. The dam of social control now has many cracks in it. It has held women back for years, but it is about to break under the strain.

Appendix II
Specimen Arguments for Study and Analysis

The Student Traffic Court

Southern University has as one of its oldest and proudest traditions a strong system of student government, through which students bear the principal responsibility for making and enforcing the rules which govern their conduct in all nonacademic phases of campus life. An important part of Southern University's student government is the five person student traffic court. The court has long had as one of its principal functions final jurisdiction over all nonmoving traffic violations that occur on the campus involving faculty and staff, as well as members of the student body. These include meter violations, parking in unauthorized areas, failure to register a car with the campus police department, etc. Fines imposed as penalties for such violations range from two dollars for a first offense to ten dollars for a third, and are payable directly to the treasurer of the student body rather than passing through regular university channels. The money thus collected is used to support a wide range of student government activities.

While the student traffic court is responsible for adjudicating the sorts of traffic violations just described, the rules governing all aspects of automobile use on campus are set by a committee of three students and four faculty members acting in an advisory capacity to the dean of students. The campus police are employees of the university rather than of the student government and are ultimately responsible to the president. They receive their paychecks from the university business office.

Although the system worked reasonably well for many years, more recently, with the greatly increased number of automobiles being brought to campus, a problem has arisen. Specifically, during the past few months morale among the members of the campus police force has suffered badly, and seven officers out of a total of sixteen have left the university to accept appointments in the county sheriff's office, although this change in position means no increase in pay.

Upon investigation, it has become apparent that the reason for the drop in morale and the consequent resignations is the fact that the officers feel they are not receiving sufficient support from the student traffic court in carrying out their assigned duties. The court, they claim, not only is far behind in hearing the cases on its docket, but is failing to levy fines against some of the most flagrant and persistent violators of traffic regulations.

As one example they point to a student who, though he has a total of thirty-two recorded violations during the current academic year, has never received a fine or reprimand. Another student, upon receiving a ticket, said to the policeman, "Go ahead and ticket me. I've got friends on the student traffic court, and they'll take care of it." A third student who had received in the neighborhood of fifteen tickets told a policeman, "You can't do anything to me. You have no authority." He then proceeded to tear up the ticket and throw it at the officer. Other policemen have had similar experiences with members of the university faculty and staff.

Parking and traffic control on the campus is a serious problem. Although there are only 3879 available parking spaces, 5415 student cars are registered. In addition, there are 1203 cars belonging to the faculty and 765 belonging to members of the university staff. Compounding the problem still further is the fact that on an average schoolday some 1500 vehicles driven by visitors and other nonuniversity personnel come to the campus.

Besides their responsibilities for controlling traffic, members of the university police force patrol the campus at night, investigate thefts and break-ins, report fires, and help keep order at football games and other athletic events. They are not, however, authorized by the city or county to make arrests.

QUESTION: Should the student traffic court be abolished and the enforcement of all nonmoving traffic regulations placed in the hands of the dean of students?

The Electrical Equipment Companies

Some years ago the Department of Justice brought to trial a number of high-level executives of the major U.S. electrical equipment manufacturers. The charges were based on a long history of secret meetings at which, in clear violation of the antitrust laws, these men had allocated the share of new business their respective companies would receive and set the prices they would charge for comparable sorts of products.

Over thirty executives pleaded guilty to the charges. Many received fines of several thousand dollars, some were given suspended jail sentences, and a few served jail sentences in addition to paying fines.

Testimony before and during the trials revealed without question that other employees of these companies on the junior-executive and middle-management levels had known about the illegal actions for many years. No records, however, could be produced to show that they had reported the violations either to their corporations' legal officers or to government officials.

QUESTION: Should the persons who knew of the illegal actions have reported them?

Distribution of Student Fees

In addition to their tuition, students at Sunshine College pay an activities fee of $26.50 a semester. Of this amount, $20.00 is allocated to retiring bonds authorized by the board of trustees to build a new auditorium and fieldhouse, and is specifically set aside by the board for this purpose. The remaining $6.50 is turned over to the Office of Student Services; and the director of that office, in consultation with the dean of students, determines how this amount will be distributed among various campus activities and organizations. The director of the Office of Student Services is a full-time employee of the college.

In recent years the distribution of the fund has been as follows:

Campus newspaper	$2.00
Marching band	.50
Student Senate	1.00
Lectures and concerts	1.00
Literary magazine	.50
Infirmary	1.50
	$6.50

In order to insure reasonable continuity and to facilitate planning, the Office of Student Services has followed the policy of notifying each organization at least two years in advance of any contemplated change in its portion of the activities fee.

Reasoning from the premise that, since the fee consists of student money, students should have the final voice in determining how it is spent, a majority of the members of the student body (as revealed in a recent campus poll) believe that the present method of allocation should be replaced with a so-called check-off system. Under this system every student, as part of his regular registration procedure each semester, would be given a list of the activities presently benefiting from the fee and asked to indicate which he wished to support. He would also be free to decide how he wished to have his $6.50 distributed among the items he selected, and even to designate activities or organizations not presently eligible for funds. The money derived from the fees would then be distributed by the Office of Student Services in accordance with these directions.

QUESTION: Should the check-off system replace the present method of collecting and distributing student fees?

The Jenkins Pulp and Paper Company

The Jenkins Pulp and Paper Company is located in a small town in southern Alabama. Although it has been in business for many years, it has always remained small, and at present it employs about 250 persons. Despite its size, the Jenkins Pulp and Paper Company is the only industry in the town in which it is located, and plant officials and citizens alike recognize that the economic survival of the town is directly dependent upon it.

During the past decade, a number of factors have combined to put the Jenkins Company in a decreasingly favorable competitive position. Among these are the improved means of mass production introduced into larger mills, the increased cost of transportation, and constantly escalating wage scales. In order to meet these problems, the management of the Jenkins Company has done everything it could to increase the efficiency of its operation. It has bought what new machinery it was able to afford; it has aggressively sought new business; it has acquired three heavy-duty trucks of its own as a means of reducing in-state shipping costs.

These efforts have been relatively successful, and have enabled the company to remain in business and even to expand slightly. However, it is now confronted with a new and serious problem in the form of an antipollution ordinance passed recently by the town council and strongly supported by a local ecology group. In order to comply with this ordinance, it would be necessary for the company to revise its entire production system. This would mean scrapping most of the machinery it now has, including some of the new machines recently purchased, and replacing it with a whole new production line.

In view of the marginal nature of its operations in recent years, the management of the company is certain that it cannot bear this expense. In addition, it recognizes that such a changeover to more modern production methods, even if it were possible, would reduce the number of workers needed and probably lead to the dismissal of nearly a third of its present employees.

The company has therefore petitioned the town council either to rescind the antipollution ordinance or at least to allow a grace period of five years before the ordinance is enforced. In presenting this petition, the company does not deny that it does indeed pollute the atmosphere with noxious odors or that some of the fumes emitted may conceivably endanger the health of the citizens. It does, however, maintain that, if the ordinance is presently enforced, it will be obliged to close down permanently, leading to serious repercussions on the economy of the town and genuine hardships in the families of its 250 employees.

QUESTION: Should the town council act favorably on the company's petition?

The Babysitter

Mrs. Betty Waverly, who lives a few blocks from the campus of State University, is the mother of two small children. Because of the proximity of her home to the campus, she has always hired undergraduate girls as babysitters when she and her husband are gone for the evening.

In recent months, Mrs. Waverly regularly used as a sitter a freshman named Mary Roberts. Mary won the affection of the Waverly children, handled them well, and in all respects proved to be an excellent sitter. For her services Mrs. Waverly paid Mary $1.25 an hour, considerably above the going rate in the community. She also provided Mary with transportation to her home and back to the dormitory.

The arrangement thus worked out was a good one for both Mrs. Waverly and Mary. For Mrs. Waverly it meant a dependable sitter whom her children liked. For Mary it meant a welcome source of income, since she is one of a number of children in an underprivileged family and must earn all of the money necessary to pay for her own books, clothing, and entertainment. Through her work with the Waverly family she was able to average between seven and eight dollars a week.

A few weeks ago, however, Mrs. Waverly began to notice that small amounts of money left about the house were missing, and in addition, a ring of some value had disappeared. After some days she came to suspect that Mary might have taken them. Yet she had come to like Mary so much that she could not really believe that this was the case, and so she did not rule out the possibility that her children or some of their playmates who roamed about the house freely might be the culprits.

In any event, she decided not to continue to use Mary as a sitter, and did not call her for two weeks. Thereupon, she received a call from Mary, who told her that, because she had been invited to a formal dance for which she would have to buy a dress, she was especially anxious to earn some money. Would Mrs. Waverly, by chance, have any need for a sitter soon, Mary wondered. Because Mrs. Waverly did need a sitter for the following evening, she engaged Mary for the job. However, after talking the matter over with her husband, she decided to lay a trap.

The trap consisted of leaving ten dollars in small bills and change in her purse in the front closet, and telling Mary that if the paperboy came to collect during the evening, she would find money in her purse. When Mrs. Waverly returned, she found $1.65 missing. Mrs. Waverly accused Mary of taking this money, and Mary confessed that she had done so. However, she denied that she had taken any of the money or other items that were missing earlier.

QUESTION: Is Mrs. Waverly chiefly responsible for Mary's action in taking the $1.65?

John Poliaro

John Poliaro is thirteen years old and a student in the sixth grade at Kirby Smith School. His teacher, Ms. Hilda Jones, has had eighteen years of teaching experience, ten of them at Kirby Smith, where she has taught the second as well as the sixth grade. Ms. Jones holds a master's degree from the College of Education at the University of Nevada.

John's parents were migrant workers during the early years of his life, but finally settled in Lake City and have lived there for the past two years. Because of their earlier migrant life, however, John has attended four different elementary schools. John's father now works as a carpenter's helper; his mother takes in ironing. John has four brothers and four sisters, three older than himself. One of John's brothers quit high school before graduating; another is a college graduate. His older sister is doing well in high school, where she is a member of the debating team and an honor student. John's father drinks heavily, but this does not prevent him from holding a steady job. All of the family attend church regularly.

During the current school year, John has been absent a good deal because of illness, and he has also skipped school to go fishing on a number of occasions. When he is present, he seems to learn easily and to finish his work quickly. However, he is constantly a disruptive factor in the classroom. He talks with his neighbors, puts his feet on the desk, refuses to answer questions, and makes insulting remarks to the teacher. Recently he hit and painfully injured the girl who sits in front of him when she asked him to be quiet so she could study. Ms. Jones has repeatedly punished John for his behavior by keeping him after school and sending him to the principal's office, but this does not seem to have had any effect on his behavior.

On Wednesday, April 23, during a quiet period in which the students were supposed to be writing a story about what they had done during spring vacation, John got up from his seat and began to walk around the room, stopping at various desks and scribbling lewd words on the papers the students were writing. When Ms. Jones asked him to return to his seat, he said, "You go to hell," and kept on walking about. At this time his own story was completed, and when read later was found to be a very good composition.

When John told Ms. Jones to go to hell, she immediately grabbed a one-foot, steel-edged ruler which lay on her desk and began to beat him about the head and shoulders. He covered his head with his hands to protect himself and ran from the room. He has not returned to school since that time, and his parents have said they will not send him back if Ms. Jones continues to be his teacher. In addition, they have demanded that Ms. Jones be dismissed at the close of the current school year, and have hired a lawyer to press their case before the school board.

Prior to this time Ms. Jones has had an unblemished record so far as discipline is concerned, and she is generally regarded as a satisfactory teacher. The Lake City school board has no established policy concerning striking children in the classroom. In the past, similar instances have been dealt with individually, and have been decided in different ways.

QUESTION: Should Ms. Jones be dismissed at the close of the current school year?

A Marriage Problem

John and Mary are college students. John is twenty years old and in his junior year in engineering; Mary is nearly nineteen and a sophomore in home economics. They met about a year and a half ago at school and have been dating steadily since that time. There is no question that they are really in love. Three months ago, with the consent of the four parents, they became engaged; and they wish to be married within the next three months.

Neither John nor Mary is self-supporting. Their tuition and most of their expenses are paid by their parents, who in both cases are fairly well-to-do. It will take John two more full years, including summers, to complete his engineering degree. Mary can complete her degree in about two years, and should have no difficulty getting a job after graduation.

The parents, though not entirely happy about the marriage plans, have promised to continue supporting them until their educations are completed.

QUESTION: Should the couple marry now?

The Valley Weekly

At Pine Valley College the student newspaper, the *Valley Weekly*, receives three quarters of its annual operating expenses (about $35,000) in the form of an outright grant from the general fund of the college. The remainder it gets from the sale of advertising and subscriptions to faculty, alumni, and other interested persons. The *Valley Weekly* is distributed free to the 2500 students at the college.

In recent years the editors of the paper have been outspoken in their criticism of the administration of the college and of the educational philosophy to which it adheres. On more than one occasion they have openly asked for the resignation of the president and dean. In addition, they have regularly published material which many of the faculty regard as obscene, and have freely sprinkled their stories and editorials with four-letter words.

The administration of the college, through the offices of the president and dean, has repeatedly reprimanded the editors for their language and choice of materials. Members of the college alumni association have also been highly critical of the paper. Despite these complaints, the paper has in no way altered its policies. The editors, who are chosen each spring in an all-campus election, have argued that they are giving the students what they want, and that they have every right to criticize the administration of the college freely.

Finally, because of his own disgust with the paper and because of the very strong pressure brought on him by faculty, alumni, and friends of the college, the president announced that the college's subsidy of $35,000 was being withdrawn at the close of the current school year. In the letter announcing this decision, he pointed out that the reputation of the college was suffering, that gifts from foundations and individuals had declined sharply, and that the parents of many prospective students would not send their sons or daughters to Pine Valley.

When the withdrawal of funds was announced the editors of the *Weekly*, as well as the student body in general, claimed that the action interfered with the traditional freedom of the press as guaranteed in the First Amendment, and that by withdrawing its support the college administration had in effect killed the paper. The president denied this charge. He said that the students were still completely free to publish the *Weekly* and to criticize the college in its pages. He also said that the paper was still free to carry any material that did not violate state or federal obscenity laws. The students, however, would have to find a way to finance the paper without the traditional subsidy.

QUESTION: Did the president act properly in withdrawing the subsidy?

Index

1 2 3 4 5 6 7 8 9 10 11 12 13 14 15 16 17 18 19 20 21 22 23 24 25   82 81 80 79 78 77 76 75 74